# INDIVIDUAL AND COMMUNITY

# Individual
# and Community:

## VARIATIONS ON A THEME
## IN AMERICAN FICTION

*Edited by*
KENNETH H. BALDWIN
*and*
DAVID K. KIRBY

DUKE UNIVERSITY PRESS
*Durham, N.C. 1975*

© 1975, Duke University Press

L.C.C. card no. 74-75476
I.S.B.N. 0-8223-0319-1

PRINTED IN THE UNITED STATES
OF AMERICA BY KINGSPORT PRESS

For

CHARLES ROBERTS ANDERSON
*Caroline Donovan Professor Emeritus*
*of American Literature,*
*The Johns Hopkins University*

# CONTENTS

# INTRODUCTION

Let us regard as polarities the concept of the individual and the concept of the group, of society. Neither of these extremes can of course be the focus of the novel. Yet every novel locates itself somewhere between these extremes.

James W. Tuttleton, *The Novel of Manners in America*

Well into the adventures of Huckleberry Finn, Huck is mistaken for his old comrade Tom Sawyer by Sally and Silas Phelps. His response to the confusion is revealing: "But if they was joyful," he says, "it wasn't nothing to what I was; for it was like being born again, I was so glad to find out who I was." The question of valid identity is not central to *Huckleberry Finn* alone, of course. The history of any literature is the history of a unique series of quests, the stories of individuals in search of external community and internal harmony. Fictional characters as well as writers of fiction seek to discover or create a mode of existence that provides a common bond with others at the same time that it allows for a sense of individual autonomy. Without a sense of community, a context to authenticate his existence and ratify his identity, the individual is driven to isolation and finally to physical or spiritual destruction. Once God is dead, and each time, so to speak, he dies again, a substitute must be found, some web of shared values which will give meaning and significance to the fragile individual self.

In the early history of a nation, the establishment of the external community is paramount, and nowhere was this need greater than it was in America during the age of colonization;

divorced from all but the remotest possibilities of aid, confronted by a land rumored to be rich in precious commodities of all kinds yet harsh and forbidding on the surface, plagued by the knowledge of the failure of previous and similar colonies, the early explorers and colonizers confirmed in their thought and literature the absolute necessity of establishing a colony that was self-reliant and resolute in the face of adversity. The subjects of books centered on practical concerns—farming, industry, surveying, and military affairs—and the dominant literary modes—diary, journal, letter, and autobiography—were perfect vehicles for such matters.

Only after the wilderness had been subdued and the spiritual solidarity of the community established could the individual afford the self-indulgent luxury of the quest for internal harmony. Yet the wilderness is never subdued, and the solidarity of the community is, at any given moment, tenuous at best. Thus the establishment of the external community is a continual matter. The drive toward a national unity preached by the Romantics was violently and sharply terminated by the Civil War, a division of allegiances wholly responsible for the dormancy of Southern literature for decades and partially responsible for the rise of local color. Unable to identify with larger communities, writers drew in their boundaries and created smaller worlds, trying to turn regional landscapes and local dialects into self-contained mindscapes. A similar motivation can be detected in much of contemporary radical literature in which bonds are formed by defining individuals in terms of their racial, sexual, or political allegiances. And although no sharp line can be drawn between external and internal worlds, it is clear that the notion of "community" has steadily become less a matter of geography, consanguinity, and visible bonds and more a matter of shared psychological and spiritual states.

The nine essays contained in this collection attempt to illuminate aspects of the individual-community relationship. Though different in focus and approach, the essays themselves express a "community" of concern, a concern which includes not just the situations of characters in fictional worlds but one which touches the relationship of both novelist and reader to a world of words. This volume is concerned with fiction instead of poetry, for if poetry is the language of unity, because it not only unites but reconciles disparate elements through metaphor and simile, fiction is the language of duality, for it separates elements in order to create tension. The creation, the alternate tightening and easing, and the final resolution of the tension between elements (in this case, the individual and the community) constitutes the novel. The inherent duality of fiction can be argued from numerous viewpoints, and illustrative examples abound, as evidenced by the essays which follow.

In his study of "The Empty World of *Wieland*," J. V. Ridgely traces the Gothic horrors of Charles Brockden Brown's tale back to a separation of individuals from larger social frameworks. The inner conviction of both Wieland and his father "that God spoke directly to a single individual leads directly to a corrupted vision of one's duty toward mankind at large." The world of Wieland is empty precisely because it lacks a frame of external reference; the solipsism of the leading characters results in misinterpretation, murder, and suicide. Only Clara and Pleyel are saved, and their salvation is made possible by their movement from the dark shadows of physical and psychic isolation toward the enlightening context of a social order. Brown himself, Ridgely argues, was experiencing, at the time he composed *Wieland*, "the deprivation of a fostering social order" and he recognized America's need for "greater awareness of otherness, for some replacement for severed parental ties."

Edgar A. Dryden suggests that Hawthorne, not unlike Charles Brockden Brown, was painfully aware of the gap between the individual and the community and that the distance separating the realms of romance and reality in his works is a "thematization of the distance which Hawthorne always believed prevailed between himself and the shared world of others." *The Marble Faun*, the specific text which Dryden examines in "The Limits of Romance: A Reading of *The Marble Faun*," is seen as an exploration of various alternatives to isolation—culture, nature, religion, love, and others. The chill which "permeates the mysterious world" of the novel derives from Hawthorne's recognition "that sympathetic communication is impossible." Dryden extends his argument past a single book or author, though, to explain the way in which all readers and writers are "destined to be disenchanted by the realization that the realms of fiction and reality can never coincide."

Roy Harvey Pearce also discusses Hawthorne's quest for the perfect community in his essay "Day Dream and Fact: The Import of *The Blithedale Romance*." "When I write another romance," Hawthorne said, before composing *The Blithedale Romance*, "I shall take the Community for a subject." He did indeed treat the concept of the community, based on his own experiences at Brook Farm, in *The Blithedale Romance*, where he dealt with the impossibility of escaping from the mundane world into an Arcadian dream world. Almost without exception the characters regress, as Pearce shows, from the day-to-day adult world to the fanciful world of childhood; having given up "the option of adjusting their fantasies to the exigencies of life lived in the world proper," they are "acting like children, trying to reduce or return life to terms impossible for adults."

Mark Twain appears to have a strong sense of community precisely because he could never find his place in one. His fiction clearly indicates this ambivalence, as Louis D. Rubin, Jr. points out in " 'The Begum of Bengal': Mark Twain and the South." Twain's life and his literary efforts were strangely affected by his Southern experience. Rubin documents, for example, the way in which Twain's fascination with aristocratic characters grew out of his relationship with his own father, a man in whom the young Twain admired the heroic gesture of minor Southern aristocracy at the same time that he despised his father's ineffectiveness in the face of the practicality of a rapidly expanding democratic society. The events of Twain's early life—his boyhood in a town that was neither Southern nor Western, the collapse of the aristocratic pretensions of his family, his tenuous relation to the Southern cause in the Civil War—combined to jar him loose from his Southern heritage. Yet the separation was never total; throughout his life the forces of his creative imagination "held ferociously on, in resentment and in pride, to that faraway country of his youth." It is thus the tension between the pull of the community and the forces that separate the individual from it that is the source of Twain's art. His relationship to the society that he knew "anticipates that of the generation of writers who came to literary maturity after the first world war."

In treating Hemingway as a case of the *artist* as individual, Carlos Baker approaches the question of the individual-community polarity from a unique angle in "Hemingway's Empirical Imagination." As Baker documents through several new sources, raw experience enriched by acute powers of observation was the mainstay of Hemingway's art. The early Hemingway had a knack for reproducing stories as he heard them and incorporating them, with minimal changes, into his fiction. The later Hemingway, however, progressively withdrew from the community of fictional sources that sustained him in his work and began to listen too much to internal voices. As he turned in upon himself, in the lesser works of his final years, he upset the fine balance of "objective discernment and subjective response" that his best work displayed and he fell victim to the "implicit narcissism" that he had charged Fitzgerald and Joyce with.

In "Faulkner's 'Country' as Ideal Community," Philip Momberger identifies Faulkner's master-theme as "man's inescapable need to search for communal ties." Although Faulkner's characters typically lack "a sense of participation in a cohesive community," the opening section of his collected short stories is an exception. The six stories subtitled "The Country," Momberger explains, together define "an ideal of communal health, wholeness and peace against which the reader can measure the social and personal disintegration rendered in subsequent sections and throughout the Faulkner canon." Here Faulkner comes closest to depicting the social ideal "that lies behind all his fiction," a state of "communal wholeness within which, as within a coherent and loving family, the individual's identity would be defined, recognized, and sustained."

Faulkner's attitude seems to be considerably less sanguine in his early *Sanctuary*, as suggested by the title of James E. Miller, Jr.'s essay "*Sanctuary*: Yoknapatawpha's Waste Land." Pointing out that the novel has been much misunderstood, Miller places *Sanctuary* in the context of Faulkner's entire canon. Miller has previously written in *Quests Surd and Absurd*: "In a sense . . . each one of Faulkner's novels represents a descent into the vortex of time, a vortex created by an event that disturbs, upsets, alarms, or frightens the family or community. In moving frantically back and forth in the search for the cause and consequences of this key and singular event, Faulkner creates the structure of his novels: a whirlpool or circular structure suggesting that the secret of time (or life) is not to be found in the simple, straight chronology of one event following another, but rather in hidden corners . . . of the past." Miller makes frequent reference to Eliot's *Waste Land* in probing the hidden corners of *Sanctuary*, and the analogy in itself indicates that the idea of community in that novel is somewhat less than the pastoral ideal discussed by Momberger. Indeed the bitterness of *Sanctuary*, Miller says, lies specifically "in its insight into the hypocrisy and hollowness of both the religion and the community presented in the novel." Ironically, no one finds true sanctuary in the novel, and the "most genuine human communion" is experienced in a whore house and a jail. And the empty sky at the end of the novel emblemizes the withdrawal of God, for the season of *Sanctuary* is indeed "the season of rain and death."

Just as Faulkner's world can be compared to Eliot's wasteland, so the surrealistic works of Djuna Barnes reflect the nightmare visions of Poe, as James Baird shows in "Djuna Barnes and Surrealism: 'Backward Grief.'" Despite the fact that Djuna Barnes has aesthetic similarities to Poe, Joyce, and Stein, those writers were intent upon "a privacy of vision ending with the limits of each sovereign imagination." Barnes's art is designed to refer beyond itself. Although part of her personal life has been marked by strict seclusion, her artistic interest in universal psychic states is an attempt at "an exposition of universals." In *Ryder* and *Nightwood*, as in other efforts, she examines the relationship between our individual and collective conscious and subconscious lives. Isolated and alienated, her various fictional characters are trying to trace backward, in grief, the path that leads from a common lost childhood. For it is the child's possession of the self that we lose as adults, the "beastly inarticulate in the state of original innocence, where integration is, where human children, other creatures in a jungle world, begin uncoiling their human destinies."

According to Edward Mendelson, Thomas Pynchon's second novel, *The Crying of Lot 49*, offers an alternative to the "triviality and exitlessness" so prevalent in contemporary literature. *V.*, Pynchon's first novel, took the reader to the edge of the "unlit, motionless world of the later Beckett" whereas *Lot 49* leads to "Prospero's island and the seacoast of Bohemia." "While the processes of *V.* isolate," Mendelson says, "those of *Lot 49* create community." And just as Oedipa Maas, the protagonist of *Lot 49*, moves past narcissism to communication, Pynchon himself moves away from subjunctive fiction (works which illuminate their own language and structure) toward a new mode of indicative fiction (works which transmit information about the emotional and physical world of nonliterary experience). Pynchon's quest is a "lonely and isolated one, but it leads to a place where fiction can become less lonely, less isolated than it has been for many years."

The essays which comprise this volume are not intended as an overview of American literature. They are intended, though, to point to the continuity of an important theme in American fiction and to offer insight into the variety of philosophical and literary strategies utilized in significant works of significant authors in dealing with the question of the individual and the community. The essays of Ridgely and Baker caution against too much isolation; those of Pearce, Dryden, and Rubin, while not disputing the admonition, demonstrate the difficulty in establishing solidarity between individual and community. While Miller and Baird locate new Wastelands on the literary landscape, Momberger explores a lost pastoral community; Mendelson suggests a way in which a new vision can redeem an incoherent world. The permutations on the theme of the individual and the community are many; the same tensions and polarities which have occasioned the essays that follow apply explicitly to many novels and novelists and implicitly to all.

This volume is offered as a professional and personal tribute to Charles Roberts Anderson, Caroline Donovan Professor Emeritus of American Literature, The Johns Hopkins University. In his long and distinguished career Professor Anderson has helped to shape our approach to nineteenth-century American literature, fostered an appreciation of American literature abroad, and, perhaps most significantly, served as mentor for several generations of teachers and scholars. The contributors to this collection of essays are but a symbolic fraction of the impressive total whom Charles Anderson has enlightened and inspired as teacher or colleague.

Even a partial description of his bibliography gives sufficient indication of the debt that is owed him by all students of American literature. His major publications include three ground-breaking studies: *Melville in the South Seas*; *Emily Dickinson's Poetry: Stairway of Surprise*, winner of a Christian Gauss Award; and *The Magic Circle of Walden*. Among the works which he has edited are the ten-volume *Centennial Edition of Sidney Lanier*; the two-volume *American Literary Masters*; *Thoreau's World: Miniatures from his Journal*; and the Greylock Edition of *Typee*. His numerous articles feature important examinations of Robert Penn Warren, Faulkner, Henry James, Frost, and Hemingway as well as a cluster of essays on the special features of Southern literature. For an indication of

Charles Anderson's true *curriculum vitae*, his bibliography would have to be augmented by a variety of other achievements and awards. He has served, for example, on the editorial boards of *American Literature, Journal of American Literature* and *Modern Language Notes*. Rosenwald, Fulbright, Huntington, Guggenheim and other Fellowships have punctuated his career as have a sizeable number of Visiting Professorships in the United States, Europe, and the Orient. He is a past President of the Melville Society of America and former Chairman of the American Literature Group of the Modern Language Association; among his special lectures are the Barrow Lecture at the University of Georgia and the Lamar Memorial Lecture at Wesleyan College. That so many of his honors have been matters of election or invitation provides special testament to the esteem in which he is held by his peers.

Although his academic career began with an appointment at the University of Georgia, followed by more than a decade at Duke University, it is with The Johns Hopkins University that the name of Charles Anderson has been associated since 1941, a tenure which includes six years as Chairman of the English Department. The same spirit that led him, as a young man, to trace Melville's South Sea journey has continued to inform his professional life. Professor Anderson's contribution to the graduate training of other scholars, the depth and breadth of his own completed scholarship and criticism, and the promise of the works which he is presently completing signify that he has not only inherited the Hopkins tradition but also become a part of that tradition.

KENNETH H. BALDWIN
*University of Maryland*
*Baltimore County*
DAVID K. KIRBY
*Florida State University*

# INDIVIDUAL AND COMMUNITY

# THE EMPTY WORLD OF *WIELAND*


*Wieland* is a nocturnal tale, a nervous melodrama played out in
the uncertain illumination of candle, lamp, fire, moon, stars.
To a degree, of course, Brown's darkened stage set is a literary
convention; in folk tale as well as in the contemporary Gothic
novel of terror, night is the time when creatures of mystery and
danger are expected to walk abroad. But Charles Brockden
Brown was a self-proclaimed novelist of purpose, and the titil-
lating shudder, though he employed it as a time-tested lure for
readership, he condemned as an end in itself. In his preface he
announced that he aimed at no less than the "illustration of some
important branches of the moral constitution of man,"[1] and he
attached a didactic tag to the end of the novel to assure that no
one could underestimate his fundamental seriousness. Unfortunately, this conclusion can too lazily be taken as a sufficient
summation of the tale's entire import. Certainly, as recent criticism has made us aware, *Wieland* is far more complex in structure and in meaning than its narrator, Clara Wieland, intimates
by moralizing in her final sentences only on the "errors" of the
Stuarts, of Wieland, and of herself. For, as Brown himself pro-
claims, Man is the protagonist; and the theme is conceived as
universal: when the light of reason becomes dimmed or is
extinguished by superstition, by trickery, or by unusual experience which is misconstrued as preternatural, horror is loosed in
the world. This horror is that of man's darkened mind; and its
state may be externalized, as here, by false appearance, by the
urge to destroy reason in others, by murder, by self-destruction.
*Wieland* is a warning to beware of the quality of sense per-

1. *Wieland or The Transformation,* ed. Fred Lewis Pattee, Hafner Library
of Classics (New York, 1958), p. 3. All subsequent references are to this
edition, which follows closely the first printing of 1798, and are included in
the text.

ceptions, an appeal to cultivate and protect the light of reason; for, once benighted, some men may not find their way back out of the blackness.

This is Brown's manifest message; but, as several recent commentators[2] have argued, Brown's apparent dedication to Lockean sensationalist psychology is compromised by other ramifications of the tale. Thus Larzer Ziff sees Brown as the first American novelist "to face the confusion of sentiment and an optimistic psychology, both of which flowed through the chink in the Puritan dike, and to represent American progress away from a doctrine of depravity as a very mixed blessing indeed."[3] William M. Manley, disputing Ziff's focus on sentimental-seduction materials in the novel, still finds that the "astonishing intensity which Brown generates . . . reflects his ability to convey through a first-person narrator the shifting instability of a mind swayed between objective logic and subjective terror, creating thereby a tension which is not resolved until the final pages."[4] And Donald A. Ringe summarizes: "To show that Brown made use of sensationalist psychology in his book does not necessarily mean that he accepted it uncritically, for the developing action of the novel calls its validity into serious question."[5] Despite their different emphases, all three critics reach what is certainly a valid conclusion: the manifest and the latent content of *Wieland* appear to be at odds. Yet all, in arriving at this point, overlook an aspect that is an even more fundamental peculiarity of the tale. For the world of *Wieland* is not only nocturnal; it is also a remarkably empty one. Confined to a few characters and some set locales, it is curiously without a wider social reference: state, city, church—even other families—remain mere shadows lurking in the general gloom. It is this world devoid of those authori-

2. See Larzer Ziff, "A Reading of *Wieland*," *PMLA*, 77 (March, 1962), 51–57; William M. Manly, "The Importance of Point of View in Brockden Brown's Wieland," *American Literature*, 35 (Nov., 1963), 311–321; Donald A. Ringe, *Charles Brockden Brown* (New York, 1966), pp. 25–48.

3. Op. cit., p. 54.

4. Op. cit., pp. 311–312.

5. Op. cit., p. 27.

tative institutions by which sense impressions could be weighed and judged which I wish later to emphasize. But I would like, first, to demonstrate just how Brown brings each of his principal characters—Clara, Pleyel, and Wieland—to the ultimate state of dangerous illusion, to that "transformation" to which the subtitle refers.

I

As several critics have correctly emphasized, an early comment of Clara's furnishes the key to Brown's method of putting his leading players to the test. "The will," writes Clara, "is the tool of the understanding, which must fashion its conclusions on the notices of sense." And, she continues sententiously, "If the senses be depraved it is impossible to calculate the evils which may flow from the consequent deductions of the understanding" (39). These maxim-like statements provide the philosophical basis for Brown's employment of light and dark patterns. For if "depravity" of the senses is crucial it is but a step to positing that the light of full day may be linked with the light of unclouded reason; or, to formulate the principle in the reverse manner, that if the senses are required to function in natural gloom, in artificial (hence "false") light, or in darkness, mental perception is correspondingly obscured. The degree and the quality of illumination, then, are all-important. It is this point which Wieland, Pleyel, and finally Clara spectacularly fail to comprehend.

Brown's narrative ultimately depends for force upon the cumulative effect of misapprehended experience; but, for purposes of discussion, it may be divided into four main parts: (1) *a prolog*, dealing with the elder Wieland's background in Europe and with his death in Pennsylvania; (2) *a central action*, constructed around the eight voices produced by the ventriloquist Carwin and reaching a climax in Clara's discovery of the body of Wieland's wife; (3) *a denouement*, in which Clara learns that Wieland has murdered his family and that

Carwin is the agent of the voices; and in which Carwin's confession, Wieland's threat of death to her and his suicide bring on her mental collapse; (4) *an epilog*, written in France three years after these last events, in which Clara tells of her restoration to rationality and of her union with Pleyel. What now follows is a synoptic analysis of *Wieland* in accordance with this structure, with particular reference to Brown's schematic employment of light-dark contrasts.

1. The Prolog (chs. I–II). The elder Wieland, convinced that his religion has been "expressly prescribed to him" (14), builds a classical temple to his deity and retires there for worship each noon and midnight (the midpoints of light and darkness). His religion has the appearance of the light of reason (the classical temple and midday), but it is also associated with the darkness of unreason (revelation and midnight). On the final evening of his life he goes alone to his shrine. There his "fancy" pictures a "person bearing a lamp" and at the same moment a "spark" lights upon and consumes his clothes. Watching from a window, his wife and her brother (Clara's uncle) see "gleams" and "rays." Running to the temple, the uncle discovers that the elder Wieland's body is scorched; before his death he describes the fiery doom that had overtaken him. This harrowing event, occurring during Clara's childhood, becomes obsessively the subject of her thoughts. Two explanations are presented to her: either the "Divine Ruler interferes in human affairs" or "the [dangerous] condition of [her father's] thoughts" caused a natural physical reaction—i.e., spontaneous combustion, a "scientific" theory supported by her uncle (a surgeon) and by Brown himself in a footnote. The circumstances of the death (fire, night) set up the light-dark structure for the whole book and underscore Brown's use of the temple as a locale for misapprehended experience.

2. The Central Action (chs. III–XVII). Left orphans, Clara and Wieland grow up on isolated properties outside Phila-

delphia. Since her education was modeled on "no religious standard" but rather left to the guidance of her own "understanding," Clara leans to the deistic. Her brother, though, scholarly, speculative, and moody like his father, pursues "the history of religious opinions" (26). These views are scoffed at by his friend Pleyel, "the champion of intellectual liberty, and [one who] rejected all guidance but that of his reason" (28). Upon Wieland's marriage to Pleyel's sister Catharine, Clara moves to a house nearby, but all meet regularly in the temple for intellectual amusements.

*First voice*: Wieland goes at night to the temple to retrieve a letter. The moon is for a moment hidden by a cloud (his senses are darkened) and he sees a "glimmering" (false light) that reminds him of the fate of his father (36). It is then that he hears a voice, which he takes to be that of his wife, warning him of danger ahead and urging him to return to the house. The voice, as we learn later, is projected by Carwin; but as the bright moon comes out again Wieland sees no one. Back in the house, he is told that his wife has not stirred, and Pleyel attributes hearing of the voice to a "deception of the senses" (38).

*Second voice*: Some time later, Clara and Catharine are sitting at home awaiting the return of Wieland and Pleyel. As the clock strikes midnight, the men enter and relate that while talking in the temple they have heard Catharine's voice informing them that Pleyel's intended bride is dead. The experience shakes Pleyel's rationalism; it only confirms Wieland's belief in revelation.

*Third voice*: Carwin now makes his first open appearance. Dressed as a rustic but speaking with a musical and educated voice he is initially seen by Clara in afternoon sunlight. But next day arises in "darkness and storm" (61), a signal that though Carwin is outwardly a man of reason (his arrival in daylight) he is dark and perverted within. As night returns, the storm ceases; Clara spends "the darksome hours" (62) musing on death. Retiring to bed, she listens to the clock (which her father had owned) striking twelve; then she hears voices at her bed's head whispering threats of murder. In panic she flees to Wieland's house, where she faints.

*Fourth voice*: A voice of "piercing shrillness" (68) calls the occupants to Clara's aid. As she recovers, Clara reflects on the occurrences of the voice; she can no longer doubt its reality. But she fails to realize that it has always been heard in semidarkness and that the understanding may thus have been duped.

*Fifth voice*: Clara goes at sundown to her summerhouse near the river and falls asleep. She dreams that as she is walking to her brother's house in twilight she comes upon a deep pit; beyond it her brother beckons her forward. As she is about to step into the abyss, someone catches her from behind and a voice cries "Hold! hold!" She awakens in "deepest darkness," with her "faculties still too confused" for her to find her way up the bank. Then comes a voice, which she recognizes as one of those which whispered near her bed. It promises her safety if she will avoid the summerhouse and not reveal what has happened. Without "the faintest gleam" to guide her steps, she remains motionless till she sees a "ray" (71–72). The "first visitings of this light [call] up a train of horrors," as she thinks of her father's end and of the warning voice (flickering light is associated with superstition). But now a "new and stronger illumination" (73) bursts upon her; it is Pleyel bearing a lantern. Confused, she tells him nothing of her experience.

Next evening Clara meets Carwin at Wieland's and learns that Pleyel had known him in Europe. The "voices" become a main topic for their discourse and three conflicting theories emerge: (1) Carwin holds for a "ready and plausible solution" (natural causes), but conceals his own role (reason deceiving by partial truth); (2) Wieland again maintains "the probability of celestial interference"; (3) Pleyel still accepts no testimony but that of his senses (83–85).

*Sixth voice*: In her bedroom, Clara goes to a closet; inexplicably a voice again cries "Hold! hold!" Terrified, she searches for its source, but in the faint moonlight from the windows she can discover no one. "Dark is less fertile of images than the feeble lustre of the moon," she muses (96–97). Suddenly recalling her dream, she now first consciously associates danger with her brother; and in a "phrenzy" she calls for him to come forth. But it is of course Carwin who emerges from the closet; and, dissembling for his own purposes, he says that he had come to ravish her but that the voice of warning had saved her. Actually, he has been prowling through her effects and has no intention of sexual attack. Carwin leaves in moonlight, and Clara is left to her "bewildering ideas" (105).

*Seventh voice:* Pleyel tells Wieland that he has heard voices which have convinced him that Clara has given herself to Carwin; later, in his own home, he relates to Clara his experience while denouncing her supposed fall from virtue. He had been on his way to tell her that Carwin was a fugitive from justice; as he passed her summerhouse in moonlight he became aware of voices he took to be Clara's and Carwin's. "My sight was of no use to me. Beneath so thick an umbrage, the darkness was intense," he recalls—not comprehending that he should have mistrusted his *other* senses. Sadly he tells her, "I yielded not but to evidence which took away the power to withhold my faith" (154). Clara protests vainly; as Pleyel stalks out of the room, she notices that "the light was declining" (155). The light of reason has now been dimmed in Pleyel too.

*Eighth voice:* Carwin writes asking for an 11 P.M. interview at Clara's house to explain his threat of rape. Though Clara thinks, with justice, that "the writer had surely been bereft of his reason" (156), she decides to return home. Arriving, she arms herself with a penknife and starts up the stairs. But again there is a cry of "*hold! hold!*" and she is confronted by a mysterious face, which then vanishes. Remarkably continuing up the stairs anyway, she enters her room. She discovers not Carwin but a note from him warning of a horrible sight to come. Carrying a light "in order to dispel any illusive mists that might have hovered" before her eyes (170), she comes upon the body of Catharine. Her death Clara immediately attributes to Carwin; and when Wieland enters in a distracted state she mourns the "extinction of a mind the most luminous and penetrating that ever dignified the human form" (174)—supposing that grief has driven him mad. With these two erroneous conclusions of Clara's the pattern of mystification in the novel ends.

3. The Denouement (chs. XVIII–XXVI). Clara, discovering next that Wieland's entire family has been murdered, sinks into delirium. As she recovers, she puts the blame upon Carwin, but her uncle gives her some documents to read, informing her that the "execution was another's" (182). The death-dealing hand was Wieland's own, she learns. In his confession, light and dark are again given their schematic roles. Before the court Wieland recalls his moment of "illumination." Having gone to Clara's house in search of her, he had entered her darkened room. Satisfied of her absence, he turned to leave; but on the stairs he was "dazzled" by a "lustre" which burst upon his vision: "I opened my eyes and found all about me luminous and glowing. It was the element of heaven that flowed around. Nothing but a fiery stream was at first visible; but, anon, a shrill voice from behind me called upon me to attend" (188). A visage, he continues, now beamed upon his sight and he was enjoined to kill his wife and (later) his children as sacrifices. The intensity and quality of this false light are important; they signify the force of his delusion.

Reading through this account, Clara cannot at first realize that the voice which Wieland heard was *not* that which had addressed herself and the others on previous occasions. Told by her uncle that Wieland was a victim of religious mania, she counters that "this madness, if madness it were, had affected Pleyel and myself as well as Wieland" (202).

Clara is not long left in doubt. Returning to her bedroom in order to destroy her journal, she sits in the twilight of her closed house, the darkness "suiting the colour of [her] thoughts" (218).

As she contemplates suicide, Carwin enters and confesses to being the source of the eight voices through his power of "biloquism" (225–241). His hidden motivation (which Brown reveals more fully in *Memoirs of Carwin, the Biloquist*) derives from his association with a secret anarchistic order like the Illuminati; what he tells Clara is: "I cannot justify my conduct, yet my only crime was curiosity" (231). Emphatically he denies any responsibility for the "voice of God" heard by Wieland or for the murders. While Clara is pondering these explanations, Wieland, having escaped from prison, rushes in and tells her she is the predestined final victim demanded by his "angel." But Clara points at Carwin and charges him with being the source of the "angel" voice. Wieland challenges him, but Carwin will admit only to some deception. Wieland orders him out and is able for a moment to see part of the truth: "If I erred, it was not my judgment that deceived me, but my senses" (251–252). He thanks God for this last "illumination"—i.e., knowledge of Carwin's power to defraud. However, suddenly irrational again, he argues that though the messenger was evil the commissions must have come from God, and he will carry out the final order. Carwin reenters, unseen by Wieland, and for the ninth and last time in the novel he employs his feigned voice. Crying "*hold!*" he stays Wieland's hand; then he orders him to "ascend into rational and human": "not heaven or hell, but thy senses have misled thee to commit these acts." Wieland is shaken: "A beam appeared to be darted into his mind." This beam is the emblem of right reason, for he is "restored to perception of truth" (257–259). But his recovered rationality brings immediate awareness that he cannot live in the world of daylight, and he commits suicide.

4. The Epilog (ch. XXVII): written in France by Clara three years later. After Wieland's suicide, Clara's will to live was destroyed and she sank into a heedless state. But one night she was shocked into awareness by a light-filled dream: "Sometimes I was swallowed up by whirlpools, or caught up in the air. . . .

Sometimes gleams of light were shot into a dark abyss, on the verge of which I was standing, and enabled me to discover, for a moment, its enormous depth and hideous precipices. Anon, I was transported to some ridge of Aetna, and made a terrified spectator of its fiery torments and its pillars of smoke" (264). Coming out of this phantasmagoria, Clara realized the house was ablaze; and, in a scene in which Brown draws obvious parallels with the death of her father, she was rescued. But whereas the inner fire of his delusion destroyed him, actual flame was for Clara a purifying agent. She now agreed to her uncle's plea to leave the nightmare-producing scene behind; together they have come to live in France, the home of the Enlightenment.

Brown now clumsily drags in the Stuart-Conway-Maxwell subplot which he had introduced early and neglected—but not before he restores Pleyel too. Pleyel had married his foreign bride, but she has conveniently died in childbirth. Now, having heard from Carwin the truth about Clara, he comes back to her; and Brown is able to marry restored reason to reason in fact as well as symbol.

## II

As I have said, Brown is content in his conclusion simply to let Clara bemoan the "errors" of passion and foresight which had brought catastrophe to the Stuart and Wieland families. But these errors, as we have seen in detail, are really the result of the immediate granting of ultimate authority to the last recorded sensory data. Quite unaccountably, Brown does not allow Clara to ponder the process by which she and Pleyel have been able to restore themselves: it is by a return to society, by the recognition that one must verify sense impressions in the context of a world which is broader than the limiting locales of the central action.

Brown does, indeed, sketch in for the reader all the necessary background. As the extended prolog makes evident, a fatal pattern has been initiated in previous generations, on both the paternal and maternal sides of Clara's family; and the human danger in this fallacy is pointed up by the early and isolated deaths of the fathers. The paternal grandfather married beneath his social level, cut himself from familial ties, devoted himself to literature and music, and "died in the bloom of his life" (7). His son, Clara and Wieland's father, was taken under the protection of a London merchant, given duties that were "laborious and mechanical," and "spent all his time pent up in a gloomy apartment," where he devoted himself to dismal religious speculation. His only attempt at broader social contact—a move to America in an effort to become a missionary of his faith to the Indians—was a failure. He then married a "woman of a meek and quiet disposition" and eventually retired to his sequestered farm with his small family. Clara herself underscores the ultimate isolation from the wider world which his religious fanaticism produces: "He allied himself with no sect, because he perfectly agreed with none. Social worship is that by which they are all distinguished; but this article found no place in his creed. He rigidly interpreted that precept which enjoins us, when we worship, to retire into solitude, and shut out every species of society" (12). The deadly consequences of his act are thus foreordained: testing his sense of a divine proscription given to himself alone against no established religious body, he goes to the solitary and fiery death which is brought on, as Clara surmises, by the "condition of his thoughts." In a later scene, Clara's uncle reveals to her the similarly spectacular demise of her maternal grandfather: believing that his own end "would be inevitably consequent on that of his brother, [he] waited from day to day in expectation of the stroke which he predicted was speedily to fall upon him." Finally, the "summons" comes and he throws himself from a cliff (201–202). His illusions Clara's uncle simply classifies as "maniacal."

Brown would have us understand, then, that a tendency toward a private belief which leads to insane conclusions is inherent in the Wieland family: it is a trait which is to be

revived in the younger Wieland, Clara's brother. In the pre-
ferred isolation of his country home, Wieland devotes himself
to "long and abstruse deductions from the system of divine
government and the laws of our intellectual constitution"
(39–40), and his only diversion is meeting with the limited
family circle which gathers in the temple where his father had
died. It is Clara who first sees the family propensity reemerging:
"There was an obvious resemblance between him and my
father, in their conceptions of the importance of certain topics,
and in the light in which the vicissitudes of human life were
accustomed to be viewed" (26). Both in his own and his father's
cases an inner conviction that God speaks directly to a single
individual leads to a corrupted vision of one's duty toward
mankind at large. As Wieland boasts in his confession, "my
contemplations soared above earth and its inhabitants" (187).

This familial predisposition toward damaging introspection
accounts not only for Clara's solitary intellectual pursuits but
also for her obsessive dwelling on her father's fate and for the
intuitive dread of Wieland which is released in her dreams.
Indeed, the death of the father is clearly represented as the key
incident which drives the family into a mistaken sense of its
own uniqueness: "We gradually withdrew ourselves from the
society of others, and found every moment irksome that was
not devoted to each other" (23). Like her father and brother,
Clara is eventually led by her untested perceptions into mental
disorientation. Yet she alone has the means for survival. Both
the love which she has felt for Pleyel and the disturbing fact
of the intrusion of an outsider, Carwin, prove to be her salvation. As she tells us, the shock of Wieland's murderous actions
and his own suicide drove her to seek the seclusion of her house
and to communicate with no one. Only gradually, she remarks
in her postscript, did she become aware that continued obsessive
brooding on her family's fate and refusal to reenter society would
have proved fatal to her as well:

> I now see the infatuation and injustice of my conduct in
> its true colours. I reflect upon the sensations and reasonings

of that period with wonder and humiliation. That I should be insensible to the claims and tears of my friends; that I should overlook the suggestions of duty, and fly from that post in which only I could be instrumental to the benefit of others; that the exercise of the social and beneficent affections, the contemplation of nature and the acquisition of wisdom should not be seen to be means of happiness still within my reach, is, at this time, scarcely credible. (263–264)

For the fire which demolished her home had also destroyed her past:

This incident, disastrous as it may at first seem, had, in reality, a beneficial effect upon my feelings. I was, in some degree, roused from the stupor which had seized my faculties. The monotonous and gloomy series of my thoughts was broken. My habitation was levelled with the ground and I was obliged to seek a new one. A new train of images, disconnected with the fate of my family forced itself on my attention, and a belief insensibly sprung up, that tranquillity, if not happiness, was still within my reach. Notwithstanding the shocks which my frame had endured, the anguish of my thoughts no sooner abated that I recovered my health. (265–266)

Clara's "transformation" back to normality is, of course, completed by her union with Pleyel, that alleged man of reason who also too easily trusted to his unverified sense perceptions. Through her uncle's efforts, Pleyel is at last brought to hear Carwin's confession of his unseen role, and Clara is immediately restored to Pleyel's "good opinion." But why did Pleyel on his own never think of confronting Carwin? Why, when all his memories of Clara cried out against belief in her sexual fall, did he refuse to accept her own denials? The answer is that, though he had wider social contacts and interests than did the Wieland family, he had been infected by an unfounded pride in his intellect as sole judge of the truth; like the others, he admitted of no institutions by which he might have challenged his erroneous perceptions. Now, in the settled society of Europe, amid contacts which emphasize man's role as social animal, his mind functions as it should.

We may ask, finally, whether Brown intends some deeply significant contrast between young open America and old crowded Europe in the final scenes set in France. The question is difficult to answer with assurance, because the intrusion of the Maxwell-Stuart subplot obfuscates what might have been clear-cut definition. But it may well be that, writing in a decade which followed upon the sundering of America from the parent country, Brown himself was experiencing the deprivation of a fostering social order, of those traditional institutions by which the individual self attempts to gauge its proper role. True, some intellectual comfort could be found in optimistic sensationalist psychology, in the *tabula rasa* with which each individual started anew: America's slate too had scarcely been scratched. Yet the terrible emptiness of the world of *Wieland* and the demonstrable falsity of dependence upon unmediated sensory perception suggest that Brown perceived America's need for greater awareness of otherness, for some replacement for severed parental ties. Perhaps even more strongly than the Wieland family did their literary creator feel the loss of the father.

J. V. RIDGELY
*Columbia University*

# THE LIMITS OF ROMANCE: A READING

# OF *THE MARBLE FAUN*

Fiction is to the grown man what play is to the
child; it is there that he changes the atmosphere
and tenor of his life; and when the game so
chimes with his fancy that he can join in it with
all his heart, when it pleases him with every
turn, when he loves to recall it and dwells upon
its recollection with entire delight, fiction is
called romance.

> Robert Louis Stevenson, "A Gossip on Ro-
> mance," quoted by Miriam Allott, *Novelists
> on the Novel* (New York, 1966), p. 54.

There are thus two interpretations of interpretation. . . . The one seeks to decipher, dreams
of deciphering, a truth or an origin which is free
from freeplay and from the order of the sign,
and lives like an exile the necessity of interpretation. The other, which is no longer turned
toward the origin, affirms freeplay and tries to
pass beyond man and humanism. . . .

> Jacques Derrida, "Structure, Sign, and Play
> in the Discourse of the Human Sciences,"
> in *The Languages of Criticism and the
> Sciences of Man*, ed. Richard Macksey and
> Eugenio Donato (Baltimore, 1970), p. 264.

I

The student of the novel will find it helpful to remember that
the act of reading precedes the act of interpretation, for the
special attractions which novels hold for readers provide some

clues to their nature. For example, the expressions which we habitually use to describe our encounter with the novel sufficiently show its uniqueness. When we say that we are "caught up by a book," that we "lose ourselves in it," that we are "overwhelmed by it," "enveloped by it," we are identifying a particular spell cast over us by the fictive world. And let no one doubt that it is a spell, an enchantment as mystifying as the games of childhood, for as long as we breathe the hallucinating atmosphere of this world, which is, after all, no more than black marks on a page, we lose the sense of our own identities, our own world, and give ourselves over to a realm which does not exist. It is the pleasure we derive from this experience which causes us to wish that the book would never end and which produces in us that disappointment we always feel when we turn the final page of a novel. For, unfortunately, if fiction resembles the games of childhood, it recalls too those experiences most often associated with the loss of childhood innocence. While some novels are longer than others (and committed novel readers always prefer the longer ones) all must end sooner or later, and with the end comes disenchantment, a sense that one has lost something that will exist now only in the form of a nostalgic memory.

To confront the problem of disenchantment is to uncover the central issues raised by the novel's form, for it is present at the beginnings of fictions as well as at their ends.

But a certain kind of sensibility can be made very uncomfortable by a recognition of the arbitrariness of physical facts and the inability to accept their finality. Take France, for example: France is shaped like a tea pot, and Italy is shaped like a boot. Well, okay. But the idea that that's the only way it's ever going to be, that they'll never be shaped like anything else—that can get to you after a while. Robert Louis Stevenson could never get used to the fact that people had two ears, funny-looking things, and eye-balls in their heads; he said it's enough to make you scream. I agree. And it seems to me that this emotion, which is a kind of metaphysical emotion, goes almost to the heart of what art is, at least some kinds of art, and this impulse to imagine alternatives to the world can become a driving impulse for writers. I confess that it is for me. So that what you really want to do is re-invent philosophy and the rest— make up your own whole history of the world.[1]

For John Barth the creative act is both the result and the expression of a radical philosophical freedom. Like his heroes he finds fulfillment in the discovery of new worlds. For him "reality is a drag," a "nice place to visit but you wouldn't want to live there" (11). And his use of "yarns," "elaborate lies" (4) and "flabbergasting plots" (4) is evidence enough that he feels free to take leave of reality. But the freedom one finds in the Barthian world of farcical adventure has two sides, one a blessing, the other a curse, for while it makes possible the search for the new and fantastic, it implies a rejection of the absolute validity of the old. Indeed, the explorative impulse is instigated by an emotional conviction of the absolute untenability of existence: "Who sets me goals to turn my back on" asks Burlingame in *The Sot-Weed Factor*, and then adds, "had I a home I'd likely leave it; a family alive or dead I'd likely scorn it, and wander a stranger in alien towns."[2]

Neither the novelist nor the hero is satisfied with reality. Both, like Don Quixote, sally forth in quest of adventure motivated by the will to alter reality or to imagine alternatives to it. Such a quest is filled with difficulties and dangers. To begin with, it implies a stubborn resistance not only to the pressures of society, its customs and usages, but also to what Ortega calls the "barbarous, brutal, mute, meaningless reality of things."[3] The freedom claimed by the novelist and in the novelistic world by his hero calls into being a series of realities which differ from

1. "John Barth: An Interview," *Wisconsin Studies in Contemporary Literature*, 6 (1965), 8.
2. Barth, *The Sot-Weed Factor* (New York, 1964), p. 145.
3. José Ortega y Gasset, *Meditations on Quixote* (New York, 1965), p. 145.

nature and with respect to which they are fictions. And from
the conflict between these planes emerges the dark side of the
novelistic enterprise, for it makes explicit the inevitable dis-
junction between imagination and perception. Creating the distance which separates the novelist's dreams from materiality is
a desire, the nature of which precludes the possibility of any
satisfaction. Barth, of course, accepts with wry amusement the
distance between willing-to-be and believing-that-one-already-is
and uses it to generate a literature of exhaustion. This is not the
case with some of his nineteenth-century predecessors. For them
the distance was no less important and far more painful. Indeed
it is the original impulse or basic theme in those American novels
we have come to call Romances and is in part responsible for
the eccentricities of form we associate with those books.

The works of Cooper, Poe, Melville, and Hawthorne are
nostalgic parodies of lost heroic and autonomous forms, the
creations of imaginations which have lost their innocence and
are seeking to replace it. As such they alternate between enchantment and disenchantment and focus persistently—even
morbidly—on their own origins. The effect of this focus, however, is not to emphasize beginnings but endings, for the in-
vestigation of sources leads to the discovery of the nature of the
illusion causing it to vanish with the quickness of a mirage. The
disenchantment can, of course, occur in various ways, with a
bang or a whimper. In *A. Gordon Pym* and *The Confidence
Man* the revelation that the literary work is founded on absurd
premises is properly followed by apocalypse while the enchanted
realms of *The House of the Seven Gables* and *The Last of the
Mohicans* are demystified by conclusions which subversively
ridicule them.

In these books, then, the novelists' primary burden is one of
simply sustaining the illusion. However, if "the sense of an
ending" is especially acute for these writers it is a problem they
share to some extent with all novelists. It is, for example, present
in *Don Quixote*, the ancestor of all novels, which, here, as
always, is exemplary. In chapter twenty of part I of *Don Quixote*

Sancho overcomes his fear of unknown sounds issuing from an impenetrable darkness and amuses his master with a story. It concerns a certain goatherd who, as a result of an unsuccessful love affair, has decided to leave the country. To do so he must cross a river. It is at this point that we pick up Sancho's tale:

"As he was looking about, he saw a fisherman alongside a boat so small that it would only hold one person and a goat, but, nevertheless, he spoke to the man, who agreed to take the shepherd and his flock of three hundred to the opposite bank. The fisherman would climb into the boat and row one of the animals across and then return for another, and he kept this up, rowing across with a goat and coming back, rowing across and coming back—Your Grace must be sure to keep count of the goats that the fisherman rowed across the stream, for if a single one of them escapes your memory, the story is ended and it will not be possible to tell another word of it.

"I will go on, then, and tell you that the landing place on the other side was full of mud and slippery, and it took the fisherman a good while to make the trip each time; but in spite of that, he came back for another goat, and another, and another—"

"Just say he rowed them across," said Don Quixote; "you need not be coming and going in that manner, or it will take you a year to get them all on the other side."

"How many have gone across up to now?" Sancho demanded.

"How the devil should I know?" replied Don Quixote.

"There, what did I tell you? You should have kept better count. Well, then, by God, the story's ended, for there is no going on with it."

"How can that be?" said the knight. "Is it so essential to know the exact number of goats that if I lose count of one of them you cannot tell the rest of the tale?"

"No, sir, I cannot by any means," said Sancho; "for when

> I asked your Grace to tell me how many goats had been
> rowed across and you replied that you did not know, at that
> very instant everything I was about to say slipped my
> memory. . . ."[4]

Sancho's story, quite clearly, depends upon something external
to itself. For it to continue there must be some contact with
empirical reality which furnishes its ground. Hence when Don
Quixote loses count of the goats, he robs the story of its supporting substance causing it immediately to vanish from Sancho's
memory. " 'I know that there is nothing more to be told,' "
Sancho says, " 'for it ends when you begin to lose count of the
number of goats that have crossed' " (151).

But the full implications of this abbreviated story are not
revealed until four chapters later when the knight is treated to
another story, an account by the Ragged One of his enormous
misfortunes.

> "If, gentlemen," he said to them then, "you would like me
> to tell you briefly how enormous the misfortunes are that
> I have suffered, you must promise that you will not inter-
> rupt with questions, or in any other manner, the thread of
> my mournful tale, for the moment you do it will come to
> an end."
> This remark reminded Don Quixote of the story his
> squire had told him, when the knight had been unable to
> remember the number of goats that had crossed the river
> and the tale had been left hanging in the air. (189)

In spite of the warning, Don Quixote is unable to restrain himself when the narrator introduces the subject of chivalry. He
interrupts; the story ends; and the Ragged One's madness, which
had been momentarily suspended, returns, and he attacks the
unsuspecting knight. Here, obviously, is a kind of fiction which

4. Miguel de Cervantes, *Don Quixote*, trans. Samuel Putnam (New York,
1949), pp. 150–151.

is the antithesis of Sancho's, for it implies an autonomous view of art. The story ends when its protective seal is broken and externality enters. Sancho's story, on the other hand, demands that the knight make it a part of his life, that his interest in the goats be equal to that of the man whose livelihood depends upon them. Its fragile structure is unable to tolerate the suggestion that it differs from life in any way, and it vanishes like a mirage when Don Quixote conceptualizes its details. The story of the Ragged One, however, resembles Don Pedro's puppet show, for in this case disenchantment follows the intrusion of reality. These fictive worlds depend for their existence on their isolation from real people and objects. With the intrusion of reality (which comes, ironically, as a result of the knight's being enchanted by the fiction) the magic of the fiction is neutralized, and everything undergoes a reduction of scale; the noble Cordenio is transformed once again into the Ragged Madman and the puppets are revealed as cardboard and sawdust.

These two stories bring together and dramatize the common problem of readers and novelists, for they demonstrate that the relationship between fictive worlds and externality is discontinuous. Neither a microcosmic mode based on analogous correspondences nor a mode based on mimetic representation can provide a secure ground for the fictive, with the result that both teller and auditor, writer and reader, are destined to be disenchanted by the realization that the realms of fiction and reality can never coincide. The search for such a ground together with an ironic realization that it will never be found provides, I believe, the shaping impulse of the Romance in nineteenth-century America. But it is in the work of Nathaniel Hawthorne that the quest appears in its most complicated form. Here the distance separating the realms of romance and reality is a thematization of the distance which Hawthorne always believed prevailed between himself and the shared world of others. Consequently, in his writing, what J. Hillis Miller calls the "ontological basis" of fictional form is particularly clear, thereby

giving it an exemplary quality which makes it especially interesting for the student of the American novel.[5]

## II

Hawthorne, no less than his romantic contemporaries, dreams of
a time of lost plenitude, of a "Golden Age, before mankind was
burthened with sin and sorrow. . . ."[6] His work is permeated
with a sense of nostalgia for lost origins and natural innocence
and with a Rousseauistic sense of the distance which separates
that lost time of immediateness from the present moment. But it
is in *The Marble Faun*, the last and darkest of his Romances,
that the theme of loss or absence receives its fullest treatment.
It is a book of precipices and chasms, of perspectives and dis-
tances. The characters are separated one from the other by a
"voiceless gulf" (113); each finds himself an "alien in the
world" with a "wholly unsympathetic medium betwixt himself
and those whom he yearns to meet" (92). Other people are
"within . . . view" and yet "beyond . . . reach" (66), enveloped by a "strange distance and unapproachableness" (89).
"They might gaze at one another from the opposite sides [of a
chasm], but without the possibility of ever meeting more . . ."
(207). Because there is an "insuperable gap" between "man
and man" (285), the primary need in the world is for some
form of mediation, some way of reaching across the "immeasurable distance" (410) which separates man from God, nature,
and his fellow man. *The Marble Faun* explores various alternatives for fulfilling that need, of finding some substitute for that
lost world of sympathetic involvement.

One of Hawthorne's models for his imaginings of that lost
happiness is natural man, a "beautiful creature, standing betwixt

5. See *The Form of Victorian Fiction* (Notre Dame, 1968), pp. 29–48.
6. *The Marble Faun*, eds. William Charvat and Roy Harvey Pearce
(Columbus, 1968), p. 84. Unless otherwise indicated all references to Hawthorne's works will be to the Ohio State edition. For convenience, the following abbreviations are used: SL, *The Scarlet Letter*; HSG, *The House of
the Seven Gables*; BR, *The Blithedale Romance*; MF, *The Marble Faun*.

man and animal, sympathizing with each, comprehending the speech of either race, and interpreting the whole existence of one to the other" (13). Speaking in the "original voice and utterance of the natural man" (248), which has since been "laid aside and forgotten by other men, now that words have been feebly substituted in the place of sign and symbol" (77–78), this creature is free of the burden of interpretation. "Before the sophistication of the human intellect formed what we now call language" (248), the world interpreted itself "without the aid of words" (258). In the place of language which seeks through endless analogies to mediate the distance which now exists between man and nature, there once existed a power of sympathy which brought all parts of existence together and allowed them to communicate instantly and completely: "he was believed to possess gifts by which he could associate himself with the wild things of the forests, and with the fowls of the air, and could feel a sympathy even with the trees, among which it was his joy to dwell" (235).

But as Donatello's adventures make clear, that state of sympathy which once united man to his milieu no longer exists. The young primitive loses that "power of sympathy" (320) which binds him to the natural world, and he finds it impossible to live the life of his forefathers. "He could not live their healthy life of animal spirits, in sympathy with Nature, and brotherhood with all that breathed around them. Nature, in beast, fowl, and tree, and earth, flood, and sky, is what it was of old; but sin, care, and self-consciousness have set the human portion of the world askew; and thus the simplest character is ever the surest to go astray" (239–240). Nor is it possible to discover the source or origin of that lost unity: "It would have been as difficult . . . to follow up the stream of Donatello's ancestry to its dim source, as travellers have found it, to reach the mysterious fountains of the Nile" (231). He who undertakes the journey "must needs follow his own guidance, and arrive nowhither at last" (231). Heralds trace the family to the "early morn of Christendom" but at that "venerable distance" give up "in despair."

Nevertheless, where the written record leaves the genealogy of Monte Beni, tradition takes it up and carries it back to the "sylvan life of Etruria" where it was "supposed to have had its origin" (232). But this explanation is "altogether mythical" (232) and at best can provide only a "shadowy and whimsical semblance of explanation for the likeness, which he, with Miriam and Hilda, had seen, or fancied, between Donatello and the Faun of Praxiteles" (232–233).

The unbridgeable distance between the present moment and that lost moment of beginning is implied, too, by the fact that Donatello seems to his companions to resemble, not a faun, but the representation of one, and that representation, moreover, is the expression of rather than the solution to a mystery. "Praxiteles has subtlely diffused, throughout his work, that mute mystery which so hopelessly perplexes us, whenever we attempt to gain an intellectual or a sympathetic knowledge of the lower forms of creation" (10). The meaning of the statue, in short, is in the form of a "riddle," an unanswered question, which is the sign of a primeval origin, lost forever, and available now only in the form of the "poet's reminiscence of a period when man's affinity with Nature was more strict, and his fellowship with every living thing more intimate and dear" (11).

Art, however, cannot provide a cure for the man lost in the alienation of his separation from his source. Hawthorne, it is well to remember, dramatizes the essential loss at the level of culture as well as of nature. Hilda's initial innocence is not the Arcadian unselfconsciousness of the Old World pagan and does not manifest itself in the form of an enjoyment of the "warm, senuous, earthly side of nature" (13). As a "daughter of the Puritans" (54), she is "perplex[ed]" by Donatello's apparent affinity with nature. Her innocence is the result of a special relationship with divinity; she looks at "humanity with angel's eyes" (53). She is a "poor, lonely girl, whom God has set here in an evil world, and given her only a white robe, and bid her wear it back to Him, as white as when she first put it on" (208). Her innocence, therefore, takes the form of a "silent sympathy" not with nature but with the paintings of the Old Masters, those products which are at once the expression of man's highest accomplishments and the "true symbol of the glories of the better world, where a celestial radiance will be inherent in all things and persons, and render each continually transparent to the sight of all" (304). By the use of a "guiding light of sympathy, she went straight to the central point, in which the Master had conceived his work. Thus, she viewed it, as it were, with his own eyes, and hence her comprehension of any picture was perfect" (57).

It is Hilda's sympathetic insight which lies behind her skill as a copyist, allowing her, as it does, to penetrate to the "spirit and essence" of the picture and to represent it on her own canvas. Moreover, she is able to use this same insight to open the eyes of others: even her "silent sympathy was so powerful that it drew your own along with it, endowing you with a second-sight that enabled you to see excellences with almost the depth and delicacy of her own perceptions" (62).

For Hilda, as for Donatello, interpretation at first imposes no problem. Other copyists work "entirely from the outside" and seek "only to reproduce the surface" (60), thereby representing the painting's superficial design but missing the inner core of meaning, while Hilda, on the other hand, is able to "interpret what the feeling is, that gives [the] picture such a mysterious force" (65).

Her interpretive powers derive, of course, from her special relationship to God—"I had only God to take care of me, and be my closest friend" (359)—a relationship which validates the religious themes of the "mighty Italian Masters" (336). The crime which she witnesses, however, destroys this relationship: "the terrible, terrible crime, which I have revealed to you, thrust itself between Him and me; so that I groped for Him in the darkness as it were, and found Him not—found nothing but a dreadful solitude, and this crime in the midst of it" (359). And with the loss of her special relationship to God comes a "dimness of insight," a loss of her powers of "self-surrender . . . and sympathy" (335). In the place of that lost sympathy, moreover, is substituted a "keen intellectual perception" which produces "irreverent" rather than sympathetic criticism, and Hilda grows "sadly critical." "Heretofore, her sympathy went deeply into a picture, yet seemed to leave a depth which it was inadequate to sound; now, on the contrary, her perceptive faculty penetrated the canvas like a steel probe, and found but a crust of paint over an emptiness" (341). Hilda's knowledge of Donatello and Miriam's crime makes an innocent interpretation impossible for her. The process of understanding a painting is now one which necessarily does violence to it. Even worse, the interpretive act which destroys the surface does not reveal a core of hidden meaning but instead an absence which implies that the "pictorial art" might be "altogether a delusion" (336) and her earlier response to it, therefore, the result of a mystification.

Hilda approaches, at this point, a vision of culture very similar to the one voiced by the more pessimistic Miriam. "The chasm was merely one of those orifices of that pit of blackness that lies beneath us, everywhere. The firmest substance of human happiness is but a thin crust spread over it, with just reality enough to bear up the illusive stage-scenery amid which we tread. It needs no earthquake to open the chasm. A footstep, a little heavier than ordinary, will serve; and we must step very daintily, not to break through the crust, at any moment" (161–162). From Miriam's Conradian perspective, human life seems permeated by an artificiality which robs it of durability and significance. Surrounded by the ruins of Rome she becomes aware of the "transitoriness of all things" (150) and comes to believe that her own culture is doomed to go the way of the cultures of the past, for in Rome one looks "through a vista of century beyond century—through much shadow, and a little sunshine—through barbarism and civilization, alternating with one another, like actors that have prearranged their parts. . . . Your own life is as nothing when compared with that immeasurable distance . . . (410).

The ruins of Rome, in fact, point to the same emptiness

which the disenchanted Hilda finds beneath the paint-covered canvases of the Old Masters and which the more bitter Miriam senses beneath everything. The ruins are not so much symbols of human accomplishment and survival as they are ominous reminders of man's mortality. For Hawthorne, material ruins always imply—often contain—decayed human ruins; hence Rome is a "sepulchral store-house of the past," (436) a "vast tomb" (24) containing a "long decaying corpse" (325). The forms of culture, in short, are as fragile as man himself, his memorials symbols of oblivion rather than a protection from it. The tombs of the Appian Way, for example, built by men "ambitious of everlasting remembrance" (420), have lost their human meaning and now, retaining nothing "except their massiveness," they are "alien from human sympathies" (419). Monuments originally designed as memorials perpetuating memories have become instead reminders of a lost significance, an abandoned cult, a vanished god, a forgotten family.[7]

For Hawthorne as for Ortega "culture is memories and promises, an irreversible past, a dreamed future,"[8] but for the American writer, the future as well as the past suggests neglect and desertion. Seen from the perspective of Rome's ruins, culture no longer represents the noble dream of the reconciliation of spirit and the world but stands as an example of the distance which separates man from his lost origins. "We who are born into the world's artificial system can never adequately know how little in our present state and circumstances is natural, and how much is the interpolation of the perverted mind and the heart of man. Art has become a second and stronger nature; she is a stepmother, whose crafty tenderness has taught us to despise the bountiful and wholesome ministrations of our true parent."[9]

---

7. I am indebted here to Jean Starobinski's discussion of ruins in *The Invention of Liberty 1700–1789*, trans. Bernard C. Swift (Geneva, 1964), p. 180.

8. Ortega, p. 145.

9. *The Complete Works of Nathaniel Hawthorne* (Cambridge, 1883), II, 279. All subsequent references to this edition of Hawthorne's work will be indicated in the text by the abbreviation CW.

Man, it seems, has managed to transform almost the entire earth from its natural state into something useful to him. Everything bears the "footprints of his wanderings and the results of his toil" (279). The most glaring example of this condition is the "thick, foggy, stifled elements of cities" (BR, 146). Here one can perceive most clearly the "marks and tear, and unrenewed decay, which distinguish the works of man from the growth of nature," for man's "artificial system . . . is implied in every lamp post and each brick of the houses" (CW, II, 281–282). And, of course, Rome, the Eternal City, expresses best this unnatural aspect of human life for here "whenever man has once hewn a stone, Nature forthwith relinquishes her right to it, and never lays her finger on it again. Age after age finds it bare and naked, in the barren sunshine, and leave it so" (MF, 165). Surrounded by the "smell of ruin, and decaying generations" (74) the resident of Rome is unable to find comfort anywhere. No aspect of human life remains meaningful: "all that is dreary in domestic life seems magnified and multiplied" (325). All social roles and levels seem equally ugly and corrupt.

But no matter how dark this critique seems at first to be, it does hold open a possibility of escape. Perhaps man can direct his labor in such a way that he works with rather than against nature. Certainly the grounds of the Villa Borghese seem to imply such an answer, for man has arranged the landscape so artfully here that his transforming powers seem to bring him closer to nature rather than to separate him from it. Here there is "enough of human care . . . bestowed long ago, and still bestowed, to prevent wildness from growing into deformity; and the result is an ideal landscape, a woodland scene, that seems to have been projected out of a poet's mind" (72). Here the "soft turf of a beautiful seclusion" (70) offers welcomed relief from the "stony-hearted streets" (75) of Rome. Here the "ancient dust, the mouldiness of Rome . . . the hard pavements, the smell of ruin, and decaying generations; the chill palaces, the convent-bells, the heavy incense of altars . . . [rise] from . . . con-

sciousness like a cloud . . ." (74). Consequently, people of all
social ranks and nationalities may meet and celebrate their
shared freedom. Because each person seems equal to the rest,
they are able to participate in a "sylvan dance" which celebrates
a new transparency and total reciprocity:

> Here, as it seemed, had the Golden Age come back again,
> within the precincts of this sunny glade; thawing mankind
> out of their cold formalities; releasing them from irksome
> restraint; mingling them together in such childlike gaiety,
> that new flowers . . . sprang up beneath their footsteps.
> (88)

Unfortunately, however, such visions of harmony are the result of a mystification produced by the hallucinating air of a
present freed from its ties to past and future. " 'Tomorrow will
be time enough to come back to my reality,' " Miriam decides.
" 'Is the past so indestructible?—the future so immitigable' "
(82)? And as she gives herself up to the "magic" (87) of the
moment, reality seems transformed into fantasy. But this enchantment is no more than a delusion. The grounds of the
"Suburban Villa" do not duplicate the landscape of the unfallen
world. Just the reverse is true: "Scattered here and there, with
careless artifice, stand old alters, bearing Roman inscriptions.
. . . But even these sportive imitations, wrought by man in
emulations of what Time has done to temples and palaces, are
perhaps centuries old, and, beginning as illusions, have grown
to be venerable in sober earnest" (72–73). As a result of this
artifice, the grounds are "pensive, lovely, dreamlike, enjoyable,
and sad" (73). And adding to the "dreamlike melancholy that
haunts the spot" (73) is malaria, a curse which insures that it
will never be the "home-scenery of any human being" (73),
for it can be safely visited only in winter and early spring.

Initially, then, the grounds were the product of a vision which
sought a partial reconciliation of man and nature through the
employment of a mild irony. They were designed not as a
Quixotic attempt to recover the moment of lost plenitude but in

an attempt to come to terms with that loss by reflecting on it. The result is the creation of a place where man seeks partially to alleviate his alienation by indulging in a gentle nostalgia for the lost unity. His "sportive" imitations of the effects of time seem to place him outside those effects and to protect him from them. This possibility, however, is put into question by the narrator's description of the final moments of the Sylvan dance.

> Or it [the dance] was like the sculptured scene on the front and sides of a sarcophagus, where, as often as any other device, a festive procession mocks the ashes and white bones that are treasured up, within. You might take it for a marriage-pageant; but, after awhile, if you look attentively at these merry-makers, following them from end to end of the marble coffin, you doubt whether their gay movement is leading them to a happy close. . . . Always, some tragic incident is shadowed forth, or thrust sidelong into the spectacle; and when once it has caught your eye, you can look no more at the festal portions of the scene, except with reference to this one slightly suggested doom and sorrow. (88–89)

Here art clearly is relegated to the status of a mystified defensive strategy which seeks to avoid the temporal predicament that renders man's life meaningless. Like the succession of discontinuous movements of the sylvan dance—"each vanished with the moment that gave it birth, and was effaced from memory by another" (85)—the figures on the sarcophagus seem to imply the supremacy of art over nature through the transcendence of the effects of temporal duration. The "unweariable steps" (88) of the dancers mock the "Demon of Weariness" (336) who haunts the streets of Rome in the same way that the figures on the sarcophagus mock the "ashes and white bones" it contains. However, at the very moment man is celebrating his powers of renewal, the destructive powers of time are secretly at work. The dance is moving toward its conclusion as inevitably as the figures in the marriage-pageant are toward the "ashes and white bones" they at first seem to transcend. From the point of view of death all human activity has the "character of fantasy" (90).

> The spell being broken, it was now only that old tract of pleasure-ground, close by the people's gate of Rome; a tract where crimes and calamities of ages, the many battles, blood recklessly poured out, and deaths of myriads, have corrupted all the soil, creating an influence that makes the air deadly to human lungs. (90)

The "suburban gardens," then, can offer no real escape from the threatening atmosphere of Rome. The "enchanted ground" (75) at best can provide no more than a moment's mystification, and the disenchantment which inevitably follows it invalidates the mildly ironic vision which produced the grounds in the first place. The pleasant nostalgia for a lost relationship between man and nature which the grounds are intended to evoke is replaced at the moment of disenchantment with a painful intersubjective problem.

> A moment afterwards [after the appearance of Miriam's model], Donatello was aware that she had retired from the dance. He hastened towards her and flung himself on the grass, beside the stone-bench on which Miriam was sitting. But a strange distance and unapproachableness had all at once enveloped her; and, though he saw her within reach of his arm, yet the light of her eyes seemed as far off as that of a star; nor was there any warmth in the melancholy smile with which she regarded him. (89)

Donatello and Miriam have not been able to use the natural world to bridge the "great chasm" (207) which separates them. He, it is true, is the representation of a condition which once existed between man and nature and seems able to identify himself with the nonself, but that sense of identification can never lead him toward another self. Indeed, it is his total commitment to another which destroys his sense of identification with nature. Unfortunately, however, an awareness of the distance between nature and self does not insure that interpersonal contacts will be easier to establish, although this is Donatello and Miriam's initial assumption. Their shared glance, which condemns the Model, seems to have established a "new sympathy" which "annihilated all other ties" and which "knits" their "heart-strings together" (175).

> "I feel it Miriam," said Donatello. "We draw one breath; we live one life!"
> "Only yesterday," continued Miriam; "nay, only a short half-hour ago, I shivered in icy solitude. No friendship, no sisterhood, could come near enough to keep the warmth within my heart. In an instant, all is changed. There can be no more loneliness." (175)

Like their experience in the Suburban Villa, however, this sense of wholeness is a delusion, the result of a "moment of rapture" which ends with the appearance of the corpse of the victim. At this point Miriam can no longer "bring his mind into sympathy with hers" (197), and her words of love and devotion are met with a "heavy silence" (198).

But if human separateness cannot be overcome by either distancing oneself from the destructive forces of civilization or by violating its laws of restraint, perhaps the forms and usages of civilization can themselves be used to mediate between isolated selves. Miriam and Donatello explore this possibility when they participate in the "scenic and ceremonial" (436) carnival, near the end of the novel. Having failed in their earlier attempts to transform themselves into Faun and Nymph, they adorn themselves with masks and costumes and become "The Peasant and Contadina" (439). For in the carnival there is a "sympathy of nonsense; a true and genial brotherhood and sisterhood, based on the honest purpose . . . of being foolish, all together" (439). Perhaps the "sympathetic mirth" (438) of others, the "sympathetic exhilaration of so many people's cheerfulness" (324) will enable them to bridge the distance which separates them. In contrast to the magic of the Sylvan Dance, which thaws the participants out of their cold formalities, and mingles them together in a "childlike gaiety" (88), the spell of the carnival seeks to unite men by recognizing and exaggerating the distance which separates them from nature and each other. Here one finds "orang-outangs; bear headed, bull-headed, and dog-headed individuals; faces that would have been human, but for their enormous noses . . . and all other imaginable kind of monstrosity and exaggeration" (446). These disguises hardly represent nostalgic attempts to recover that lost resemblance between man and nature. Rather they imply a comic recognition of the differences between the two realms and are an implicit affirmation of the superiority of the human. Men are brought closer together when any assertion of a resemblance between the human and natural is made to seem untenable. In a similar way the other costumes and masks, which from the point of view of unclothed nature imply human separateness and civilized restraint, in the context of the carnival suggest relief from the burdens of class and profession and protection from the dangers of the threatening gaze of others, for they allow individuals to form a "mad, merry stream of human life" (439).

However, the carnival, too, is the product of a deceitful magic which covers a "stern and black reality" with "fanciful thoughts" (428), and the "sympathetic mirth" (438) which it generates, is "like our self-deceptive pretense of jollity at a threadbare joke" (437). Hence, the sugar-plums which the participants throw at one another "were concocted mostly of lime, with a grain of oat or some other worthless kernel in the midst" (439), and the carnival flowers, which have been "gathered and tied up by sordid hands," are "wilted," "muddy," and "defiled . . . with the wicked filth of Rome" (440). The carnival, in short, is the "emptiest of mockeries" (437), composed of a host of absurd figures who in "pretending to sympathize" (446) with one another only make more obvious the absence of any real sympathy. Miriam, a participant in the "sad frolic" (446), hides a "tear-stained face" beneath her mask and speaks with a "profound sadness in her tone" (448). Appropriately, she and

Donatello are arrested by the authorities at the height of the revelry, and their arrest is misinterpreted as "some frolic of the Carnival, carried a little too far" (451).

The failure of mediated relations which the carnival episode dramatizes is implied, too, in the activities of the Catholic Church. Like the carnival, it is "traditionary not actual" (436) and is "alive this present year, only because it has existed through centuries gone by" (436). It stands, therefore, as another manifestation of the theme of absence, for it has lost the "dignity and holiness of its origins" (345). In the place of "general medicaments" (345) for the sick soul, it can offer only "cordials" (344) and "sedatives" (345). Saint Peter's Cathedral contains no "cure . . . for a sick soul, but it would make an admirable atmospheric hospital for sick bodies" (369). This tendency to reduce the spiritual to the physical, moreover, leads to a more serious and more deceptive reduction, the transformation of a theocentric relationship into an interpersonal one.[10]

> Hilda saw peasants, citizens, soldiers, nobles, women with bare heads, ladies in their silks, entering the churches, individually, kneeling for moments, or for hours, and directing their inaudible devotions to the shrine of some Saint of their own choice. In his hallowed person, they felt themselves possessed of an own friend in Heaven. They were too humble to approach the Deity directly. Conscious of their unworthiness, they asked the mediation of their sympathizing patron, who, on the score of his ancient martyrdom, and after many ages of celestial life, might venture to talk with the Divine Presence almost as friend with friend. (346–347)

The sympathy generated by such a relationship is as much a mystification as that produced by the sylvan dance and the carnival. Donatello receives the "bronze Pontiff's benediction"

---

10. I am indebted here to Paul de Man's discussion of a similar reduction in Coleridge's thought. See "The Rhetoric of Temporality" in *Interpretation: Theory and Practice*, ed. Charles Singleton (Baltimore, 1969), p. 182.

(315) as he seems by his "look and gesture" (324) to approve of the young Italian's union with Miriam, only to be separated from her and imprisoned by the "priestly rulers" (465) of Rome. Similarly, Hilda, seeking relief from her troubled conscience, receives the benediction of the old Priest who heard her confession and later becomes a "prisoner" in the convent of the Sacre-Coeur (466) watched over by that same priest. The forms of the church, in other words, no longer derive authority from something beyond them; its "mighty machinery" (345) is managed by human engineers, and it operates in a world where things have lost their analogical sense. High and low no longer indicate the direction of salvation or damnation; the Palazzo del Torre does not "sink into the earth" (400) when the lamp of the Virgin is extinguished, as a priest had insisted that it would. Hilda's tower is no more symbolic than Donatello's. One is a "dove-cote" (54), the other an "owl-tower" (252), one a shrine of the Virgin, the other a "strong-hold of times long past" (215), but both are "square," "lofty," and "massive" (51, 214), and Kenyon, standing in one tower, is reminded of the other "turret that ascended into the sky of the summer afternoon" (264). The point is, of course, that neither Hilda's tower with the shrine and doves nor Donatello's with the crucifix and death's head allows them to avoid sin or to deal with its consequences. Both structures mock man's "feeble efforts to soar upward" (256), for they imply the absence of any kind of spatial hierarchy. Donatello finds relief only when he leaves his ancestral tower for the crowded market place of Perugia, and Hilda comes "down from her old tower, to be herself enshrined and worshipped as a household Saint, in the light of her husband's fireside" (461).

The actions of the fallen innocents, then, seem to imply that the problem of distance can only be handled if it is first secularized. Perhaps the other attempts to overcome it fail because it is seen as a lack, an emptiness, the result of a loss rather than an indication of "human promise" (461). Perhaps what man has to do is to renounce the towers, and the ceremonies of the old world, which in seeking to overcome absence only succeed in signifying it, and turn with Hilda and Kenyon toward the new world.

Still, Praxiteles' classical theme is apparently also Hawthorne's; the book, his Marble Faun, provoking mysteries and riddles rather than a revelation of Donatello's true nature. His notebook entries clearly indicate that the book begins in the form of an interpretation of Praxiteles' statue.[11] Nevertheless there is evidence in the novel which suggests that his interest shifts from the meaning of the statue to the problem of interpretation itself. Donatello, to be sure, owes his existence to the sculptured figure and is in some sense an interpretation of it, but the "real" source of *The Marble Faun*, as the narrator is careful to point out, is not the Praxiteles Faun but Kenyon's bust of Donatello.

> Most spectators mistake it [Donatello's bust] for an unsuccessful attempt towards copying the features of the Faun of Praxiteles. One observer in a thousand is conscious of something more, and lingers long over this mysterious face, departing from it, reluctantly, and with many a glance thrown backward. What perplexes him is the riddle that he sees propounded there. . . . It was the contemplation of this imperfect portrait of Donatello that originally interested us in his history, and impelled us to elicit from Kenyon what he knew of his friend's adventures. (381)

The meaning of *The Marble Faun*, then, is not to be found outside itself residing in a source which generated it. Kenyon's "difficult office" is to study Donatello's characteristics and "interprete them to all men" (270), but his interpretation does not lead to a revelation of meaning but simply generates another interpretation: the narrator's. The novel in this sense is its own source, the narrator's verbal interpretation of the sculptural interpretation of one of his fictional characters by another. This reflexiveness has the effect of creating a realm which has no apparent beginning outside itself but seems made of words

11. See Claude M. Simpson's discussion of the notebook material in the "Introduction" to the Ohio State edition of *The Marble Faun*, pp. xix–xxiii.

whose meaning depends not on some reality which lies behind them but on other words. Hence the interpretive process seems an endless one with one interpretation leading always to another. Near the end of the novel, for example, Kenyon, whose interest in Donatello is the source of the narrator's, offers an interpretation of the meaning of his friend's adventures.

It seems the moral of his story, that human beings, of Donatello's character, compounded especially for happiness, have no longer any business on earth, or elsewhere. Life has grown so sadly serious, that such men must change their nature, or else perish, like the antediluvian creatures that required, as the condition of their existence, a more summer-like atmosphere than ours. (459–460)

Hilda, however, who is "hopeful and happy-natured" (460), rejects his interpretation as too dark, and Kenyon, who loves her, willingly abandons it and offers instead a reading based on Miriam's interpretation of Donatello.

"Then, here is another; take your choice!" said the sculptor, remembering what Miriam had recently suggested, in reference to the same point. "He perpetrated a great crime; and his remorse, gnawing into his soul, has awakened it; developing a thousand high capabilities, moral and intellectual, which we never should have dreamed of asking for, within the scanty compass of the Donatello whom we knew.". . .
"Sin has educated Donatello, and elevated him. Is Sin, then. . . like Sorrow, merely an element of human education, through which we struggle to a higher and purer state that we could otherwise have attained. Did Adam fall, that we might ultimately rise to a far loftier Paradise than his?" (460)

But Hilda, "shocked . . . beyond words, by a theory which makes a mockery . . . not only of all religious sentiment, but of moral law" (460), rejects this interpretation more emphatically than the first. At this point Kenyon abandons his interpretive quest altogether, faces the meaninglessness of his exiled condition, and looks to Hilda to provide a ground for his existence.

> I never did believe it [his interpretation]! But the mind wanders wild and wide; and, so lonely as I live and work, I have neither pole-star above, nor light of cottage-windows here below, to bring me home. Were you my guide, my counsellor, my inmost friend, with that white wisdom which clothes you as with a celestial garment, all would go well. Oh, Hilda, guide me home. (460–461)

Here, as at the end of *The House of the Seven Gables*, the enchantment of love is offered in the place of an unequivocal interpretation of the novel's meaning. Hilda does not solve Kenyon's problems but she smooths them away, leading him to project on the rest of the world the light of his own happiness.[12] To him the world now seems full of "human promise," and he plans to turn his back on the problem of the meaning of Donatello's adventures and return to his "own land" (461). The narrator, however, puts the lovers' happiness into question by pointing to the possibility that at their return they may discover that their "native air has lost its invigorating quality, and that life has shifted its reality to the spot where we have deemed ourselves only temporary residents" (461). The narrator recognizes, in other words, that the idea of a *home*, a "house and moderate garden-spot of one's own" (HSG, 156), is as much an ideal out of reach, as much "beyond the scope of man's actual possessions" (MF, 73) as is the possibility of an unequivocal interpretation.[13]

12. In *Septimius Felton*, describing the effect of Rose on Septimius' troubled mind, Hawthorne writes: "She reconciled him, in some secret way, to life as it was, to imperfection, to decay; without any help from her intellect, but through the influence of her character, she seemed, not to solve, but to smooth away, problems that troubled him; merely by being, by womanhood, by simplicity, she interpreted God's ways to him . . ." (CW, XI, 287–288).

13. For a discussion of the theme of homelessness in Hawthorne's work see my essay, "Hawthorne's Castle in the Air: Form and Theme in *The House of the Seven Gables*," ELH, 38 (June, 1971), 294–317.

The ending of *The Marble Faun*, then, seems to validate Kenyon's earlier assertion that the "seven-branched golden candlestick, the holy candlestick of the Jews," which is capable of providing the "whole world . . . the illumination which it needs" (370–371), is lost forever. Nor can the flickering light of the domestic "fireside" (461) serve as an adequate substitute, for it is not capable of illuminating the "sevenfold sepulchral gloom" (462) cast by the Etruscan bracelet which Miriam sends Hilda as a bridal gift.

Still there is the possibility that the narrator may know more than any of his characters. Although his position is not the privileged one of the "disembodied listener" (HSG, 30) of *The House of the Seven Gables*, since he is at times *seen* as well as *seeing*, he is able to cross the distance which separates Kenyon, Miriam, Hilda and Donatello one from the other, to view the conduct of each "from his own point of view, or from any side-point" (385). Perhaps this ability will allow him to give a final and complete interpretation of Donatello's adventures. Unfortunately, however, the narrator knows little more about his characters than they know of each other. For example, he overhears part of a private conversation between Miriam and her mysterious Model which takes place in the solitude of the Borghese Grove, but the fragments which he hears make their relationship not less but more inscrutable.

Owing, it may be, to this moral estrangment—this chill remoteness of their position—there have come to us but a few vague whisperings of what passed in Miriam's interview, that afternoon, with the sinister personage who had dogged her footsteps ever since the visit to the catacomb. In weaving these mystic utterances into a continuous scene, we undertake a task resembling, in its perplexity, that of gathering up and piecing together the fragments of a letter, which has been torn and scattered to the winds. Many words of deep significance—many entire sentences, and those possibly the most important ones—have flown too far, on the winged breeze, to be recovered. If we insert our own

conjectural amendments, we perhaps give a purport ut-
terly at variance with the true one. Yet, unless we attempt
something in this way, there must remain an unsightly gap,
and a lack of continuousness and dependence in our narrative; so that it would arrive at certain inevitable catas-
trophes without due warning of their imminence. (92–93)

Hawthorne's use in this passage of the image of his narrative as
a woven tapestry raises a number of interesting interpretive
problems.[14] The "tapestry," although "woven with the best of
the artist's skill, and cunningly arranged with a view to the
harmonious exhibition of its colours" (455), does not possess a
pattern of meaning which is immediately accessible to the
reader. Its "threads" (455) are "Fragmentary Sentences" (92),
signs of a meaning scattered, dispersed, and lost forever. The
novelist himself is not able to begin with an unequivocal core
of meaning but must be content with something that is already
an interpretation, and an incomplete one at that. His task is that
of piecing together "fragments of a letter" parts of which are
gone forever, a task whose very nature precludes the possibility
of the emergence of any final meaning. Consequently, the narrator's interpretation of his text, when he finally offers it, is in
the form of a plea to the reader to abandon the interpretive
enterprise altogether.

The Gentle Reader, we trust, would not thank us for one
of those minute elucidations, which are so tedious, and,
after all, so unsatisfactory, in clearing up the romantic
mysteries of a story. He is too wise to insist upon looking
closely at the wrong side of the tapestry, after the right one
has been sufficiently displayed to him, woven with the
best of the artist's skill. . . . If any brilliant or beautiful, or
even tolerable, effect have been produced, this pattern of

14. For two related discussions of the image of the literary text as a woven
cloth see J. Hillis Miller, *Thomas Hardy: Distance and Desire* (Cambridge,
1970), pp. viii–xvi and "The Interpretation of *Lord Jim*" in *The Interpretation of Narrative: Theory and Practice*, ed. Morton W. Bloomfield (Cambridge, 1970), pp. 211–215.

kindly Readers will accept it at its worth, without tearing
the web apart, with the idle purpose of discovering how its
threads have been knit together. . . . (455)

To seek the meaning of his tapestry, Hawthorne implies here,
is to violate it in some way, to tear it, perhaps, change it. And
yet, an eye which never penetrates the surface of a text is bound
to miss that "indefinable nothing, that inestimable something,
that constitutes [its] life and soul" (60). It is this "inner mystery
of a work of genius" (391) which is the source of both its
beauty and value. Moreover, the "beautiful . . . effect" which
the writer seeks to produce invites the very violence he deplores,
for it is that "gleam of beauty" which "induce[s] the beholder
to start unravelling it" (306). Adding to this sense of contradiction is the realization that Hawthorne no longer believes in
the "Gentle Reader" to whom the narrator addresses himself
here. That "all sympathizing critic" (1), that "Gentle, Kind,
Benevolent, Indulgent, and most Beloved and Honored Reader"
who "once did exist" has now "withdrawn to the Paradise of
Gentle Readers. . . . If I find him at all it will probably be
under some mossy grave-stone, inscribed with a half-obliterated
name, which I shall never recognize" (2). Gone now is that
"apprehensive sympathy" (2) which once bound writer and
reader together and in its place that same "unsympathetic
medium" which prevents the narrator from fully knowing his
characters.

The death of the Gentle Reader is the equivalent, for the
narrator, of the loss of sympathy experienced by Donatello and
Hilda, a loss which in his case as in theirs complicates the
problem of authorship. He, too, is an exile who depends on
"ceremony" (2) to replace that lost unity and looks to "ruin"
(3) as the source of his creativity.

In spite of these similarities, however, the problem of sympathy is more complicated for the narrator than for his characters. For Hawthorne, as we have seen, it is the power of sympathy which draws the things of his world together. Happiness

for him is that condition where men find themselves united to nature and other men by the waves of sympathy which flow through them all. At these moments of union they feel themselves not only a part of the "surging stream of human sympathy" (HSG, 165), "mankind's warm and sympathetic life" (CW, XI, 287) but "in sympathy with nature as well, in brotherhood with all that breathed around them" (MF, 235). But Hawthorne gives this familiar eighteenth century theme a peculiar twist by making sympathy the primary force in a world to which he does not belong.[15] In his case a peculiar preference for solitude combines with "some witchcraft or other"[16] to break his tie with the chain of humanity. Like Wakefield, he senses that it is his "unprecedented fate to retain his original share of human sympathies, and to be still involved in human interests, while he had lost his reciprocal influence on them" (CW, I, 162). The peculiar circumstances of his youth, he believed, had conditioned him in such a way that he could exist without the "oxygen of sympathy" required to sustain the lives of ordinary men.

> But I am of somewhat sterner stuff and tougher fibre . . . and the dark seclusion—the atmosphere without any oxygen of sympathy—in which I spent all the years of my youthful manhood, has enabled me to do almost as well without as with it.[17]

Hawthorne, apparently, does not require the reciprocity which sustains the worlds of other men. As a result of his own peculiar circumstances the waves of sympathy which flow from

15. Compare, for example, Georges Poulet's discussion of the theme of sympathy in Rousseau. See *The Metamorphoses of the Circle*, trans. Carley Dawson and Elliott Coleman (Baltimore, 1966), pp. 70–90.

16. "By some witchcraft or other," Hawthorne writes to Longfellow in 1837, "for I cannot assign any reasonable why and wherefore—I have been carried apart from the main current of life, and find it impossible to get back again." Letter dated Salem, June 4th, 1837 in *The Portable Hawthorne*, ed. Malcolm Cowley (New York, 1969), p. 669.

17. *The English Notebooks*, ed. Randall Stewart (New York, 1962), p. 256.

the center of his sphere are not the expression of personal or particular feelings which require a sympathetic response, but a sympathetic description of human nature in general. "And when people think that I am pouring myself out in a tale or an essay, I am merely telling what is common to human nature, not what is peculiar to myself. I sympathise with them—not they with me."[18] Fiction, then, is a way of opening "an intercourse with the world" (CW, I, 16) only in the sense that it is an appeal to "sensibilities . . . such as are diffused among us all. So far as I am a man of really individual attributes I veil my face; nor am I . . . one of those supremely hospitable people who serve up their own hearts, delicately fried, with brain sauce, as a tidbit for their beloved public" (CW, II, 44). Hence in "The Custom House" he rejects the practice of those writers who "indulge themselves in such confidential depths of revelation as could fittingly be addressed, only and exclusively, to the one heart and mind of perfect sympathy; as if the printed book, thrown at large on the wide world, were certain to find out the divided segment of the writer's own nature, and complete the circle of his existence by bringing him into communication with it" (SL, 3–4). Still, as Hawthorne recognizes, communication demands that the "speaker stand in some true relation with his audience" (4). Therefore he creates a fictional surrogate for himself out of the superficial and surface aspects of his life which are already known by the "most indifferent observer" (CW, III, 385).

There is no harm, but, on the contrary, good, in arraying some of the ordinary facts of life in a slightly idealized and artistic guise. I have taken facts which relate to myself, because they chance to be nearest at hand, and likewise are my own property. And, as for egotism, a person, who has been burrowing, to his utmost ability, into the depths of our common nature, for the purpose of psychological ro-

18. *Love Letters of Nathaniel Hawthorne 1841–1863* (Chicago, 1907). Letter dated Salem, Feb. 27th, 1842, p. 80.

mance,—and who pursues his researches in that dusky
region, as he needs must, as well by the tact of sympathy as
by the light of observation—will smile at incurring such an
imputation in virtue of a little preliminary talk about his
external habits, his abode, his casual associates, and other
matters entirely upon the surface. These things hide the
man, instead of displaying him. You must make quite another kind of inquest, and look through the whole range of
his fictitious characters, good and evil, in order to detect any
of his essential traits. (CW, III, 386)

This passage expresses Hawthorne's curious ambivalence
towards detachment which constitutes his point of departure
and determines his relation to the world. On the one hand, his
interest in other people distinguishes him from the romantic
recluse who withdraws from the world to carry on an exclusive
commerce with himself, but, on the other, his personal peculiari-
ties set him apart from those who idealize the shared intimacy
of life with other people. For him the "most desirable mode of
existence . . . [is] that of a spiritualized Paul Pry, hovering invisible round man and woman, witnessing their deeds, reaching
into their hearts, borrowing brightness from their felicity and
love and shade from their sorrow, and retaining no emotion peculiar to himself" (CW, I, 220). The perfect state of existence
is one where man is free from the burdens of both the subjective
and objective worlds. Paul Pry is not only invisible; he is also
without any emotion peculiar to himself. The lights and shadows
of his "inward sky"[19] are borrowed from the people whose lives
he is able to enter. There is no doubt that Hawthorne possessed
a remarkable faculty for "throwing [himself] mentally into situations foreign to [his] own, and detecting with a cheerful eye, the
desirable circumstances of each" (CW, I, 394). Both his wife
and son remark on his ability to make "himself all things to all

19. *Love Letters of Nathaniel Hawthorne 1839-1841* (Chicago, 1907).
Letter dated Boston, May 19th, 1840, p. 192.

men" (CW, XI, 469),[20] and he endows many of the artist figures in his fiction with this important quality. Coverdale, for example, speaks of his impulse "to live in other lives, or to endeavor— by generous sympathies, delicate intuitions . . .—[to bring] my human spirit into manifold accordance with companions whom God assigned me," to "melt into the scene, as a wreath of vapor melts into a larger cloud" (BR, 160, 207).

As Hawthorne recognizes, however, the ideal circumstances described in the Paul Pry passage are impossible. Man is not invisible; nor is he able completely to empty himself, to become a pure consciousness of others. He has a body which is at once his point of view upon the world and at the same time the object which makes him visible to other people. Consequently, if he is to approach the spiritualized Paul Pry ideal, he must find a way to watch others without being seen himself. His attempt to accomplish such a goal is expressed by the recurrent motif of spying in his fiction, and it is also present in his idea of the literary text as a veil which conceals more than it reveals. Images of spying and concealment, however, suggest a world where human relations are based on distance and mutual distrust and hence discredit the idea that the literary text has a manifest meaning which the sympathetic reader will immediately and fully intuit. Such a world requires that the meaning of a text, like the meaning of the mysterious manuscript which Septimius Felton works so hard to "decipher and interpret" (CW, XI, 336) be "lock[ed] up for safety in a sort of coffer, of which diligence and insight should be the key, and the keen intelligence with which the meaning was sought should be the test of the seeker's being entitled to possess the secret treasure" (337). The hidden

---

20. Julian Hawthorne wrote of his father: "Now Hawthorne, both by nature and by training, was of a disposition to throw himself imaginatively into the shoes (as the phrase is) of whatever person happened to be his companion. For the time being, he would seem to take their point of view and to speak their language . . ." (*Hawthorne and His Wife* [Cambridge, 1884], I, 88). See also Sophia's discussion of this same ability in Rose Hawthorne Lathrop's *Memories of Hawthorne* (Boston, 1897) pp. 198–200.

meaning will not resemble the superficial, surface one, which in Septimius' manuscript (and in some of Hawthorne's fiction) takes the form of a "digested synopsis of some old philosopher's wise rules of conduct" (337). This is not to say, however, that the hidden meaning will be "discordant with rules of social morality" (337). As a matter of fact, the "truth" which Septimius finally discovers does not manifest itself as a kernel of meaning but in the form of "something left out" (337), an invisible frost which makes the "buds of happiness curl up like tender leaves . . ." and chills the "heart . . . out of the reader" (338). A similar chill permeates the mysterious world of *The Marble Faun*, a chill which derives from Hawthorne's recognition that sympathetic communication is impossible. The literary enterprise resembles the work of the disillusioned copyist. It is derivative, the product of a probing interpretive act which focuses on something which is already an interpretation, and it generates in the reader not a gentle and sympathetic interest but a desire to question and probe—that is to say interpret. Hence, the nature of the text prevents any illusory identification with a mystified world and puts an end to the possibility of a disenchantment which takes the form of a nostalgic memory of a happy moment of mystification. For Hawthorne, at this point, writing and criticism are identical in that both involve hard work and lead, finally, to despair. The games of childhood have become the sign of the exiled adult.

EDGAR A. DRYDEN
*State University of New York
at Buffalo*

# DAY-DREAM AND FACT: THE IMPORT
## OF *THE BLITHEDALE ROMANCE*

### I

Much of the difficulty we have with *The Blithedale Romance* inevitably derives from the fact of its matrix in Hawthorne's participation in the Brook Farm venture. Granting even his prefatory disclaimers about the relationship of the romance to its "origins" in his experience, we still must insist that the book is an "anti-utopia" and consequently feel obliged to demand of it that it should have qualities of exact and exacting socio-cultural observations appropriate to that "genre"; that it should be less melodramatic and more satirical; that its first-person narrator must be either altogether in control of his narrative or altogether its victim—not, as is the actual case, somewhere between the two postures. Anti-utopian writing, we conclude, should not be all *that* ambiguous. And in our interpretations of *The Blithedale Romance* we tend on the one hand to second-guess Hawthorne and to demonstrate how much better the book would be were it not so ambiguous in its anti-utopianism, or, on the other, to strain to make a case out for it not as an anti-utopia but as an almost perfected romance of protest against things as they were and are—with Coverdale, not Zenobia, the real suicide in the whole affair.

Surely it is crucial for *The Blithedale Romance* that it grows out of Hawthorne's Brook Farm experience. What is centrally at issue—or should be—is his particular interpretation of that experience and his rendering of the interpretation, his sense of the "utopianism" he was doubting, not ours. One way into understanding what he was about is to recall the history of his labors on the text as that history helps clarify the role that his

Brook Farm experience played in its conception and composition.[1]

Hawthorne had finished writing *The House of the Seven
Gables* in late January, 1851, did little or no writing for the
next six months, began to worry about a proper subject for his
next book in July and (so his correspondence indicates) abruptly
made up his mind. For he wrote to a friend, "When I write
another romance, I shall take the Community for a subject, and
shall give some of my experiences and observations at Brook
Farm." Still, he did not set himself to writing until November
and subsequently recorded in his notebook that he wrote the
last page of the book he came, after some hesitation, to call
*The Blithedale Romance* on April 30, 1852, finished the preface
on May 1, and began to see proof on May 14. On May 2 he had
sent the manuscript to his friend E. P. Whipple, asking for
advice. It appears likely that Whipple advised Hawthorne to
soften the original ending, so as to give it that measure of "geni-
ality" which he—like Hawthorne's publisher Fields—seems always to have felt Hawthorne's work needed. What is of interest
in all this is the evidence it suggests of Hawthorne's abiding
professionalism; needing money, he was willing to take mar-
keting advice from those whom he trusted, while still insisting
that he must stick to his own last. Meantime Fields was in
England and undertook to arrange for publication of *The Blithedale Romance* there; he was successful in negotiating with
Chapman and Hall, and sold the British rights for 200 pounds,
a sum much higher than Hawthorne expected. The English
edition appeared shortly before July 7; the American edition on
July 14. The book sold well at first; but subsequent impressions
were small in number. In all, after its initial flurry, the book
was no great seller. Fields, particularly disappointed, at one point
wrote, "I hope Hawthorne will give us no more Blithedales."

One guesses—and there is a good deal of evidence to make
the guess worthwhile—that the book sold well initially not only

1. What follows derives from my historical introduction to *The Blithedale
Romance*, Centenary Edition, III, xvii–xxvi.

because it was Hawthorne's but because its first readers expected
—as do its present ones—an insider's account of Brook Farm and
its inhabitants. But things just did not work out that way.
Hawthorne seems to have begun with the intention of sticking
fairly closely to his recollections of Brook Farm, but to have
gradually moved away from these recollections in order to give
himself the freedom which his gift for the Romance demanded
of him. As noted, his first intention was to "take the Community
for a subject." A notebook entry of July 30, 1851, shows that he
had borrowed some volumes of Fourier, "with a view to my next
Romance." The matter was clear enough to Fields, who wrote
Bayard Taylor, June 5, 1852, that the scene of Hawthorne's new
Romance "is laid at Brook Farm!" (The exclamation point indicates, I think, that Fields too was expecting an insider's account.) Nevertheless, Hawthorne could justifiably write to
George W. Curtis, who had belonged to the Community, "Do
not read [The Blithedale Romance] as if it had anything to do
with Brook Farm (which essentially it has not) but merely for
its own story and characters." He wrote more bluntly to an un-
named autograph seeker in 1852: "As regards the degree in
which the "Blithedale Romance" has a foundation in fact, the
preface to the book gives a correct statement."

The preface, then, becomes a critical point of entry—or com-
mencement—for an approach to The Blithedale Romance.
Claiming that his recollections of Brook Farm are but incidental
to his story, Hawthorne is explicit as to his intentions:

In short, his present concern with the Socialist Community is merely to establish a theatre, a little removed from
the highway of ordinary travel, where the creatures of his
brain may play their phantasmagorical antics, without
exposing them to too close a comparison with the actual
events of real lives.

He would claim the privileges of the romancer who needs a
"Faery Land, so like the real world, that, in a suitable remote-

ness, one cannot well tell the difference, but with an atmosphere of strange enchantment, beheld through which the inhabitants have a propriety of their own." It follows that his characters are not to be understood as real Brook Farmers but as types entirely appropriate to a romance: "The self-concentrated Philanthropist; the high-spirited Woman, bruising herself against the narrow limitations of her sex; the weakly Maiden, whose tremulous nerves endow her with Sibylline attributes; the Minor Poet, beginning life with strenuous aspirations which die out with his youthful fervor. . . ."

These sentiments and these claims are of course analogous to those in the preface to *The House of the Seven Gables*. And they derive from a problem common to the two romances—indeed, to virtually all of Hawthorne's work after *The Scarlet Letter*: that he set himself increasingly to treating of contemporaneous life and so found himself increasingly concerned with the sort of materials which the novel as a literary form had been evolved to comprehend: the experience of life as interesting, demanding, and valuable precisely as it could be conceived of in terms lived through day-to-day. The romancer's problem was in effect to get such perspective on that experience as would free him of the novelist's regular commitment to evoke it in its own terms, so to be in some ultimate sense at least a "realist." Hawthorne's means to this end in *The House of the Seven Gables* had been to conceive of himself as a historian whose special knowledge of the history of the Pyncheons gave him a power of psychological perception such that he could function as romancer.

The problem in *The Blithedale Romance*, granting its matrix in Hawthorne's Brook Farm experience, granting his dubiety about that experience (itself quite evident in opinions expressed when he was actually at Brook Farm), is a particularly difficult one. For it is immanently necessary in anti-utopian writings—as in the utopian writings which call them forth—that there be a strong quality of novelistic treatment. This derives from the nature of the utopian enterprise itself, in which revolutionary fantasies are rendered as though realizable in quite concrete, particular, immediate, and realistic terms.

Henry James's contrast of the real and the romantic—especially because it comes in the midst of his lucubrations on Hawthorne—is useful here:

> The real represents to my perception the things we cannot possibly *not* know, sooner or late, in one way or another; it being but one of the accidents of our hampered state, and one of the incidents of their quantity and number, that particular instances have not yet come our way. The romantic stands, on the other hand, for the things that, with all the facilities in the world, all the wealth and all the courage and all the wit and the adventure, we never *can* directly know; the things that can reach us only through the beautiful circuit and subterfuge of our thought and our desire.

Hope for a utopian society may well be rooted in the romantic impulse as James defines it. But its realization, ironically enough, depends upon a bringing into full play the realistic impulse. As it were, "particular instances" must not be just generally, exotically, or allegorically desiderated, but rather forced to "come our way"—forced into being in concrete and particular "quantity and number." And when what is in question is anti-utopian writing, the burden of the novelistic is all the greater. For then there is a further formal problem, that of satire. (And as it has recently been demonstrated, utopia, anti-utopia, and satire are, as literary modes, in their origin and development, as well as in their form and function, integrally related one with another.[2]) Behind James's discomfort with *The Blithedale Romance* in his little book on Hawthorne lie the problems he sets for himself in his later preface to the New York edition version of *The American*. And James's discomfort has of course been that of many

2. See particularly Robert Elliott, "Saturnalia, Satire, and Utopia," *The Shape of Utopia: Studies in a Literary Genre* (Chicago, 1970), pp. 3–24.

critics who have come after him. That discomfort is at the root
of our difficulty with *The Blithedale Romance*.


II

The primary intention of Hawthorne's Preface to *The Blithedale Romance*, then, is to assuage that discomfort and to find a
way around that difficulty. Hawthorne is insisting not that we
forget about the "real" Brook Farm but rather that we should let
ourselves be guided into an acceptance of what he has made
out of his experience there:

> This ["Faery Land"] atmosphere is what the American ro-
> mancer needs. In its absence, the beings of imagination
> are compelled to show themselves in the same category as
> actually living mortals; a necessity that generally renders
> the paint and pasteboard of their composition but too pain-
> fully discernible. With the idea of partially obviating this
> difficulty (the sense of which has always pressed very
> heavily upon him), the author has ventured to make free
> with his old, and affectionately remembered home, at
> BROOK FARM, as being, certainly, the most romantic
> episode of his own life—essentially a day-dream, and yet
> a fact—and thus offering an available foothold between
> fiction and reality. Furthermore, the scene was in good
> keeping with the personages whom he desired to introduce.

The principal personage so introduced is Miles Coverdale. Hawthorne compounds his formal problem and complicates our
comprehending his point-of-view by introducing Coverdale as a
first-person narrator—sometimes unreliable—in whose vocabu-
lary, as Hawthorne creates it for him, terms like "day-dream"
and its analogues are prime instruments of understanding and
interpretation. Hawthorne's critique of Brook Farm, one concludes, is a critique of a day-dream made out to be rendered by
a day-dreamer, a recollection of a fantasy by a compulsive
fantast, an anti-utopia told by a failed utopian.

The task accordingly set for the interpreter of *The Blithedale Romance* is to ascertain the particular utopian quality of Blithedale, not of Brook Farm. That quality, in a word, is Arcadian: a version of what A. O. Lovejoy long ago analyzed as Western Man's overwhelming yearning to return to what he was sure must have been an earlier, simpler state of affairs, "soft primitivism"; what we can describe, in psychological terms, as a compulsion to idyllic regression. Hawthorne does have Coverdale and the others—when they are brought to confront this state of affairs—speak ironically, though most often their irony is directed not at themselves but at their fellows, as though each thinks that the other, not himself, is guilty of Arcadianism. Moreover, in the particular case of Coverdale (and the particular case is integral with his being a first-person narrator whose style as thinker is perilously close to that of his creator as it is set forth in the Preface), there is evidence of what we might best call a manifest and a latent Arcadianism. In the first instance, Coverdale habitually mocks the utopian aspirations of those at Blithedale, often including himself. In the second instance, however, Hawthorne makes him, all-unknowing, reveal his own regressive qualities; herein he is—especially in the last third of the romance—the arch peeping-tom, the voyeur who, hoping to find a means of simplifying his life to the uttermost, longs for an Arcadia beyond the ken of that his fellows are trying to create, an Arcadia of the solitary. It might well be that in creating Coverdale Hawthorne is trying to exorcise out of himself a fundamental drive in his own character, as in creating Blithedale and its special society, he is trying to come to see as "fact" a long-gone "day-dream," and so come to grips with a vital portion of his own history. At any rate, what is centrally at issue in *The Blithedale Romance*—what is central to its import—is utopianism as Arcadianism.

The motif is sharply delineated early in the narrative, in Chapter VIII—"A Modern Arcadia." Coverdale emerges from his sick-room on May-Day, and, as the narrative progresses, for the first time begins to see the relationship which obtains among

Zenobia, Priscilla, and Hollingsworth. He finds Zenobia and Priscilla "a Maying together," and, as Hollingsworth appears, realizes how Priscilla is torn between her devotion to the other two. He sees the whole scene as somehow vitalizing and now senses that at Blithedale he can undergo a kind of rebirth:

> My fit of illness had been an avenue between two existences; the low-arched and darksome doorway, through which I had crept out of a life of old conventionalisms, on my hands and knees, as it were, and gained admittance into the freer region that lay beyond. In this respect, it was like death. And, as with death, too, it was good to have gone through it. Not otherwise could I have rid myself of a thousand follies, fripperies, prejudices, habits, and other such worldly dust as inevitably settles upon the crowd along the broad highway, giving them all one sordid aspect, before noon-time, however freshly they may have begun their pilgrimage, in the dewy morning. The very substance upon my bones had not been fit to live with, in any better, truer, or more energetic mode than that to which I was accustomed. So it was taken off me and flung aside, like any other worn out or unseasonable garment; and, after shivering a little while in my skeleton, I began to be clothed anew, and much more satisfactorily than in my previous suit. In literal and physical truth, I was quite another man.

And so he is led to meditate upon the forces which make Blithedale operative. Above all, he decides, his life and that of his fellows is now no longer artificially ordered, its conventions now being set by the fundamental laws of "Nature." The rationale is the traditional one in Arcadian-primitivistic thought. As "Arcadians," he writes, those at Blithedale—individualists all —are nonetheless not "the pastoral people of poetry and the stage." Rather, they live a "yeoman life." And at this point he can afford to be ironic—this time concerning the difficulties confronting Arcadians when they would set themselves to physical labor. The irony, so it develops as the narrative continues, is also sensed by Zenobia and Hollingsworth, whom he reports as being amused at the sight of a minor poet turned yeoman. Hollingsworth at least·approves. Coverdale reports him as commenting: "There is at least this good in a life of toil, that it takes the nonsense and fancy-work out of a man, and leaves nothing but what truly belongs to him." At this point, Zenobia accepts Hollingsworth's truth as her own, and Coverdale—now with them a committed Arcadian—does not gainsay them.

Chapter VIII serves as an initial focal point for the Arcadian motifs in *The Blithedale Romance*. The motifs, however, are highlighted throughout the romance. In Chapter III, Coverdale recalls his proclaiming his intention to begin writing a new kind of poetry—"true, strong, natural, and sweet, as is the life we are going to lead. . . ." In this chapter too he remembers his discovering that Zenobia can be another Eve, as life at Blithedale will not be "artificial." In Chapter IV there is the record of Hollingsworth's declaration that the coming of Priscilla indeed marks a new beginning of things, and in Chapter V of his insistence that his utopia, his "socialist scheme," will be wholly altruistic. In Chapter V too there is reported the discussion of the search for a name for the colony; "Utopia," presumably because it calls to mind "artificial" arrangements, is "unanimously scouted down" and Blithedale is agreed upon—all this on an evening when Coverdale must report, with an irony whose full implications he cannot foresee, "How cold an Arcadia was this!" In Chapter IX Coverdale comments that it was in the nature of Blithedale to incline all "to the soft affections of the Golden Age" and later Zenobia is reported as describing events at Blithedale (here again there is an irony whose eventual implications are not foreseen) as the playing out of a "pastoral." In Chapter X Coverdale says that in the view of visitors to Blithedale, "we were as poetical as Arcadians, besides being as practical as the hardest-fisted husbandmen in Massachusetts." And so it goes—until toward the end, when in Chapter XX, Zenobia, in town, annoyed at Coverdale's spying on her, is reported as speaking of "such Arcadian freedom of falling in love as we lately have enjoyed . . . ," and when in Chapter XXIII Coverdale, looking back, can say only of his earlier Arcadian hopes for his time at Blithedale, ". . . it had enabled me to pass the summer in a novel and agreeable way, had afforded me some grotesque specimens of artificial simplicity. . . ."

The movement, as regards the Arcadian motifs, is from naive commitment to amused irony to disillusionment. But there is a degree of ambiguity at all points—an ambiguity deriving in good part from Coverdale's being continually caught between the realms of day-dream and fact. The turning-point, if it can justifiably be called that, perhaps comes toward the middle of the narrative, in Chapter XV, after Coverdale has at long last begun to realize the terrible complications of the relationships among Zenobia, Priscilla, and Hollingsworth. It is in this chapter that Hollingsworth first manifests himself for what he is—single-mindedly devoted to his version of utopia, altogether careless of the aspirations of others. In the course of their conversation Coverdale begins to have his doubts about the perdurability of Blithedale and all that it stands for. He sees that death must inevitably come to someone in this Arcadia:

"I wonder, Hollingsworth, who, of all these strong men, and fair women and maidens, is doomed the first to die. Would it not be well, even before we have the absolute need of it, to fix upon a spot for a cemetery? Let us choose the rudest, roughest, most uncultivable spot, for Death's garden-ground; and Death shall teach us to beautify it, grave by grave."

There is portrayed here a crisis (and the chapter is called "A Crisis") not only in Hollingsworth's relationships with his fellows but in Coverdale's sense of the whole Arcadian enterprise that is Blithedale. But here again, Hawthorne is writing according to the Arcadian tradition. For this episode derives—whether or not consciously on Hawthorne's part, it is impossible to say—from the traditional "Et in Arcadia ego" topos, in which the presence of death is found to be ineluctable in the Arcadian scheme of things.³ And the "Et in Arcadia ego" topos is affirmed, at almost the very end, in Chapter XXVII, when Coverdale must meditate on the "ugly circumstances" of Zenobia's suicide and of the injury to her body done in the process of recovering it. He somehow cannot believe that Zenobia would have drowned herself if she had realized how indecorous she would have looked in death. For, he writes, "in Zenobia's case there was some tint of the Arcadian affectation that had been visible enough in all our lives, for a few months past."

III

The Arcadian mode was indeed an affectation in Hawthorne's view of things. He has Coverdale, in exhausted retrospect, write of Blithedale in the last "confessional" chapter: "The experiment, so far as its original projectors were concerned, proved, long ago a failure; first lapsing into Fourierism, and dying, as it well deserved, for this infidelity to its own higher spirit." Hawthorne, indeed, believed whole-heartedly in that "higher spirit," but could nonetheless find it, for people like Coverdale and the rest, an affectation. It was an affectation for such as them, because it was a "higher spirit" appropriate only to children. And what is centrally involved in *The Blithedale Romance*—what gives it its special import—is Hawthorne's conviction that willy-nilly Coverdale and the rest are acting like children, trying to reduce—or to return—life to terms impossible for adults. Surely Coverdale's voyeurism, including its sexual aspects as his attitude toward Zenobia reveals them, has something to do with his failure to grow up.

At this point some historical considerations are again worth noting. *The Blithedale Romance* is a project Hawthorne undertook at that point in his life when at long last he was doing what he had committed himself to do as early as 1838, retelling Greek

3. The classical study on the topos of course is Erwin Panofsky, "*Et in Arcadia Ego*: Poussin and the Elegiac Tradition," *Meaning in the Visual Arts* (New York, 1955), pp. 295–320.

myths in a style appropriate to children. The chronology is important.[4] On January 1, 1851, Hawthorne finished *The House of the Seven Gables*. On April 7, 1851, he reported to a correspondent that he was planning *A Wonder-Book*. On May 3, 1851, he reported that *A Wonder-Book* was in fact designed. On July 15, 1851, *A Wonder-Book* was in his publisher Fields's hands. On July 24, 1851, he reported that he had decided to write a book based on his Brook Farm experiences. On November 8, 1851, *A Wonder-Book* was published. Around November 23, 1851, he reported that he had begun to write the book which became *The Blithedale Romance*. On May 2, 1852, he sent the manuscript of *The Blithedale Romance* to Whipple. On June 8, 1852, he reported that he was thinking about writing a continuation of *A Wonder-Book* (this became *Tanglewood Tales*). He was stalled in this enterprise subsequently, because he agreed to write Franklin Pierce's campaign biography and then involved himself in the campaign itself. In November, 1852, with Pierce elected, he knew that he would get the consulship at Liverpool; and on March 15, 1853, he could report that he was working on the continuation of *A Wonder-Book*. *Tanglewood Tales* was published in England and the United States in August 1853.

The point of the chronologizing is to emphasize the fact that *The Blithedale Romance* was written at a time when Hawthorne was most deeply concerned to demonstrate that Arcadianism was quite properly a stage in the development of the child's life. Both *A Wonder-Book* and *Tanglewood Tales* center on that notion. Hawthorne has a young collegian, Eustace Bright, retell Greek myths from a child's perspective. More important to the present argument, he is persuaded that the myths, as he has them retold, are pure not only from the child's point-of-view but from an historical point-of-view. Hawthorne went to standard learned sources, took the myths as they had come down to him, but felt bound to take into account the fact that over the

4. What follows derives from my historical introduction to Hawthorne's writings for children, Centenary Edition, VI, 287–311.

ages they had accreted to themselves the complications and corruptions of adult life—complications and corruptions which he
made clear were inevitable but nonetheless were not integral to
the myths in their "pure" state. This is yet another version of his
obsession with *felix culpa*.

The best summary of his view occurs in the preface to *Tanglewood Tales*, in which he speaks in his own person:

> . . . Eustace told me that these myths were the most
> singular things in the world, and that he was invariably
> astonished, whenever he began to relate one, by the readi-
> ness with which it adapted itself to the childish purity of his
> auditors. The objectionable characteristics seem to be a
> parasitical growth, having no essential connection with the
> original fable. . . . When the first poet or romancer told
> these marvellous legends (such was Eustace Bright's opin-
> ion), it was still the Golden Age. Evil had never yet
> existed; and sorrow, misfortune, crime, were mere shadows
> which the mind fancifully created for itself, as a shelter
> against too sunny realities; or, at most, but prophetic
> dreams, to which the dreamer himself did not yield a
> waking credence. Children are now the only representa-
> tives of the men and women of that happy era; and there-
> fore it is that we must raise the intellect and the fancy to
> the levels of childhood, in order to re-create the original
> myths.

Hawthorne is here eulogizing the sort of world which he
perforce treated dyslogistically in *The Blithedale Romance*. For
the Arcadian world of Blithedale is essentially—and for Hawthorne's purposes, inappropriately—a child's world—not the sort
of utopia of which Emerson wrote so cheerfully in "New England Reformers" (1844): "What a fertility of projects for the
salvation of the world!" Rather the world of Blithedale is one to
which all concerned willy-nilly regress in their desperate attempt
to find a place where what they take to be their gifts and com-
mitments can be realized. It is a Land of Cockaigne in which

the Identity Crisis (the critic needs the concepts of ego psychology if he is to be a proper literary historian) can be forever postponed.

Early in the romance, Hawthorne writes: "As for Zenobia, there was a glow in her cheeks that made me think of Pandora, fresh from Vulcan's workshop, and full of the celestial warmth by dint of which he had tempered and moulded her." In *A Wonder-Book* Hawthorne retells the Pandora myth in a story called "The Paradise of Children." Pandora, in this piece, is a child, as is Epithemeus, her husband in traditional versions of the story. She fusses at length over the mysterious box which Mercury has left, does not realize that her existence is idyllic, and finally opens the box, releasing a multitude of evils on the world, but also releasing Hope. In the middle of the story, Hawthorne comments thus on his Pandora:

> It might have been better for Pandora if she had a little work to do, or anything to employ her mind upon, so as not to be so constantly thinking of [opening the box]. But children led so easy a life, before any Troubles came into the world, that they really had a great deal too much leisure. . . . When life is all sport, toil is the real play. . . .

Those in residence at Blithedale, it will be recalled, do in fact "toil, but, once they discover that toil is in fact not play, not enthusiastically." What they *really* wish, Hawthorne is suggesting, is that regressive state of life wherein they will be free to realize themselves in a way the conditions of life lived day-to-day in society will not allow. With the exception of Zenobia —and this is what makes her, as James first pointed out, Hawthorne's most realized woman—they have rejected the option of adjusting their fantasies to the exigencies of life lived in the world proper. She is the exception, because such an option does not altogether exist for her. But she is nonetheless not quite right, since she could have changed her name and her life-style to that, not of Margaret Fuller, but of Elizabeth or Mary Peabody. She remains, however, a passionate *Sophia* Peabody. And that is her tragedy, the only one in *The Blithedale Romance*. The rest is pathos.

It could have been more. Hawthorne, I believe, did not have sufficient perspective on his own commitment to the notion that childhood, however Arcadian, was also a stage in growing up and into the world, a world which could not be that of the romance. Still, I think the tone of the book—mocking in its irony, not satirical—is justified by its intention and its import. My own historical fantasy as regards the place of *The Blithedale Romance* in Hawthorne's *oeuvre* is that the young collegian, Eustace Bright, who tells the stories in *A Wonder-Book* and *Tanglewood Tales*, finished college, tried his hand at literature, could not bring himself to face the practicalities of the life of the writer as his friend Nathaniel Hawthorne had done, with Hawthorne went to Brook Farm, and never recovered from the experience, precisely because the experience was for him, as it was not for Hawthorne, an abiding fact rather than a kind of day-dream. Later—as I reconstruct the inside story of *The Blithedale Romance*—he recounted his adventures, hopes, and aspirations to Hawthorne and agreed that his friend might tell them, if only his name were changed. From Bright to Coverdale. Any literary historian—with some etymological training— would understand.

ROY HARVEY PEARCE
*University of California,
San Diego*

# "THE BEGUM OF BENGAL": MARK TWAIN
# AND THE SOUTH

Of all the Southern writers who produced books in that long period between the end of the Civil War and the beginnings of the Southern Literary Renascence of the Twentieth Century, only one, Mark Twain, was able to escape the cultural shock of defeat in war. So much so, indeed, that many readers do not think of him as a "Southern" writer at all—which was precisely what he would appear to have desired, for a while at least. He came onto the postwar American literary scene by way of the Far West. He joyfully published the memoirs of General Grant. He denounced the "United States of Lyncherdom," and he filled the later pages of *Life on the Mississippi* with scathing comments on Southern romanticism and Southern addiction to the chivalric nonsense of Sir Walter Scott. He was born in the South, he used to say, but almost always insisted quickly that he had since learned better.

Yet the matter is not so easily disposed of as that. Not only was he born there: he grew up in the South, he even enlisted in the military defence in 1861, and he wrote his greatest books about the life he had known there. Furthermore, his style of humor came directly out of a literary genre that reached its greatest popularity in the South, and his art remained throughout his life strongly marked by his Southern experience. It is this experience, as it relates to his writings, that I wish to consider here.

Discussions of whether Clemens's literary imagination was importantly Southern or not tend too often to get involved in what are really irrelevancies. Was Hannibal, Missouri, a Southern or Western town when Sam Clemens was living there? Was a pilot's life on the Mississippi before 1861 Southern in its forms, or was it Western? How serious was Clemens's ideological involvement with the Marion Rangers? Does Mark Twain use the English language the way William Faulkner does, or more as Sherwood Anderson and Ernest Hemingway do? Is the theme of the revolt from the village a Southern or a Midwestern theme? And so on. These matters have their bearing on the problem, but are not central to it. What is central is the forms that the imagination took, and how the imagination was formed.

We tend, when we begin speaking about the South as a social entity, to think in terms of a part of the South, and then to treat that part as the whole. Politically there has been some justification for doing this, though it seems to be vanishing, but in most other respects it is a dubious business. C. Hugh Holman identifies three distinct modes of Southern consciousness, related to three distinct subregions, and he cautions us that "however shadowy the lines of demarcation among them may be and however similar many of their attitudes were, they dreamed different dreams, formulated different social structures, and worshipped different gods. These differences have persisted for a century and a half and they give evidence of being qualities permanent to their various locales."[1] Mr. Holman defines these subregions as the Tidewater, the Deep South, and the Piedmont South. In the last-named, he says, the "society is in many ways more nearly American and less distinctively Southern, except for its grotesquerie," than in the Tidewater and the Deep South, and he points out that unlike the writers of the latter two locales, the writers of the Piedmont have judged their homeland by a standard which, "whether it be that of social justice, or religious order, or of moral imagination, has always been an outer and different standard from that embraced by the local inhabitants." He notes Thomas Wolfe's use of the standards of the Middle Western writers. "Freed from the deep emotional commitment typical of the Tidewater and the Deep South," he declares, "Wolfe could look calmly and critically at his region, deplore its

1. C. Hugh Holman, *Three Modes of Modern Southern Fiction* (Athens, Ga., 1966), p. 6.

weaknesses, and love its strengths, without indulging in the emotional upheaval over this ambivalent attitude which Quentin Compson suffers in *Absalom, Absalom!*"[2]

Though Mr. Holman would not include Samuel L. Clemens within the geographic boundaries of his Southern tryptych, he has given us an interesting access to Mark Twain. The farmlands of eastern Missouri are not part of the Piedmont, but in the days when Samuel L. Clemens was growing up there, they were surely the border South. Hannibal, Missouri, was settled by Southerners, it was linked economically to the river and was dependent upon the trade up and down the river, it was a slaveholding community, and when the war broke out it was largely secessionist in sentiment. Its interests, tastes, and attitudes, if we are to believe Dixon Wecter and others who have studied its life, were notably Southern—even to the extent that its bookshops offered for sale the *Southern Literary Messenger*, which the *Hannibal Journal* described in 1848 as being far superior to "the wishy washy concerns that issue from the Eastern cities."[3] Hannibal was certainly not part of the Tidewater or the Deep South; it was part of the westward migration from those places. But as DeLancey Ferguson reminds us, "Mark Twain was also a son of the South. To think of him in terms of the Nevada mining camps where he made his first literary reputation, to think of his youthful homes as they look to a New Yorker of today—as too many critics have done—is to miss the strongest forces of his life. Hannibal, Missouri, cannot be interpreted in terms of that rebellion against village and farm which began with Ed Howe in the 1880s and Hamlin Garland in the 1890s. The society Mark Twain lived in was not ours; it must be thought of in terms of its own dreams, not ours."[4]

Samuel Clemens's father, John Marshall Clemens, was a

2. Ibid., pp. 55–57.
3. Dixon Wecter, *Sam Clemens of Hannibal* (Boston, 1952), p. 209.
4. Delancey Ferguson, *Mark Twain: Man and Legend* (Indianapolis, 1943), p. 15.

Virginian and a Whig, who before coming to Missouri lived in Kentucky and Tennessee, holding in the last-named state title to considerable land which to his dying day he expected would one day make his family rich. Jane Lampson Clemens, Sam Clemens's mother, was of Kentucky stock. Like her husband she believed in the rightness of slavery throughout her life. "She had never heard it assailed in any pulpit," her son tells us, "but she had heard it defended and sanctified in a thousand; her ears were familiar with Bible texts that approved it, but if there were any that disapproved it they had not been quoted by her pastors; as far as her experience went, the wise and the good and the holy were unanimous in the conviction that slavery was right, righteous, sacred, the particular pet of the Deity, and a condition which the slave himself ought to be daily and nightly thankful for."[5]

In a notable passage in *The Flush Times of Alabama and Mississippi*, Joseph Glover Baldwin describes the difficulties that the Virginians had in the frontier South of the 1830s and 1840s, set down as they were, men of honor and pride, among the less scrupulous and less prideful plain folk. "Superior to many of the settlers in manners and general intelligence," Baldwin writes, "it was the weakness of the Virginian to imagine he was superior too in the essential art of being able to hold his hand and make his way in a new country, and especially *such* a country, and at *such* a time."[6] In many respects Baldwin might have been writing about John Marshall Clemens. Dignified, reserved, a man of probity and a high sense of civic role, conscious of his status and of his ancestry, he was respected by his fellow Missouri villagers, but he met financial ruin when he involved himself with a man of considerably humbler origins and stature who however was able to inveigle Clemens into a disastrous business transaction. Clemens had owned a few slaves: ulti-

5. Mark Twain, *Mark Twain's Autobiography*, I, *Complete Works of Mark Twain: Authorized Edition* (New York: Harper and Bros., 1924), 123.
6. Joseph G. Baldwin, *The Flush Times of Alabama and Mississippi* (New York, 1957), p. 66.

mately he was forced to sell them all. He wasted two hundred dollars of the family's money on a fruitless trip to Tennessee and Mississippi to collect a debt: he could not bear to foreclose on a man who owed him money (and who was apparently fairly well off), but he had no qualms about taking a slave along and disposing of him for ten barrels of tar.[7] When his wife reproached him upon his return for his failure, he tried to justify himself and then, with a "hopeless expression" on his face, added, "I am not able to dig in the streets."[8] But his eldest son, Orion, was forced to go to work as apprentice in a print shop, and at first the comedown involved in having to perform manual labor chagrined the son. As for Sam Clemens, he was too young to go to work then, but when his father died in 1847 he found a job as helper in a print shop.

I have no intention of reciting Samuel L. Clemens's biography, but I would make the point that right here at the outset, in the boyhood of Sam Clemens's life, we have the situation that would become the hallmark of his humor: the awareness of status and the effort to maintain it. Here is the Southern family of good standing, minor aristocracy fallen upon evil days, seeking to hold to status and _noblesse oblige_ in a more crass and democratic society where aristocratic pose comes close to being quixotic gesture and high-minded scruples of honor the vulnerability whereby the vernacular land speculator with no such scruples could bring the man of honor down to poverty and ruin. And here is the youth Sam Clemens, admiring and wanting to believe in the heroic gesture, the aristocratic pose, and yet observing its practical ineffectiveness and its weakness, and experiencing the deprivation and embarrassment that it brought to those dependent upon it. In Mark Twain's work the public pose, the claim of the gentleman's privileges to special treatment and respect, is always being contrasted with the levelling processes of a disrespectful vernacular society. In his writings, so

7. Wecter, pp. 74–76.
8. Ibid., p. 77.

much that happens in the fiction and the fact (and the "fact" is often fictionalized) revolves around the question of status, and more particularly the public recognition of status. Colonel Sellers always maintains his role, at whatever cost to credibility. Tom Sawyer constantly strives to "be somebody" in the eyes of the community, and stakes everything on the "theatrical gorgeousness" of his performance. "We can't let you into the gang if you ain't respectable, you know," he warns Huck. In *Life on the Mississippi* the town boys envy the deckhand his privileged status, and the cub pilot covets the rank and dignity of the estate of piloting. In *Huckleberry Finn* a poor white boy finds it difficult to humble himself before a black man; two rogues pretend to be visiting nobility; a colonel stares down a lynch mob and berates their commonness. In *A Connecticut Yankee* a master mechanic from Connecticut becomes The Boss and takes down the king and knights of England a step or two. In *The Prince and the Pauper* an urchin changes places with a king. In *Pudd'nhead Wilson* the York Leicester Driscolls, Percy Northumberland Driscolls and Cecil Burleigh Essexes cling to their privileged roles as best possible, while a slave woman brags to her mulatto son that he comes from the best blood of Virginia.[9]

Mark Twain constantly makes humor out of this consciousness of status. "Who *is* I? Who *is* I?" declares a black man at a New Orleans dance in *Life on the Mississippi*, "I let you know mighty quick who I is! I want you niggers to understan' dat I fires de middle do on de *Aleck Scott!*"[10] But it was no joke that led the noted humorist Samuel Clemens to reply, when Howells cautioned him not to write "up" to the prestigious *Atlantic Monthly* readership, that "it isn't the Atlantic audience that distresses me; for *it* is the only audience that I sit down to in perfect serenity (for the simple reason that it don't require a

9. Arlin Turner, in "Mark Twain and the South: An Affair of Love and Anger," *Southern Review*, n.s., 4 (1968), 493–519, has thoroughly discussed the relationship of *Pudd'nhead Wilson* to Mark Twain's Southern origins.
10. Mark Twain, *Life on the Mississippi, Complete Works of Mark Twain: Authorized Edition*, VII (New York, 1924), 122.

'humorist' to paint himself striped and stand on his head every fifteen minutes)."[11]

*He* was no coarse funnyman; he was a writer of taste and refinement, he assured Howells. And there was the night when, having made an audience roar with delight all evening, he groaned to his tour companion George W. Cable that "Oh, Cable, I am demeaning myself. I am allowing myself to be a mere buffoon. It's ghastly. I can't endure it any longer."[12]

To the end of his life he openly sought the limelight, the public recognition that he was something grand and special. Happily he recounted how the policeman in Vienna recognized him and ordered him past the barricade, saying "For God's sake let him pass. Don't you see it's Herr Mark Twain?"[13] When he received his honorary degree from Oxford he wore his scarlet doctoral robe proudly, and thereafter displayed it on every possible occasion, remarking that he wished he could wear it around all the time. All through his life he required the external signs of privileged position to keep him convinced that his rank and dignity were real. "His favorite recreation in New York," Justin Kaplan tells us, "when he was not playing billiards was to stroll up and down Fifth Avenue in his white suit, chat with the police, and be stared at."[14] It was as if he never quite believed it, was never completely assured of his status. The doubt, and the need to prove his claim to importance, stayed with him to the finish. He confessed as much, albeit obliquely, in his speech at the farewell dinner tendered him in 1907 by the Lord Mayor of Liverpool when he quoted Richard Henry Dana's anecdote of the skipper of the little coaster sloop who had a habit of hailing all passing ships "just to hear himself talk and air his small grandeur," and who hailed an inbound Indiaman, only to hear its majestic identification of itself, "the *Begum*, of Bengal, one

11. Quoted in Henry Nash Smith, *Mark Twain: The Development of a Writer* (Cambridge, Mass., 1962), p. 93.

12. Quoted in Guy A. Cardwell, *Twain of Genius* (London, 1962), p. 25.

13. Justin Kaplan, *Mr. Clemens and Mark Twain* (New York, 1966), p. 353.

14. Ibid., p. 380.

hundred and forty-two days out from Canton, homeward bound. What ship is that?" The skipper of the sloop could only squeak back humbly, "Only the *Mary Ann*, fourteen hours out from Boston, bound for Kittery Point—with nothing to speak of!" For an hour of each twenty-four, Mark Twain told his English well-wishers, he lay alone at night with the realization that he was only the *Mary Ann*, fourteen hours out, with vegetables and tinware, but

> during all the twenty-three hours my vain self-complacency rides high on the white crest of your approval, and then I am a stately Indiaman, ploughing the great seas under a cloud of canvas and laden with the kindest words that have ever been vouchsafed to any wandering alien in this world, I think; then my twenty-six fortunate days on this old mother soil seem to be multiplied by six, and I *am* the Begum of Bengal, one hundred and forty-two days out from Canton, homeward bound![15]

It is a beautiful conclusion, and the imagery is revealing, for Samuel Clemens sometimes saw himself very well.

It requires no Freudian psychologist to suggest how importantly the figure of John Marshall Clemens, the proud Virginia-born father unable "to dig in the streets," whose life ended with his family moved in over a friend's drugstore and the family furniture sold to pay debts, possesses his son's imagination. We see him repeatedly in Samuel Clemens's fiction: as the pathetic and amiable Colonel Sellers, as the masterful but blood-feuding figures of aristocracy in *Pudd'nhead Wilson*, and elsewhere. Tom Sawyer, of course, has no living father; his only competition for the limelight is with his brother Sid. Huck Finn's father is a vicious old poor-white reprobate, who however is satisfactorily killed in mid-novel, though Huck is spared the knowledge until the close. Of Sam Clemens's relationship with

15. Mark Twain, "The Last Lotus Club Speech," in *Mark Twain's Speeches, Complete Works of Mark Twain: Authorized Edition,* XXIV (New York, 1923), 373–374.

his own father we know that it was distant: "a sort of armed neutrality, so to speak," he described it. His father, he says, only whipped him twice, and then not heavily.[16] But Mark Twain's lifelong love-hate fascination with men of aristocratic bearing, especially when Southerners, surely grows out of that relationship. Of Judge Driscoll in *Pudd'nhead Wilson* he writes that "In Missouri a recognized superiority attached to any person who hailed from Old Virginia; and this person was exalted to supremacy when a person of such nativity could also prove descent from the First Families of the great commonwealth." The Virginian, he says, "must keep his honor spotless . . . Honor stood first. . . ."[17] But honor was no protection against the willingness of one Ira Stout to use the bankruptcy law and ruin the Clemens family,[18] and honor did not prevent Orion and then Sam from going to work in a print shop, and honor caused a slave girl who had been in the Clemens family for years to be sold down the river. Honor, especially when viewed in retrospect, clearly had its limitations.

In Huckleberry Finn we encounter Colonel Grangerford: "His hands was long and thin, and every day of his life he put on a clean shirt and a full suit from head to foot made out of linen so white it hurt your eyes to look at it. . . . There warn't no frivolishness about him, not a bit, and he warn't ever loud. He was as kind as he could be—you could feel that, you know, and so you had confidence. Sometimes he smiled, and it was good to see; but when he straightened himself up like a liberty-pole, and the lightning begun to flicker out from under his eyebrows, you wanted to climb a tree first, and find out what the matter was afterwards."[19] But this same Colonel Grangerford

16. Quoted in Wecter, p. 67.
17. Mark Twain, *Pudd'nhead Wilson and Those Extraordinary Twins*, facsimile of the first edition (San Francisco: Chandler Publishing Co., 1968), p. 156.
18. Wecter reports that town records show no record of such an incident, but he notes that various places of evidence do indicate the likelihood that something of the sort occurred. Wecter, p. 67.
19. Mark Twain, *The Adventures of Huckleberry Finn*, "Introduction" by Lionel Trilling (New York: Rinehart and Co., 1948), p. 105.

could take part in a stupid and bloody feud against the Shepherdsons, killing young men and boys, without concerning himself with the human consequences. John Marshall Clemens could serve as judge and justice of the peace, a pillar of rectitude, but he could sell a slave downriver, and trade another for ten barrels of tar. It was, in short, splendid to be a Virginian and an aristocrat—if you had no conscience to plague you for your sins.

As for the son, *he* had a conscience, all right; he felt guilt constantly, tormenting himself with it even when no guilt actually existed. Guilt for having given matches to an old drunk in jail, who promptly set fire to the jail and was burned to death; guilt for burlesquing old Captain Isaiah Sellers's newspaper column in New Orleans and shaming the old man into stopping his harmless pontification; guilt for having allowed his badly burned younger brother Henry to be given too large a dose of morphine after the *Pennsylvania* explosion, so that he died; guilt for having violated the purity of Livy Langdon Clemens's Elmira existence with his rough, uncouth, un-genteel way of life; guilt for having taken his young son Langdon out driving, so that he contracted "diphtheria" and died; guilt for having squandered Livy's inheritance and his earnings so that he had to plead bankruptcy; guilt for having fathered Susy Clemens so that she could die a horrible death of meningitis, and Jean Clemens so that she could die of epilepsy; guilt for having once believed in slavery; guilt for the insult to Emerson, Longfellow and Holmes in the Whittier Birthday Dinner address; guilt for the loss of his literary powers; guilt for being a member of the "damned human race"—small wonder that Sam Clemens raged against his Presbyterian conscience, slew it in print so often, and in "The Mysterious Stranger" brought Little Satan to Hannibal (moved to Germany for the occasion) in order that the son of Arch-fiend might teach Tom and Huck that the absurdity known as the "moral sense" was at the root of all men's suffering. "No one, I think," Bernard DeVoto has written of Clemens's paper entitled *What Is Man?*, "can read this wearisomely repeated argument without feeling the terrible force of an inner cry: Do not blame me, for it was not my fault."[20]

Literary psychologists have expended considerable effort attempting to trace down the sources of Samuel L. Clemens's lifelong affinity for feeling guilty. The official biographer, Albert Bigelow Paine, describes a scene at the time of John Marshall Clemens's death. His son, says Paine, was fairly broken down. "Remorse which always dealt with him unsparingly, laid a heavy hand on him now. Wildness, disobedience, indifference to his father's wishes, all were remembered; a hundred things, in themselves trifling, became ghastly and heart-wringing in the knowledge that they could never be undone." Jane Clemens took her son up to the room where his father lay, told him that what had happened did not matter now, and asked him to promise her to be a faithful and industrious man, like his father. That night Jane Clemens and her daughter were awakened to find a form in white entering their room. "Presently a hand was laid on the coverlet, first at the foot, then at the head of the bed." It was Sam, sleepwalking. "He had risen and thrown a sheet around him in his dreams. He walked in his sleep several nights in succession after that."[21] What Paine does not say is that apparently young Sam Clemens, peeping through a keyhole, had watched a doctor perform a post-mortem on his father. As Wecter notes, doubtless the shock of the death and the guilty secret of the post-mortem had more to do with the "heavy hand" of remorse and the somnambulism than any deathbed promise to his mother to be a good boy.[22]

What I am attempting to establish is not the nature of the guilt[23] so much as the fact that evidently it had considerable to

20. Bernard DeVoto, "Symbols of Despair," *Mark Twain at Work* (Cambridge, Mass., 1942), p. 116.

21. Albert Bigelow Paine, *Mark Twain: A Biography*, I (New York, 1912), 74–75.

22. Wecter, pp. 117–118.

23. For a survey of the long history of critical dispute over the nature of Mark Twain's "wound," see Lewis Leary, "Mark Twain's Wound: Standing with Reluctant Feet," in Leary, *Southern Excursions: Essays on Mark Twain and Others* (Baton Rouge, La., 1971), pp. 42–74.

do with Samuel Clemens's ambivalent feelings toward John Marshall Clemens. The consciousness of his "wildness, disobedience, indifference to his father's wishes," the "hundred things, in themselves trifling," which could nevermore be undone, must indeed have made him feel his inability to feel proper respect for his father's Stoic dignity and to emulate it. He feared his father, he resented his father, and if he felt awe and admiration he also felt contempt. Sam Clemens could not muster, for the memory of John Marshall Clemens and what he stood for, the kind of unquestioning respect that he shows Colonel Grangerford as receiving in *Huckleberry Finn*. He did not believe in it, or in any case believe in it enough to live by it. His father was not only the lordly Colonel Grangerford; he was also the impractical Squire Hawkins and the unworldly Colonel Sellers of *The Gilded Age*, and the judge of *Huckleberry Finn* whose sentimentality delivered Huck over to his father's sordid brutality; and the credulous King Arthur of *A Connecticut Yankee* who allowed Merlin to hoodwink him so thoroughly; and every other gentleman of aristocratic pretensions who proved either culpable or vulnerable or both, in a wicked world.

In Mark Twain's day there was a literary tradition, or more precisely a subliterary, journalistic tradition, which was based squarely on the humor implicit in the confrontation of gentlemanly refinement and breeding with the vernacular shrewdness and realism of the new country beyond the Appalachians. The tradition had moved westward with the Southern frontier— from Longstreet's rural Georgia to Baldwin's flush times in Alabama and Mississippi to Thorpe's big bear of Arkansas. It was not the Literature of the Old South and the Northeast; it did not draw on the plantation stereotype and the chivalry of Sir Walter Scott; its language convention was not that of the historical romance. But it was equally a part of the Southern experience, and always had been. It was to this literary mode that Samuel Clemens instinctively turned, composing squibs in the print shop of Orion Clemens's newspaper, and later scribbling tales while in various places West, East, and South, as well as in the

pilot house of steamboats on the river. He was always writing
something, his teacher and crony Horace Bixby remembered.
And had Clemens been only a journalist, only a Southwestern
funnyman, that is doubtless the vein he would have worked the
rest of his life. But he was not merely a comic journalist. He was
Samuel L. Clemens, for whom being funny was not enough. He
went West for a few years, then East, and each of his books, as
Henry Nash Smith shows so convincingly, steadily deepened
their exposure to the values that lay beneath the comedy upon
the surface.[24]

The little village of Hannibal became St. Petersburg, and
then Dawson's Landing and Hadleyburg, and finally Eseldorf.
The gap between the real and the ideal, at first merely humorous, grew into a chasm that laughter could not longer bridge,
until the rage at its failure to do so turned into a desperate effort
for transcendence, the attempt to convince oneself that "you
perceive, *now*, that these things are all impossible, except in a
dream. You perceive that they are pure and puerile insanities,
the silly creations of an imagination that is not conscious of its
freaks—in a word, that they are a dream, and you the maker of
it."[25] At such times the best thing to do is to solace oneself with
the thought that, for twenty-three hours a day at least, in the
eyes of the world one is no small thing, but the *Begum*, of
Bengal, one hundred and forty-two days out from Canton, homeward bound.

What has this vision to do with the South? Simply everything. For what we have is a situation in which the private
experience of the writer matches so perfectly the public meaning
of the time and place that the concerns of one serve to exemplify
and embody the concerns of the other. Henry Nash Smith has
shown how the art of Mark Twain involves a developing exploration of the potentialities of the vernacular democratic

24. *Mark Twain: The Development of a Writer*, op. cit.
25. Mark Twain, "No. 44, The Mysterious Stranger," in *Mark Twain's
Mysterious Stranger Manuscripts*, ed. William M. Gibson (Berkeley and Los
Angeles: Univ. of California Press, 1969), p. 405.

culture as a replacement for the Official Culture, and of how this exploration was embodied in language. In an early work such as *Innocents Abroad*, the vernacular values of the narrator clash with traditional cultural attitudes toward the art, history, and sacred institutions of the Old World. In *Tom Sawyer* the genteel narrator serves only as a frame, with the chief narrator focus placed on the direct description of Tom's experience in the village. In *Huckleberry Finn*, through using for persona the viewpoint of a youth whose relationship to polite society is peripheral and disaffiliated, Mark Twain moves into a critique of the professed values of the society. The contradictions between the idealistic pieties and inflated rhetoric and the realities of selfishness, repression, sentimentality and brutality are given ever more savage exposure, until the story threatens to turn into a tragedy, so that the author must yank it back into burlesque. Is not this process, with its developing tension between aristocratic and democratic, genteel and vernacular, Romantic and realistic modes, exemplified on their personal level in the child Sam Clemens's mixed admiration and contempt for the Virginian John Marshall Clemens? And on the historical, political level in the movement of the border South away from the aristocratic ideal of the old Tidewater? And does not the progressive discovery of the possibilities of the plain style, the "language of truth," as Lionel Trilling will have it,[26] embody in language the dynamics of the breakthrough from the windblown metaphor and ornate literary diction of so much Old South writing?

Mark Twain did not have to invent his style out of nowhere. The model was at hand—but in the subliterature and journalism of the Old Southwest humor. What he did was to intensify and elevate that style into the full imaginative ordering of literature. This was his triumph, his great contribution to the development of American fiction. The Midwest realists of the 1890s and thereafter would adopt it for their purposes, but would use it for purposes of deliberate understatement; they would turn its sim-

26. Lionel Trilling, "Introduction," *The Adventures of Huckleberry Finn*, p. xviii.

plicity into a means of depicting innocence betrayed, which was never Mark Twain's approach and was not what Huck Finn was about at all. The twentieth-century Southerners would use it to cut away the excesses of the old high style and give new sinew and strength to the sensuous documentation of experience. It is impossible to read a work such as "Spotted Horses" or "The Bear," or the better stories of Flannery O'Connor, for example, without seeing the example of the prose style of Mark Twain. With each step away from the literary language of genteel society, Mark Twain moves away from the official pieties and values of the community toward a searching scrutiny of those values. To cite only one example of many such, the joyful community affirmation of the church service in *Tom Sawyer*, in which the congregation choruses "Old Hundred" when the supposedly drowned youths return in glory, becomes, when seen through Huck's eyes and with Huck's language, the hypocrisy of Miss Watson at prayer and the orgiastic sentimentality of the King at the camp-meeting (a scene drawn directly from Southwestern humor by way of Sut Lovingood).

We might profitably compare the camp meeting scene to William Faulkner's portrayal of the Reverend Hightower and his relationship with the congregation in *Light in August*. Hightower perceives, at the end of the novel, that "that which is destroying the Church is not the outward groping of those within it nor the inward groping of those without, but the professionals who control it and who have removed the bells from the steeples . . ."[27] Faulkner criticizes the perversion and prostitution of the religious values by those entrusted with their affirmation, but Mark Twain suggests that religion and piety themselves are hypocrisy and selfishness; when Huck decides that "All right, then, I'll go to hell!" it is organized religion itself that is found wanting. But here Mr. Holman's distinction is useful. Faulkner is of the Deep South, whose writers, like those of the Tidewater, "have found the standards to judge their societies

27. William Faulkner, *Light in August* (New York: Modern Library, 1950), p. 426.

in the ideals of their citizens, however little these ideals found firm expression" within the society itself, while Mark Twain is of the border South, where "the standard by which it is judged, whether it be that of social justice, of religious order, or of moral indignation, has always been an outer and different standard from that embraced by the local inhabitants."[28] The border South of which Sam Clemens was a part was engaged, in Clemen's own time, in just such a breaking away from the aristocratic ideal of the Tidewater and the Deep South as characterized the Piedmont South of a later day, toward a more generally American frame of reference; and the movement of Sam Clemens away from Hannibal and onto the river and then to West and back East embodies the process of dislodgement. Not simply the values of the society being left behind, but the tensions of the breakaway itself, are part of the Southern experience.

Yet one might well ask this: if what is important is the breaking away, the dislodgement, then at what point in the transaction does the original identity cease importantly to matter? Granted that Samuel Clemens was born into a Southern community, does he not cease, fairly early in the development of his art, to be part of it?

The answer, I believe, is that the essence of the art *is* the breaking away, and is constituted of the tension between the pull of the old community and that of the forces separating the individual from it. In the art the separation can never really be effected, since the comedy and the pathos alike of Mark Twain's work consist of the effort to separate and the effort to resist the separation, expressed not uncharacteristically in the humor of incongruity. Here we have to watch Sam Clemens very carefully, for he was a master of disguise and duplicity. Consider the famed castigation of the Old South, the diagnosis of Sir Walter Scott disease that caused fake medieval castles to be built in Baton Rouge and "created rank and caste down there, and

28. Holman, *Three Modes of Modern Southern Fiction*, p. 53.

also reverence for rank and caste, and pride and pleasure in them."[29] Huck Finn himself diagnosed the Sir Walter Scott disease in this fashion: "So then I judged that all that stuff was only just one of Tom Sawyer's lies. I reckoned he believed the A-rabs and the elephants, but as for me I think different. It had all the marks of a Sunday-school."[30]

Yet Mark Twain cannot end that novel without summoning back Tom Sawyer and his A-rabs and elephants, and in defiance of the laws of fictional probability must bring him back onto the scene for the Phelps Farm "evasion." And as for rank and caste, he has Colonel Sherburn step out into the squalor and mud of the main street of Bricksville and shoot an old drunk who abuses him, and then stand off a lynch mob, for all the world the defiant aristocrat who has contemptuously refused to be soiled by the riffraff. Sherburn tells the mob, with what can only be considered the full approval of Mark Twain (who has even shifted his persona from Huck to Sherburn for the purpose of having the speech delivered), that

I was born and raised in the South, and I've lived in the North; so I know the average all around. The average man's a coward. In the North he lets anybody walk over him that wants to, and goes home and prays for a humble spirit to bear it. In the South one man, all by himself, has stopped a stage full of men in the daytime, and robbed the lot. Your newspapers call you a brave people so much that you think you *are* braver than any other people—whereas you're just as brave, and no braver. Why don't your juries hang murderers? Because they are afraid the man's friends will shoot them in the back, in the dark—and it's just what they *would* do.[31]

The trouble with Southern writing, Samuel Clemens tells us in *Life on the Mississippi*, is that it hangs onto its old, inflated

29. *Life on the Mississippi*, p. 376.
30. *Adventures of Huckleberry Finn*, p. 14.
31. Ibid., p. 259.

style—"filled with wordy, windy, flowery 'eloquence,' romanticism, sentimentality . . ."—while the North has now discarded
it.[32] But here is a three-sentence description of sunrise on the
Mississippi from the same book:

> You have the intense green of the massed and crowded
> foliage near by; you see it paling shade by shade in front of
> you; upon the next projecting cape, a mile off or more, the
> tint has lightened to the tender young green of spring; the
> cape beyond that one has almost lost color, and the furthest
> one, miles away under the horizon, sleeps on the water a
> mere dim vapor, and hardly separable from the sky above it
> and about it. And all this stretch of river is a mirror, and
> you have the shadowy reflections of the leafage and the
> curving shores and the receding capes pictured in it. Well,
> that is all beautiful: soft and rich and beautiful; and when
> the sun gets well up, and distributes a pink flush here and a
> powder of gold yonder and a purple haze where it will yield
> the best effect, you grant that you have seen something that
> is worth remembering.[33]

It is not a bad passage at all, but it is a far cry from Huck Finn's
way of putting things, though if Tom Sawyer had written the
next book instead of Huck he would have said it pretty much
like that. The point is that when Mark Twain sounds off about
the South's reliance upon the rhetorical embellishment, he is
also chastizing an aspect of himself, and not something he has
long since put permanently behind him. Tom Sawyer's way of
building up his adventures so that they will provide "theatrical
gorgeousness" is the way of Sir Walter Scott, and though Mark
Twain pokes fun at it, the next minute he will turn around and
do the same sort of thing himself. Let us not forget that the
book that follows *Huckleberry Finn* is *A Connecticut Yankee*,
which however it satirizes feudalism involves an exploit that
Tom Sawyer would have been proud to bring off.

32. *Life on the Mississippi*, p. 377.
33. Ibid., p. 259.

It has always seemed to me that in *A Connecticut Yankee* the whole ambivalent love-hate relationship of Sam Clemens with the South is dramatized and laid out plainly. That the Arthurian England that Hank Morgan, master mechanic from Connecticut, sets out to reform is in effect the South of Clemens's youth, is clear from the very outset, as in the Yankee's description of the first town he sees: "In the town were some substantial windowless houses of stone scattered among a wilderness of thatched cabins; the streets were mere crooked alleys, and unpaved; troops of dogs and nude children played in the sun and made life and noise; hogs roamed and rooted contentedly about, and one of them lay in a reeking wallow in the middle of the main thoroughfare and suckled her family."[34] Substitute a few details, and that could be Hannibal, St. Petersburg, Bricksville, or Dawson's Landing. Hank Morgan is appalled by the squalor and the torpor, and proceeds to show the king and the knights of the Round Table what Yankee know-how and democratic egalitarianism can do toward eradicating the feudal backwardness of Old England. It is not long before he has the knights going about on their errantry wearing advertising boards and with soap commercials on the trimmings of their noble steeds. At the crisis of his battle to eradicate feudalism, he challenges a horde of armed knights to a battle to the death, and pots eleven of them with his Colt revolvers, causing the others to break and flee. "Knight-errantry was a doomed institution," he exults. "The march of civilization was begun. How did I feel? Ah you never could imagine it." Thereupon he sets out to modernize Old England, and he does pretty well:

Now look around on England. A happy and prosperous country, and strangely altered. Schools everywhere, and several colleges; a number of pretty good newspapers. Even authorship was taking a start. . . . Slavery was dead and gone; all men were equal before the law; taxation had been

34. Samuel Langhorne Clemens, *A Connecticut Yankee in King Arthur's Court*, facsimile of the first edition (San Francisco: Chandler Publishing Co., 1963), p. 28.

equalized. The telegraph, the telephone, the phonograph, the type-writer, the sewing machine, and all the thousand willing and handy servants of steam and electricity were working their way into favor . . .

Even a stock market had been instituted:

> Sir Launcelot, in his richest armor, came striding along the great hall, now, on his way to the stock-board; he was president of the stock-board, and occupied the Siege Perilous, which he had bought of Sir Galahad; for the stock-board consisted of the Knights of the Round Table, and they used the Round Table for business purposes, now. Seats at it were worth—well, you would never believe the figure, so it is no use to state it. Sir Launcelot was a bear, and he had put up a corner in one of the new lines, and was just getting ready to squeeze the shorts to-day; but what of that?[35]

As we know, however, it does not succeed. The medieval Church, with its massive authority of superstition, pronounces an Interdict. The supposedly democratized and liberated freemen revert to their former state of cowed, timid slavery. Everything is shut down, and ultimately the massed chivalry of Arthurian England marches against Hank Morgan's fortress. With horrible savagery the Yankee and his few loyal followers blow up, electrocute, and otherwise annihilate the entire establishment, their own citadel included. At the end only the Yankee is left, to sleep for eleven centuries under Merlin's spell, awakening briefly in the nineteenth century to die at last, lonely and lost, dreaming of a simple love long ago.

Henry Nash Smith has convincingly interpreted the tale as Mark Twain's fable of progress, and he identifies the terrible demolition at the close as an expression of the author's despair at the moral implications of the vernacular culture of the capitalistic nineteenth century. Because he could not finally discover a meaning for the society that has replaced what he had known

35. Ibid., pp. 515–516.

and had rejected, he blew the whole experiment to smithereens. "He had planned a fable illustrating how the advance of technology fosters the moral improvement of mankind. But when he put his belief to the test by attempting to realize it in fiction, the oracle of his imagination, his institution, the unconsciously formulated conclusions based on his observation and reading, his childhood heritage of Calvinism, at any rate some force other than his conscious intention convinced him that his belief in progress and human perfectibility was groundless."[36]

What I find interesting is the striking appropriateness of the story and its outcome to the South that Sam Clemens knew—a relevance that Smith and also James M. Cox, in *Mark Twain: The Fate of Humor*, have recognized. In effect it is a fable of the New South, as I see it. Is not the picture of the "happy and prosperous country" that Hank Morgan, the Yankee, creates out of the feudalism of Old England very much akin to the vision of the New South as advanced by Henry W. Grady, Marse Henry Watterson, and many others during Samuel Clemens's times, and which would convert the former Confederacy into a replica of the industrial Northeast where the adult Samuel Clemens lived? Factories, schools, newspapers, commerce, all the modern inventions; slavery dead and gone, and the former knight-errants become stockbrokers who "used the Round Table for business purposes, now"—this is just how he described and praised the up-to-date aspects of commercial New Orleans in *Life on the Mississippi*. Every one of the improvements is cited, and praised, even down to the newspapers and the authorship. If only the entire South, he suggests in that book, would throw off its "Walter Scott Middle-Age sham civilization," its "silliness and emptiness, sham grandeurs, sham gauds, and sham chivalries of a brainless and worthless long-vanished society," then it, like New England, might amount to something in the world.[37]

At times in *A Connecticut Yankee* he is explicit about the

36. Smith, p. 170. Smith's more extensive analysis of *A Connecticut Yankee* is *Mark Twain's Fable of Progress* (New Brunswick, N.J., 1964).
37. *Life on the Mississippi*, p. 375.

South's similarity to feudal England. Describing the callousness with which a group of pilgrims watched slaves being driven along a road, Hank Morgan comments, "They were too much hardened by lifelong every-day familiarity with slavery to notice that there was anything else in the exhibition that invited comment. That was what slavery could do, in the way of ossifying what one may call the superior lobe of human feeling; for these pilgrims were kindhearted people, and they would not have allowed a man to treat a horse like that."[38] Again, when Hank Morgan becomes disgusted with the way that oppressed peasantry instinctively sides with its noble oppressors, it "reminded me of a time thirteen centuries away, when the 'poor whites' of our South who were always despised and frequently insulted, by the slave-lords all around them, and who owed their basic condition simply to the presence of slavery in their midst, were yet pusillanimously ready to side with slave-lords in all political moves for the perpetuating of slavery, and did also finally shoulder their muskets and pour out their lives in an effort to prevent the destruction of that very institution which degraded them."[39]

Yet when the railroads and the factories and the telephones come, and the Round Table becomes a stock market and money-making replaces knight-errantry and chivalry, the outcome is not what is hoped. Not at all. So that the author's attitude toward Hank Morgan seems to change. Toward the end he becomes more callous, and when having slaughtered 25,000 knights he issues congratulatory battle communiques that burlesque those of Napoleon and the generals of the Civil War, the Yankee has changed from being an emissary of progress and freedom into a smug, conceited, cold-blooded war lord himself. He has wiped out feudalism and slavery and backwardness, but at the cost of dehumanizing himself and becoming a symbol of the nineteenth century's much more efficient brand of military destruction. The arrival of industrial capitalism in the green field of Old England has proved pretty much of a disaster.

38. *A Connecticut Yankee*, p. 262.
39. Ibid., p. 387.

One of the drawings that Dan Beard did for the original edition of *A Connecticut Yankee* is quite revealing in this respect. It illustrates an episode in which King Arthur, though he wishes to see how the common people live, refuses the Yankee's suggestion that he learn to refer to a peasant as friend or brother. "Brother!—to dirt like that?" he asks. Beard provides a three-part drawing. The first shows a fat, bloated king, before whom a peasant in chains bows his head. The second shows an equally fat, bloated Southern planter complete with wide-brimmed hat and whip, with a black slave before him wearing a halter. The third shows a smug, officious-looking nineteenth-century businessman, with a workingman standing before him. Beneath the picture of the king is a sword, beneath that of the planter is a law book, and beneath that of the industrialist a group of money bags. Under each drawing appears the identical cutline, three times repeated: "Brother!—to dirt like that?"[40]

I am not suggesting that in *A Connecticut Yankee* Samuel L. Clemens sat down to compose an allegory of the New South. What I am saying is that he envisioned feudal England in terms of the South, and set out to show how it could be made into a garden with the coming of progress, industrial development and democracy, only to realize at the end that the nineteenth-century industrial capitalism of Northeastern society was no valid alternative—whereupon he destroyed the whole thing in his rage and frustration, and ended with a lonely old man dreaming of a simpler past, and very much out of place in the modern world. The confusion of the fable, I believe, comes directly out of Samuel Clemens's Southern origins, and its roots go all the way back to the Hannibal days. We can observe the results all too clearly in the episode in which Hank Morgan tries to tutor King Arthur in the ways of imitating the manner and bearing of the peasantry. For such purposes, he says, "your soldiery stride, your lordly port—these will not do. You stand too straight, your looks are too high, too confident . . . shamble . . . . You see, the

40. Ibid., p. 363.

genuine spiritlessness is wanting; that's what's the trouble."[41]
The intent of the passage, and of several others, is to show that
the peasantry has been so beaten down by oppression that its
members are cowed and defeated. But what goes wrong is Samuel Clemens's ambivalent attitude toward aristocracy; he admires
King Arthur's dignity and manliness so much that it becomes a
matter not of upbringing but of inherent kingly character. King
Arthur is a *king*; it is inborn in him, and Samuel Clemens admires just that kingliness, even though the implications happen
to be disastrous for his social theorizing. Arthur is a king *because*
he is kingly, and thus he will not compromise. One is reminded
of Clemens's description of his father, as "Judge Carpenter," in
his unpublished "Villagers of 1840–43": "Silent, austere, of perfect probity and high principle; ungentle of manner toward his
children, but always a gentleman in his phrasing—and never
punished them—a look was enough, and more than enough."[42]
This kind of figure appears constantly in Mark Twain's fiction.

One could go on in this fashion with *A Connecticut Yankee*,
but there is no need for it. The Southern experience of Samuel
L. Clemens is so thoroughly and deeply imaged in his life and
work that one may scarcely read a chapter of any of his books
without encountering it. It was, after all, no callow youth, but a
24-year-old man, who quit the Marion Rangers and joined his
brother Orion for the journey out to the silver fields. How much
more important to Sam Clemens the issues and loyalties of the
Civil War must have been than he pretends they were in "The
Private History of a Campaign that Failed," in which the confederate enlistment is depicted simply as a lark by unthinking
boys. Surely it went deeper than that. Cox ascribes Clemens's
later zeal to identify himself as a loyal Radical Republican to the
zeal of a popular humorist to have the approval of his audience,
and his fear that such approval would be withheld if his South-

41. Ibid., pp. 361–362.
42. Mark Twain, "Villagers of 1840–43," in *Mark Twain's Hannibal,
Huck and Tom*, ed. Walter Blair (Berkeley and Los Angeles: Univ. of California Press, 1969), p. 43.

ern past were known. Until the "Private History" was published in 1885, Cox declares, "the Civil War had been the great unwritten experience in the tall tale of his past. Moreover, it had been not simply forgotten, but evaded—and evaded from the very beginning. The discovery of 'Mark Twain' in the Nevada Territory in 1863, while it had been Samuel Clemens's discovery of his genius, had quite literally been a way of escaping the Civil War past which lay behind him in Missouri. In effect, the humorous identity and personality of 'Mark Twain' was a grand evasion of the Civil War. His form, the tall tale, was a means of converting all the evasions and failures of Samuel Clemens into the invasions and excursions of Mark Twain. Thus, aspects of the innocent, the gullible, the foolish, and the incompetent 'young' Mark Twain are rehearsed by the experienced and 'old' Mark Twain. Omitted in this humorous strategy is the transition between youth and age, failure and success, innocence and knowledge."[43]

And this, I think, is largely true. For the greatest art of Mark Twain is an art of childhood—Tom Sawyer in St. Petersburg, the cub pilot learning his trade (but never practicing it), Huck Finn and Jim on the raft. "So endeth this chronicle," *Tom Sawyer* concludes. "It being strictly the history of a *boy*, it must stop here; the story could not go on much further without becoming the history of a man."[44] But into that childhood the author thrust the concerns of his adult years. Tom Sawyer is a "hymn to boyhood," but it is a boyhood in which the nostalgic image of an innocent childhood in a drowsing little town is made the scene of a young boy's determined battle for recognition and fame within the community, culminating, in heroism, success, the accolades of the leading citizens, and wealth—money let out at 6 percent. It *must* end, all right, for what else could Tom do to maintain the delusion that the A-rabs and the elephants were

43. James M. Cox, *Mark Twain: The Fate of Humor* (Princeton, N.J., 1966), p. 196.
44. Mark Twain, *The Adventures of Tom Sawyer, Complete Works of Mark Twain*, I (New York, 1922), 292.

all about him, and not just the Sunday school? The riverboat cub pilot of *Life on the Mississippi*, significantly younger and more naive than Sam Clemens was when he learned his trade, masters his craft and becomes a pilot, but there the story ends, to be resumed one page and 21 years later when the former pilot turned author comes back to inspect the river again. Besides, now that the tugboats and barges have taken over, and the pilot's association has been outmaneuvered by the boat owners, "the association and the noble science of piloting were things of the dead and pathetic past!"[45] Huck Finn, who did not believe in A-rabs and elephants, flees from the conformity and hypocrisy of the village and sets out on a long voyage downriver, his companion a runaway slave. As the journey progresses, the exploration of the corruption of the society along the banks widens, culminating in Colonel Sherburn's denunciation of the mob and then the claustrophobic, suffocating presentation of ignorant cruelty and emotion-starved sentimentality that is the Wilkes family episode. After that, Jim is sold into captivity, and Huck makes his liberating decision: to disregard the "conscience" that his society has given him to distinguish between right and wrong, and free his friend. But when he arrives at Phelps Farm, it is not really a Deep South farm that he finds: it is that of Sam Clemens's uncle John Quarles in Florida, Missouri,[46] only viewed not as the child Sam Clemens knew it but as it would appear to Huck Finn. Using Huck for his persona, Clemens can see the country of his youth without the blinders of nostalgia. But Huck cannot *act*. So along comes Tom Sawyer and the great evasion, and the terrible anticlimax at the close in which we learn that Tom has known all along that Jim was free.

Why that wretched undercutting? Why could not Mark Twain have let Tom help Huck to free the slave? Because Samuel Clemens knew only too well that the boy that Tom Sawyer symbolized could never have set a slave free. Such was the con-

45. *Life on the Mississippi*, p. 142.
46. For a discussion of the imagery of the Quarles Farm in Clemens's fiction, see Smith, *Mark Twain: The Development of a Writer*, pp. 129–132.

tinuing hold of his Southern childhood upon Samuel Clemens's imagination: Huck might assume Tom's name at the farm, but Huck, with what he knew, could never *be* Tom. Yet Mark Twain had to become Tom again in order to end the novel.

Artistically, all that follows *Huckleberry Finn* is a comedown. In *A Connecticut Yankee* the old South, with its feudalism and pseudo-chivalric ideal, is changed into the postwar industrial society of the urban Northeast, but that does not work either, and must be erased in explosion and rage. In *Pudd'nhead Wilson* the drowsing village becomes Dawson's Landing with its confused and hopeless nightmare of miscegenation, hypocrisy, and violence; black is white, white black; the upright Virginia-born judge is dishonored and murdered. It has not helped to change things around so that the enslaved man is white and the aristocrat is a Negro; for the slavewoman whose story it is, what matters in life has been destroyed: "her hurts were too deep for money to heal; the spirit in her eyes was quenched, her martial bearing departed with it, and the voice of her laughter ceased in the land. In her church and its affairs she found her only solace." Clemens is clearly unable to make any sense of the story; significantly, even the active persona of Mark Twain is missing from the scene, appearing only in the calendar entries which serve as headnotes for the chapters. We are left with Pudd'nhead Wilson's cynical maxim for summation: "October 12, the *Discovery*. It was wonderful to find America, but it would have been more wonderful to miss it."[47]

Mark Twain was born in the border South, of a Virginian father and a Kentucky-born mother. He grew up in a little slaveholding village along the river, a village very much like others in the country beyond the Tidewater and the mountains, where in his own words, "there were grades of society; people of good family, people of unclassified family, people of no family. Everybody knew everybody, and was affable to everybody, and nobody put on any visible airs; yet the class lines were quite clearly

47. *Pudd'nhead Wilson*, p. 142.

drawn, and the familiar social life of each class was restricted to that class. It was a little democracy that was full of Liberty, Equality, and Fourth of July; and sincerely so, too, yet you perceive that the aristocratic taint was there."[48] *His* family, by birth and pretension at least, was of the aristocracy, and his father a lawyer and leading citizen of the village. But in that town and in that time and place, it was not enough to be an aristocrat; for this was not Virginia, but the border South, where the land was too cheap and people too much on the move to remain within the old patterns. Unable and unwilling to lower himself, as he must have seen it, to the requirements for prospering in that new country, John Marshall Clemens failed, and left his son a legacy of decline and fall, the pride of honorable bearing and the knowledge of its pathos and its inadequacy.

Had Samuel Clemens been born in the Deep South and had things worked out there in the same way, the literary result might well have been the equivalent of the Quentin Compson of *The Sound and the Fury*, holding desperately to concepts of Southern honor in a world of Snopses and change, and finding a resolution only in tragedy. But this was the border South, and he was Sam Clemens of Missouri, who perceived the absurdity equally with the pathos.

Or to speculate further—always a risky business, to be sure— had he lived further South, the war might have caught him up in its magnitude—and surely his father would have wanted it that way for him, once Virginia had been invaded—and left him trapped in the confusion and the shock of the defeated Confederacy. Instead he went West with his brother, became a humorist, and then came East, where he flung himself gleefully into the money-making frenzy of the Gilded Age, scheming to make millions with typesetting machines and kaolin compounds in much the same way that Tom Sawyer dreamed of pirate gold. But all the while the forces of his creative imagination held ferociously on, in resentment and in pride, to that faraway coun-

48. Mark Twain, "Jane Lampson Clemens," in *Mark Twain's Hannibal, Huck and Tom*, ed. Blair, p. 46.

try of his youth. Again and again he sought in art to find in the play of his memory the order and meaning that would tell him who he was. In comedy he strove to articulate and resolve the tensions, incongruities, and contradictions that his restless self-scrutiny kept turning up. His great weapon was laughter. When finally it failed, he was left high and dry, dictating rambling memories to a secretary, along with furious but ineffective tirades against a hostile universe.

When we come to assess the place of Samuel L. Clemens in the story of Southern literature, this much seems obvious. Clemens, as no one else in Southern literature before the twentieth century, brought to bear upon the Southern experience a critical scrutiny that enabled him to search below the surface pieties and loyalties and get at the underlying conflicts and tensions within the society. It seems safe to say that he saw these things so well because they were to be found within his own heart as well as in the life around him. No other Southern writer came close to the liberation he achieved. He was able to do it for at least two reasons. The first was that by accident of time and place, he was jarred loose from the Southern community in a way that none of the others were, with the social tensions involved therein present within his family and his society. The second reason, of course, was that he was Mark Twain.

He stands, with all his genius and his shortcomings, in a relationship to the society he knew that anticipates that of the generation of writers who came to literary maturity after the first world war. Not for decades after his time would there be other Southern writers who would find themselves both tied to and dissociated from the Southern community in something like the way he was. When that day came, the twentieth-century Southern literary renascence would be under way.

In February of 1901 a gathering was held at Carnegie Hall in New York City to celebrate the 92nd birthday of Abraham Lincoln. The purpose was to raise funds for the Lincoln Memorial University at Cumberland Gap, Tennessee. Colonel

Henry Watterson, editor of the Louisville *Courier-Journal* and a leading propagandist for the New South of commerce and industry, was the featured speaker, and to introduce the noted Marse Henry the sponsors called upon a cousin of his, Samuel L. Clemens. Mark Twain opened with some humorous remarks, and then went on about how he and Henry Watterson, both of them ex-rebels, were, like thousands of other Southern boys who had fought bravely for the flag they loved, proud to pay their homage to Abraham Lincoln, remembering only that "we are now indistinguishably fused together and nameable by one common great name—Americans."[49]

It was a fairly standard reconciliation speech, one of many such made by many Southerners during those years. The curious thing, however, is the pose that Samuel L. Clemens was assuming for that occasion. "We of the South are not ashamed," he declared, of having fought against the Union, for "we did our bravest best, against despairing odds, for the cause that was precious to us and which our conscience approved; and we are proud—and you are proud—the kindred blood in your veins answers when I say it—you are proud of the record we made in those mighty collisions in the fields."[50]

Knowing what we do of the several weeks of active avoidance of all possible collisions in the fields of Missouri that marked the entire Civil War record of Lieutenant Samuel Clemens of the Marion Rangers, what are we to make of that performance? Was he being ironic? What would Huck Finn have thought of it? God only knows. I doubt very much that Mark Twain knew himself.

Louis D. Rubin, jr.
*University of North Carolina
at Chapel Hill*

49. Mark Twain, "On Lincoln's Birthday," in *Mark Twain's Speeches,* p. 231.
50. Ibid., p. 230.

# HEMINGWAY'S EMPIRICAL IMAGINATION

> "What is a course of history or philosophy, or poetry, no matter how well selected . . . compared with the discipline of looking always at what is to be seen?"
>
> Thoreau, *Walden*

> "I thought we did not deserve to live in the world if we did not see it."
>
> Hemingway, *African Journal*

## I

All readers of fiction know it. It arrives with a flash of immediate and warming recognition, like passing an open fire on a cold day. It is the assurance, felt in our very bones, that we are confronting the actual, albeit within a frame of invention. It is the impression of vital authenticity, and whether it occurs at the beginning, the middle, or the end of a story, it arrests our attention, as a real nightingale might do if we found it perched upon an artificial bough of an artificial tree somewhere in the parklands of the holy city of Byzantium.

In Kipling's "Love-o'-Women," for example, a quiet sergeant has just shot down one of his corporals at the end of morning parade. "The horror, the confusion, and the separation of the murderer from his comrades," writes Kipling, "were all over before I came. There remained only on the barrack-square the blood of man calling from the ground. The hot sun had dried it to a dusky goldbeater's-skin film, cracked lozenge-wise by the heat; and as the wind rose, each lozenge, rising a little, curled up at the edges as if it were a dumb tongue. Then a heavier gust blew all away down wind in grains of dark-coloured dust." Kipling, of course, elaborates and frames his effect with biblical analogy and anatomical simile: "the blood of man calling from the ground," and "as if it were a dumb tongue." What we do not forget are the dark-golden lozenges curling at the edges in the immense heat, cracking and blowing away in the furnace-gust of morning wind.[1]

Another example comes near the end of Hardy's *Jude the Obscure*. Arabella and Jude have just gone off to be remarried, and Tinker Taylor is offering the company his opinion of the "retread" bride. "Take her all together, limb by limb," says he, "she's not such a bad-looking piece—particular by candlelight. To be sure, halfpence that have been in circulation can't be expected to look like new ones from the mint. But . . . she's passable enough. A little bit thick in the flitch perhaps: but I like a woman that a puff o' wind won't blow down." In the midst of Hardy's rather wooden dialogue, Taylor's mundane and fleshly vulgarisms stand out in rough bas-relief. She is not "a bad-looking piece," passable enough, even though she is "thick in the flitch." The coin analogy heightens the effect by suggesting Arabella's perennial money-consciousness; and the use of the word *flitch*, normally a side of bacon, reminds us of her earthy origins as a pig-breeder's daughter.[2]

Like Hardy and Kipling, and indeed most other writers of fiction, Ernest Hemingway was always ready to make use of a story, an incident, an anecdote, or at least a few authentic sentences that he had picked up from the lips of close friends or chance acquaintances. Almost invariably, these were nonliterary people, a fact which endeared them to Hemingway, since they were not as a rule habitual readers, and what they said therefore held little or no taint of literature, no special literary trickery or embroidery. Where transformation was needed, he could always supply it, whether by some extemporaneous carpentry or more careful marquetry to make it fit the new context; or by in-

1. *Soldiers Three and Military Tales, Writings*, II (New York, 1920), 309.
2. *Jude the Obscure* (New York, 1895), pp. 456–457.

venting a framework within which it could be freshly displayed; or by recreating the whole in the general spirit of the original. For the rest, he stayed alert for stories that seemed to spring from that bedrock level of experience where he wished his own work to operate.

Such ideas often formed the burden of his avuncular exhortations to Fitzgerald. The good parts of a novel, he told his friend, might be something a writer was lucky enough to overhear.[3] Or again he said that Fitzgerald's fundamental problem lay in his failure to keep on listening to what went on around him. This was what dried a writer up. The moment he began listening again, he would sprout like dry grass after a good rain.[4]

The corollary of such a program was to invent so exactly in the spirit of the actual that the reader would be immediately convinced of the veracity of what he was being told. Many writers have espoused this position. Melville, for example, long ago defined writing as "the great Art of Telling the Truth."[5] Hemingway's French namesake, Ernest Renan, observed in 1860 that "the imagination . . . has often more chance of finding truth than a servile fidelity, content to reproduce the original accounts of the chroniclers."[6] It is clear that Hemingway would agree with this generalization, even though his fierce empiricism often led him to reproduce what he had personally experienced, or heard, or overheard, with only minimal imaginative manipulation, permutation, or interpolation. Yet he counted on imagination as an ancillary power. Even in the midst of a story probably based on fact, he would (naturally enough) turn to invention if by so doing he could make a better story of it. For all his talk of "absolute truth," he "lied" whenever he felt like it, often thereby increasing the force of his story. About this proposition he could be very forthright. "All a writer of fiction is really," he wrote in his *African Journal*, "is a congenital liar who invents from his

3. EH to FSF, Sept. 4 and 13, 1929.
4. EH to FSF, May 28, 1934.
5. "Hawthorne and his Mosses," in *Herman Melville, Representative Selections*, ed. Willard Thorp (New York, 1938), p. 334.
6. Emery Neff, trans., *The Poetry of History* (New York, 1942), p. 162.

own knowledge and that of other men. I am a writer of fiction and so I am a liar too and invent from what I know and what I've heard. . . . A man who writes a novel or a short story is a liar *ipso facto*. His only excuse is that he makes the truth as he invents it truer than it would be. That is what makes good writers or bad."[7]

II

Hemingway in his twenties made a fetish of accuracy and veracity in seeing and saying. Such a vignette as the following perfectly evokes an action and a scene: "I have watched two Senegalese soldiers in the dim light of the snake house of the Jardin des Plantes teasing the king cobra who swayed and tightened in tense erect rage as one of the little brown men crouched and feinted at him with his red fez."

What we do not at first notice is that the very style of this brief passage is itself and aspect of the imaginative reconditioning which has taken place. To achieve the concentration of this single sentence about the soldiers' harassment of the cobra, Hemingway pared out many elements of the situation—all onlookers besides himself, all the other snakes in their glass-walled pens, the dimensions of the building, the time of day, the season, the atmospheric odors and sounds, the temperature, the soldiers' uniforms, and dozens of other environmental factors. The essentials remain: two short, brown-skinned soldiers, one angry snake, the dramatic confrontation, the well-chosen active verbs —*teasing, swayed, tightened, crouched, feinted*—most of which suggest taut muscular control, and finally the red of the flapping fez, the single bright spot of color in that crepuscular light. Imagination does actually operate here through the selectivities of Hemingway's style. The result might well serve as an illustration for Coleridge's dictum that "Art would or should be the abridgment of nature." The rest is visual empirical data gathered

7. "An African Journal," *Sports Illustrated*, 35 (Dec. 20, 1971), unpaged insert.

through the intent observations of an experienced reporter.[8]
As he had advised Fitzgerald to do, he could also listen. A year
after the snake house sketch, he wrote another about an engagement between the British and the Boche in Belgium. "We were
in a garden at Mons. Young Buckley came in with his patrol
from across the river. The first German I saw climbed up over
the garden wall. We waited till he got one leg over and then
potted him. He had so much equipment on and looked awfully
surprised and fell down into the garden. Then three more came
over further down the wall. We shot them. They all came over
just like that."

These eight sentences so exactly catch the narrative manner
and even the intonations of a young and still enthusiastic British
officer that I once guessed, and Hemingway confirmed, that he
had heard such an anecdote, *viva voce*, from his Irish friend,
Eric Dorman-Smith, who had fought at Mons with the Northumberland Fusiliers before he was twenty. A few British locu-
tions provide the needful tone: "young Buckley," "potted him,"
and "awfully surprised." The rest is fact, recollected by an eye-
witness and faithfully reported by one who was "lucky enough to
overhear" it, about a shooting-gallery with human ducks in a
high-walled Belgian garden.[9]

8. The cobra incident is one of six one-sentence vignettes in "Paris, 1922,"
first published in *Ernest Hemingway: A Life Story* (New York, 1969), p. 91.
The observation by Coleridge is drawn from his essay, "On Poesy or Art,"
reprinted in *Biographia Literaria*, II, ed. J. Shawcross (London, 1949), 262.
In an article called "Two Hemingway Sources for *in our time*," *Studies in
Short Fiction*, 9 (Winter, 1972), 81–86, Dr. Michael S. Reynolds has shown
with great skill how Hemingway reworked two news-stories into arresting
vignettes for his first short-story collection, *in our time*, Paris, 1923. One
was the account of the execution of the Greek cabinet ministers in December,
1922 (*iot*, ch. 5). The other was the story of the cigar-store burglars in
Kansas City on November 19, 1917 (*iot*, ch. 8).
9. *in our time*, ch. 3. Eric Edward Dorman-Smith (July 24, 1895–May 11,
1969) was an Irish professional soldier who resumed his original family
name of Dorman-O'Gowan in 1949 after a distinguished career with the
British Army, from which he retired as Major-General, taking up residence at
the family seat in Bellamont Forest, Cootehill, County Cavan, Eire. He
appears as Hemingway's friend Chink in *Green Hills of Africa* (New York,
1935), pp. 279–280, and in the introduction to *Men at War*, (New York,
1942), p. xiv, and in *A Moveable Feast* (New York, 1964), pp. 53–54.

This habit of looking and listening, whether to what happened around him or to what someone told him, continued to engage Hemingway's loyalty well into his middle thirties. On a trip to Dry Tortugas, for example, he heard from Eddie Saunders, called Bra, the tale of a sunken Spanish liner, the *Val Banera*. It struck him with such force that he set it down as "After the Storm" following four years of intermediate marination in his well-stocked memory. Although we know the source, it is unhappily impossible now to distinguish what Hemingway invented in the finished story from what Saunders told him in 1928, since both Saunders and the only other auditor, Waldo Peirce, are dead. But we are not one page deep into Hemingway's story before we come upon yet another of those passages which smack of authenticity.

> Brother [says the narrator] that was some storm. I was the first boat out and you never saw water like that was. It was just as white as a lye barrel and coming from Eastern Harbor to Sou'west Key you couldn't recognize the shore. There was a big channel blown right out through the middle of the beach. Trees and all blown out and a channel cut through and all the water white as chalk and everything on it; branches and whole trees and dead birds and all floating. Inside the keys were all the pelicans in the world and all kinds of birds flying. They must have gone inside there when they knew it was coming.

Even in the retelling, the "right" phrases appear: "You never saw water like that was," "just as white as a lye barrel," "the water white as chalk and everything on it," "all the pelicans in the world," and "They must have gone inside there when they knew it was coming." It is obvious that young Hemingway, aged twenty-eight, had listened to Bra Saunders with complete attention. This was a story direct from life, piratical in flavor, with a built-in form of its own: the courageous embarkation in a small boat among still raging seas, the accidental discovery of a sunken liner filled with a fortune in gold bullion, repeated and unsuc-

cessful attempts to break into the hold, and finally a loss of all
he had longed for to the Greek sponge fisherman who had the
equipment and the experience that Bra had lacked. It was exactly the kind of yarn that Hemingway liked to know and tell:
one man alone against the elements, pitting his bravery and in-
genuity against almost insuperable counterforces, defeated finally
by circumstances beyond his control, yet winning that kind of
victory whose reward is simply the consciousness of having carried through a difficult operation with courage and endurance.
On April 15, 1932, he wrote his friend Waldo Peirce to keep
an eye out for the May *Cosmopolitan,* whose editors had paid
him $2700 for a story of a lone fisherman's abortive attempt
to break into a sunken liner. He was sure that Waldo Peirce
would remember that trip to Dry Tortugas in 1928 "when Bra
told it to us first."[10]

The volume *Winner Take Nothing* that contained "After the
Storm" included another story called "One Reader Writes." It
consists largely of a woman's letter to a newspaper medical
columnist, asking his advice about the wisdom of her coming "in
close contact" with her husband, a former Marine who contracted syphilis while stationed in Shanghai and who is now
being treated for it by the family physician. If the letter itself
rings with authenticity, as it seems to do, there is good reason
for it, since it is nothing but a slightly edited transcript of an
actual letter composed by a woman in Harrisburg, Pennsylvania
shortly before Christmas, 1931. The letter was one of a sheaf of
six handed over to Hemingway by his new friend, Dr. Logan

10. "After the Storm," in *The Fifth Column and the First Forty-Nine
Stories* (New York, 1938), pp. 470–471. The *Val Banera,* owned by Pinillos
Izquierda of Cadiz, was bound for Cuba and Louisiana with 400 passengers,
a crew of 88, and a cargo reputedly including millions in gold bullion. She
appeared briefly off Havana harbor on the night of Sept. 8, 1919, and then
vanished in the hurricane. About 1 P.M. on the 12th, the Key West Naval
Station picked up the ship's radio signal. On the 19th, the U.S. Coast Guard
cutter *Tuscarora* and a Navy subchaser found the wreck. The ship had
foundered with all hands in the quicksands near Rebecca Light. If Bra
Saunders's story, as told to Hemingway, was true, he was the first to locate
the sunken ship. Unable to get inside, he lost the fortune in gold to the
Greek sponge fishermen.

Clendening of Kansas City, who conducted a syndicated volume of medical advice. Apart from the minor editing, Hemingway merely added two sentences of fictional setting, and a brief concluding paragraph of internal monologue, in which the woman was made to reflect on her bad luck and her hopes that the doctor could provide her with trustworthy advice. This direct and literal transcript of a segment of human experience was probably the easiest short story that Hemingway ever wrote. His imagination was employed only in providing the simple framework within which the letter could be displayed.[11]

He was still in his thirties when he wrote the two nonfiction books, *Death in the Afternoon* and *Green Hills of Africa*. As one would expect, both of these offer much evidence of Hemingway's continuing skills in observational accuracy, with minimal use of imaginative fusion. Although it would be possible to multiply examples, two will do for illustration. The first is a single sentence, in kind not unlike the one he had written ten years before about the soldiers teasing the snake. This, too, catches small men in characteristic action: the paid representatives of the lordly matadors, assembled on the morning before a bullfight to inspect the bulls that will be fought that afternoon. "The representatives," writes Hemingway, "usually short men in caps, not yet shaven for the day, with a great variety of accents, but all with the same hard eyes, argue and discuss." The second is also brief, a moving picture of a Cape buffalo fleeing through the Tanganyika bush-country. "Then I saw the black back, the wide-swept, point-lifted horns and then the quick-moving, climbing rush of a buffalo on the other bank. He went up, his neck up and out, his head horn-heavy, his withers rounded like a

11. "One Reader Writes," in *The Fifth Column and the First Forty-Nine Stories*, pp. 518–519. Hemingway had spent the fall of 1931 in Kansas City, where his wife Pauline produced her second son, Gregory. There he met and befriended Dr. Logan Clendening, whose column, "Diet and Health," was syndicated in some 400 newspapers. His book, *The Human Body*, published by Alfred Knopf in 1927, had sold half a million copies by this date. Hemingway spoke of his admiration for Clendening in a letter to Guy Hickok on Dec. 12, 1931.

fighting bull, in fast strong-legged climb." At age thirty-five, Hemingway's eyes and ears were still alert for the sights and sounds of both men and beasts in characteristic action.[12]

It was in *Green Hills of Africa* that he recorded a literary conversation with an Austrian named Koritschoner, who was renamed Kandisky in the book, about the great figures of the nineteenth-century American literary renaissance. One of his victims was Emerson, whose works he had not read for years, if indeed ever. Yet if he had looked into "The American Scholar," Emerson's Phi Beta Kappa address of roughly a century before, he might have felt at least a momentary rush of fraternal feeling. For Emerson there clearly anticipates a position of Hemingway's in his statement that "So much only of life as I know by experience, so much of the wilderness have I vanquished and planted, or so far have I extended my being, my dominion."[13]

This we know also to have been Hemingway's view. It was the driving force behind his passion for ceaseless activity, for experience, vicarious or otherwise, was the very stuff of his fiction. In East Indian terms he could have been described as the type of the Karma Yogi, "the man who perfects and purifies himself through action," only afterwards pausing to metathesize that action for a literary end. In the preface to his collected stories of 1938, he set down the since famous statement that "in going where you have to go, and doing what you have to do, and seeing what you have to see, you dull and blunt the instrument you write with. But I would rather have it bent and dulled and know I had to put it on the grindstone again and hammer it into shape and put a whetstone to it, and know that I had something to write about, than to have it bright and shining and nothing to say, or smooth and well-oiled in the closet, but unused." In Emerson's terms, the experience of action, and the *ex post facto* use of it in literary forms, was the best way of vanquishing the wil-

12. Representatives: *Death in the Afternoon* (New York, 1932), p. 27. Buffalo: *Green Hills of Africa* (New York, 1935), p. 100.
13. Emerson, *Selected Prose and Poetry*, ed. Reginald L. Cook (New York, 1950), p. 55.

derness, of extending one's dominion over the broad reaches of the available green world. Again in Emerson's words, it is not too much to say of the bullfighters' representatives in Spain and the fleeing Cape buffalo in Tanganyika, that they came into Hemingway as "life" and "went out from him truth."[14]

## III

Like other authors of serious fiction, Hemingway must often have been struck by the curious and seemingly magical fashion in which the memory provides relevant materials when and where they are needed. Such was the case on two occasions which have not hitherto been documented. One occurs in "The Snows of Kilimanjaro" as part of the dying protagonist's internal monologue. The other appears in *For Whom the Bell Tolls* during a conversation in which Robert Jordan is explaining American social mores to Maria and Pilar. Both instances suggest that the empirical imagination in Hemingway might sometimes be defined as one of the modes of memory—but memory gone incandescent, fusing past particulars into new entities.

This was clearly the case with the yarn of the half-witted chore boy on a Montana ranch, one of "the stories that [Harry, the dying writer of 'The Snows'] had meant to write" but never did.[15] Having spent several seasons at a ranch just across the Montana border in Wyoming, Hemingway seems to have heard the account from some of the older men who served as guides and wranglers in the employ of Lawrence Nordquist, who owned the ranch in the early 1930s. One of these men was Leland Stanford Weaver, called Chub, who generously undertook to discover the real-life source of the story at my suggestion and request.[16]

14. Karma Yogi: see George Woodcock, *Mohandas Gandhi* (New York, 1971), p. 8. "In going where you have to go": Hemingway, *The Fifth Column and the First Forty-Nine Stories*, "Preface," p. vii. Emerson, op. cit., p. 51.
15. *The Fifth Column and The First Forty-Nine Stories*, pp. 169–170.
16. L. S. Weaver is mentioned as Chub in *For Whom the Bell Tolls* (New York, 1940), pp. 337, 381.

About April 1, 1912, as Mr. Weaver found, a Mr. Gilbert was the owner of what later became the Nordquist ranch, and he had hired as a chore boy a retarded youngster named Tony Rodicheck. "It seems," wrote Mr. Weaver, that "Gilbert was going to Cody and told Tony . . . not to let a Mr. Smith have any hay. On the way to Cody, Gilbert happened to meet Smith at Crandall Creek and gave Smith permission to get the hay. Tony was unaware of this. When Smith drove up to the barn the half-wit was in the hayloft with a gun. According to Tony, he told Smith he could not have any hay and told him to get back to his ranch. Instead of leaving, Smith got off the sled and started for the barn. Tony shot him, got down from the loft, and was going to help him. Smith refused any help and as a result bled to death. Tony just let him lay and the dogs ate off an arm. Word got out to Cody that something had happened to Smith, so the Sheriff and Mr. Gilbert went back to the ranch. They found Smith where he'd been shot. Tony was still at the house so they had him help take Smith's body to Cody. Tony had no idea he'd done anything but what he'd been told to do. In Cody he was put in jail and later sent to the asylum for life."[17]

Hemingway's version of the story elaborates somewhat on Weaver's succinct account. The visitor is called "that old bastard from the Forks who had beaten the boy when he had worked for him." When the boy denies him cattle-feed, the old man threatens to beat him again. The body lies frozen in the corral for a full week, and the dogs eat "part of him." Then the boy and Hemingway's Harry wrap the dead man in a blanket, lash the bundle to a sled, and haul it "sixty miles down to town." There the boy is said to weep when the sheriff snaps the handcuffs on his wrists, a detail missing from the Weaver version. Still, the story is substantially the same that Hemingway picked up at the Nordquist ranch in 1930 or 1932, roughly twenty years after the fact. It rose in time from the depths of his memory to claim a place in his fiction.

17. L. S. Weaver to Carlos Baker, July 22, 1967. I am much indebted to Mr. Weaver, who went to considerable trouble to run down the story of Tony Rodicheck.

Another example of Hemingway's empirical imagination at
work in the partial metamorphosis of hearsay evidence occurs in
*For Whom the Bell Tolls*. Robert Jordan interrupts Pilar's
memorable account of the massacre of the Spanish fascists with
a story about his own vicarious experience of mob action. At
age seven, as he tells Maria and Pilar, he went with his mother
to a wedding in Ohio in which he was to be one of the flower
children. The house where the ceremony took place stood on a
street-corner illuminated by an arc-light. Peering through the
window-blind, the small boy watched a mob of townspeople
hang a Negro to the arc-light. The hoisting mechanism broke,
and the mob was just hauling the victim up for another try
when Mrs. Jordan pulled her son away from the window and
he saw no more, although he later heard that the Negro's body
was not only hanged but also burned.[18]

The actual incident on which Jordan's story was based occurred in Oxford, Ohio on the evening of October 1, 1903.
Although Hemingway himself was not there, his sister Marcelline, then nearly six, had come to Ohio with her mother to be
flower-girl in the wedding of her uncle, Dr. Willoughby
Hemingway, who was marrying Mary E. Williams, daughter
of a medical missionary to China.[19] The wedding day happened
to coincide with the Fourth Annual Street Fair and Farmer's
Exposition, held in a park in the center of town. Around six
that evening, two white brothers from Kentucky became so
drunk and obstreperous that the Town Marshall and his deputy
attempted to quiet them down. Without warning, the drunks
shot both the officers and seriously wounded a bystanding student. The Kentuckians were overpowered and jailed, one of
them being seriously wounded in the melée.

Rumors now circulated that the three natives of Oxford
would probably die. An enraged mob of two or three hundred
broke into the jail, seized the unwounded brother, and dragged

18. *For Whom the Bell Tolls*, pp. 116–117.
19. Dr. Willoughby Hemingway followed his father-in-law as medical
missionary to China and a long and useful career which ended with his
death in 1932 at age 58.

him to the town park and a large elm called "the nigger tree," where two blacks had recently been lynched. There, while a crowded merry-go-round continued to do business in the immediate background, the supposed murderer was hauled off the ground three times, being let down once to write his wife, again to say his prayers, and at last when a courageous deputy sheriff from Hamilton, the county seat, managed to yank him free of the noose and run him back to jail. While various public officials pacified the crowd, the deputy spirited the brothers into a carriage and drove them to Hamilton in the dead of night. The three wounded Oxford men presently recovered, the second brother died of his wounds, and the happiest result of the whole affair was the decision by the residents of Oxford to cut down the lynching elm.[20]

News of the terrible riot on the evening of Uncle Will's wedding must obviously have been brought home to Oak Park by Marcelline and her mother, and subsequently discussed within the family circle. Although Ernest himself was only four at the time, either then or later he picked up enough of the story to serve his purposes more than thirty-five years afterwards when he imagined the situation in which Robert Jordan had been involved as a child spectator, and then introduced it into his novel as a kind of American parallel to the mob-action of the Spanish Republicans in the early stages of the Spanish Civil War.[21]

Neither of these incidents as Hemingway handles them can

20. This summary closely follows a full account of the attempted Oxford lynching most generously provided by Professor Richard S. Donnell in response to a query of mine. (Donnell to author, July 16, 1967.) He names as his chief sources the article, "Hanged Three Times!" *Hamilton Evening Sun*, October 2, 1903, p. 1, and "All Victims of Oxford Riot in a Fair Way to Recovery," *Republican-News* (Hamilton, Ohio), Oct. 2, 1903, pp. 1, 5, 8. Both papers carried follow-up stories on Oct. 5 and 6, and both printed the announcement of the Hemingway-Williams wedding on October 1.

21. This will acknowledge my debt to the late Mrs. Marcelline Hemingway Sanford, who first pointed out to me that it was she, not her brother, who had been a flower-bearer at Uncle Willoughby's wedding, and that Hemingway had used the incident of the attempted lynching in garbled form in his novel. Mrs. Sanford to author, personal interview at Grosse Pointe, Michigan, January 19, 1963.

be said to echo with quite that degree of authenticity which Kipling and Hardy managed to infuse into their accounts of a parade-ground murder in British India or Tinker Taylor's portrait of Jude Fawley's *bête noire*, Arabella. Yet all four examples point to the wisdom of Wallace Stevens's observation, "The real is only the base, but it is the base."[22]

## IV

It was also Wallace Stevens who brilliantly summarized the task of transmutation that the imagination can perform upon the materials experience provides. In one of his poems, "Description Without Place," he speaks for all artists in referring to "the difference that we make in what we see / And our memorials of that difference." Just so. No one looks at a scene, an incident, a person, an animal, or a total Gestalt experience from quite the same angle as another would do. Upon each he brings to bear the totality of his social and psychological preconditioning, a set of attitudes and beliefs that are as native to him as his fingerprints. When the thing seen emerges in literary form, it shows a measurable difference from what another person would see, and the literary expression itself is an incarnation—or in Stevens's words, a memorial—of that difference. Another poet, Robert Browning, makes a similar observation in *The Ring and the Book*. The great trick in developing an art form from an empirical base, he says, is to mingle the gold of the actual with a suitable imaginative alloy, and then, "duly tempering both," to produce a "manageable mass" for the artificer to work upon, as he could not do if the gold were left in its soft and too easily malleable state. Browning's elaborate metaphor is yet another way of describing the manner in which "prime nature" takes on an "added artistry" through the permeative powers of the artist's imagination.[23]

22. Wallace Stevens, *Opus Posthumous*, ed. Samuel French Morse (New York, 1957), p. 160.
23. Wallace Stevens, *Collected Poems* (New York, 1955), p. 344. Robert Browning, *The Ring and the Book*, Bk. 1, lines 8–29.

There seems to be general agreement that something happened to Hemingway in his later career: a gradual change in perspective that softened and sentimentalized what had formerly been as hard as a gem and as objectively accurate as some of the examples we have been citing from his earlier work. One legitimate speculation about the causes of this change might be to say that it came about because he began listening to his internal voices too much rather than too little, with the inevitable result that he began to pay less attention to those other voices babbling on around him—exactly the fate, ironically enough, against which he had warned Fitzgerald in 1934.

This is another way of saying that if the empirical imagination is not to become stagnant, it requires the constant refreshment of new sense impressions, like a lake fed by living springs. By his middle fifties, at any rate, Hemingway himself seems to have realized that his powers of observation, once so acute, were beginning to show signs of partial atrophy. In his *African Journal*, based on his adventures on safari in 1953–1954, he wrote regretfully of his failure to notice the birds around the Kimana Swamp campground. His attention was so strongly focussed on the larger predators that he "only half saw" the small birds as "moving bits of color." He was ready to call this failure a moral fault, though it may have been partly physical. "This looking and not seeing things was a great sin," he wrote, "and one that was easy to fall into. It was always the beginning of something bad and I thought that we did not deserve to live in the world if we did not see it." He blamed this great sin on too much reading and drinking, since he customarily used both as anodynes after the "concentration of serious hunting." He even spoke of drinking as "a purposeful dulling" of an observational receptivity so sharp and "highly sensitized" that it might otherwise have become unbearable. But this last statement may have been a form of whistling in the dark. The gradual failure of the arts of observation in which he had so long and proudly excelled, and on which his empirical imagination had counted so heavily for renewal and refreshment, may rather have been owing to such natural causes as advancing age and increasing fatigue.[24]

The passage in *An African Journal*, written in the fall of 1954, may be more significant than might at first appear in accounting for the partial deterioration of power which many critics have noticed in Hemingway's later work. One recent study discusses his "general decline" from a previous high point, at which he conveyed emotions to the reader in concrete terms, to a low point, as in *Across the River and into the Trees*, when he sought to engage the reader's sympathetic emotional response by abstract statement. It was if he were operating under an internal compulsion not only to "state the emotion," but also to "revel in it, relish it," as he had rarely done in the earlier days of tightlipped control and understatement. When Colonel Cantwell meets the head waiter at the Gritti Palace Hotel, for example, Hemingway tells us that "contact was made between two old inhabitants of the Veneto, both men, and brothers in their membership in the human race, the only club that either one paid dues to, and brothers, too, in their love of an old country." The point is that Hemingway would once have described the meeting in swift and graphic terms, allowing the reader to draw his own inferences. Now he preaches about it, and in a tone from which sentimentality is not entirely absent.[25]

This is one way of analyzing the problem. Another, not too distant, is to say that in some of the later works, such as *Across the River, Islands in the Stream*, and even *The Old Man and the Sea*, one finds an ulterior and perhaps subconscious tendency to exploit his personal experiences not objectively, to enrich his prose from the empirical springs, but subjectively, as a means of justifying himself and his actions in the eyes of the great world. It was exactly the tendency he had deplored in a significant fragment on Joyce's *Ulysses* written in 1924. "That was the weakness of Joyce," he wrote. "Daedalus [sic] in Ulysses was

24. Hemingway, *An African Journal*, Part II, "Miss Mary's Lion," *Sports Illustrated*, 36 (Jan. 3, 1972), unpaged insert.

25. Floyd C. Watkins, *The Flesh and the Word* (Nashville, Tenn., 1971), p. 163. Hemingway, *Across the River and into the Trees* (New York, 1950), p. 55.

Joyce himself, so he was terrible. Joyce was so damn romantic and intellectual about him." The trouble with Colonel Cantwell, Thomas Hudson, and even at times Santiago is that Hemingway allowed himself to be "damn romantic" and not so much intellectual as sentimental about them—a variation on the trap of implicit narcissism into which he believed that Joyce had fallen.[26]

Depending on the manner in which nostalgia is employed by a writer, it can strengthen or weaken his work. In the two genuine masterpieces among his novels, *A Farewell to Arms* and *For Whom the Bell Tolls*, nostalgia was among the forces that strengthened and sustained Hemingway. In the lesser works of his final years, however, nostalgia drove him to the point of exploiting his personal idiosyncrasies, as if he hoped to persuade readers to accept these in lieu of that powerful union of objective discernment and subjective response which he had once been able to achieve. Certain adumbrations of the new imbalance began to be evident as early as 1937. Even though the change seems to have been very gradual, and even though he never altogether lost that tight grip an observational accuracy which we have noticed as one distinguishing feature of his earlier work, a change of emphasis does nevertheless become evident, and it has a bearing on our answer to the question about what happened to his empirical imagination in the later work. What happened specifically, to return to Browning's metaphor, was nothing quite so simple as using more imaginative alloy and less empirical gold in the fiction he wrote from 1949 until his death in 1961. It was not so much a quantitative as a qualitative problem. For the gold, though certainly not spurious, was too often mined from the depths of his own psyche rather than from enabling sources outside himself, while the alloy of imagination in many ways softened, rather than hardening, the

26. Hemingway on Joyce: from an internal monologue by Nick Adams in the original conclusion to "Big Two-Hearted River," which Hemingway deleted before publication. Printed in part in *Ernest Hemingway: A Life Story* (New York, 1969), p. 131, and in full in *The Nick Adams Stories* (New York, 1972), pp. 233–241.

composition with which he had to work. In short, a delicate formulaic balance, hitherto so well maintained, was upset if not destroyed, and the loss is ours as much as it was Hemingway's.

CARLOS BAKER
*Princeton University*

# FAULKNER'S "COUNTRY" AS
# IDEAL COMMUNITY

Faulkner's master-theme is man's inescapable need to search for communal ties, a search on which the individual's achievement of authentic selfhood depends. If he is to complete himself, the Faulkner hero must move from his initial solitude toward some form of social engagement. He must accept the risks of involvement in the lives of his fellows, for only in so doing can he feel himself to be an integral part of "a human family, of the human family."[1] Faulkner's metaphor points to the larger social ideal that lies behind all his fiction: a state of communal wholeness within which, as within a coherent and loving family, the individual's identity would be defined, recognized, and sustained.

It is precisely this sense of participation in a cohesive community that is lacking, however, in the lives of nearly all Faulkner's characters. In his fiction the ideal state of communal wholeness is usually implied by its absence, in the dramatization of its opposite. From the urban chaos depicted in his early New Orleans sketches (1925) through the anarchic violence rendered in the Snopes Trilogy (1940–1959), the fragmented world confronted by Faulkner's typical protagonist offers him no acceptable role, no sense of participation or purpose, and no religious or moral tradition that can guide and support him. Estranged from everything outside himself, a Darl Bundren, a Quentin Compson, or a Joe Christmas can look to no external authority for recognition and validation of his selfhood. Faulkner's recurrent dramatization of the decay of families—e.g., the deterioration of the Compson, Sutpen, and Sartoris lines—is an

1. Faulkner's phrase, in a comment on Thomas Sutpen quoted in Frederick L. Gwynn and Joseph L. Blotner, eds., *Faulkner in the University* (New York, 1965), p. 80.

expression in the domestic sphere of a more general, public dis-integration: the collapse of the ideal of "human family" in the modern world and the resulting deracination of the individual. Only in section I of his *Collected Stories* (1950), subtitled "The Country," does Faulkner reverse his usual strategy. In these stories he offers an extended rendering of an organic com-munity in which his social ideal is given positive definition and complete institutional embodiment. Here Faulkner assembles six tales set in rural areas of Yoknapatawpha County, four of them in the southeastern quarter near Frenchman's Bend. "Barn Burning" heads the group, followed by "Shingles for the Lord," "The Tall Men," "A Bear Hunt," "Two Soldiers," and "Shall Not Perish."[2] Of these pieces, first published in magazines between 1934 and 1943, only "Barn Burning" has enjoyed much attention for its literary art. The others have occasionally been discussed, though chiefly in sociological terms.

Challenging the conventional premise that the population of Yoknapatawpha County is divisible into three social classes—aristocratic planters and their descendants, degraded "white trash," and Negroes—Cleanth Brooks and others have shown that the inhabitants of "The Country" constitute a fourth group rarely noticed by Faulkner's critics.[3] The small landowners of these stories represent the proudly independent "plain folk" of

2. *Collected Stories* (New York: Random House, 1950). Page references for quotations from this text will be given in parentheses in the body of the essay. For the sake of expository consistency, the verbs in passages quoted will be transposed from past to present tense, with all such changes indicated by brackets.

3. Brooks, *William Faulkner: The Yoknapatawpha Country* (New Haven,. 1962), ch. 2; see also M. E. Bradford, "Faulkner and the Jeffersonian Dream: Nationalism in 'Two Soldiers' and 'Shall Not Perish,' " *Mississippi Quarterly,. 18 (1965), 94–100; "Faulkner's 'Tall Men,' " *South Atlantic Quarterly,* 61 (1962), 29–39; "Faulkner's 'Tomorrow' and the Plain People," *Studies in Short Fiction,* 2 (1965), 235–240; Elmo Howell, "Faulkner's *Sartoris* and the Mississippi Country People," *Southern Folklore Quarterly,* 25 (1961), 136–146; "William Faulkner and the New Deal," *Midwest Quarterly,* 5 (1964),. 323–332; "William Faulkner and the Plain People of Yoknapatawpha County," *Journal of Mississippi History,* 24 (1962), 73–87; and John M. MacLachlan, "William Faulkner and the Southern Folk," *Southern Folklore Quarterly,* 9 (1945), 153–167.

the rural South, adherents to a simple code of decency, personal honor, and self-discipline, and to the imperative of earning one's own way. As Frank L. Owsley, Bell Wiley, and other historians were demonstrating during the period when these stories were written, the people in this class had long played an honorable role in the history of Faulkner's region.[4] The yeoman, not the glamorized planter, had been the economic mainstay of the antebellum South. It was he who had sacrificed most during the Civil War and who had subsequently given his defeated homeland the measure of economic and social stability necessary to postwar recovery.

Faulkner's admiration of the Southern yeoman was often revealed in his rather wishful description of himself as a "farmer" or "countryman"; and whether or not Faulkner had read any of the historians cited above, his stories show full awareness of the role this class had played in the Southern past and intimate acquaintance with the yeoman's idiom, attitudes, and customs. Occasional critical praise for the accuracy of Faulkner's depiction of the "plain folk" has suggested that the primary value of these tales is their contribution to a descriptive chronicle of the Southern experience.

To take that approach to the stories of the Country, however,

4. Of the many appraisals of the "plain folk" and their role in Southern history that appeared during the decade when Faulkner was publishing his stories of the Country, the following are noteworthy: Blanche Henry Clark, *The Tennessee Yeomen, 1840–1860* (Nashville, Tenn., 1942); Harry L. Coles, Jr., "Some Notes on Slaveownership and Landownership in Louisiana, 1850–1860," *Journal of Southern History*, 9 (1943), 380–394; Avery O. Craven, *The Coming of the Civil War* (Chicago, 1942), ch. 2; A. J. N. den Hollander, "The Tradition of the Poor White," in W. T. Couch, ed., *Culture in the South* (Chapel Hill, N.C., 1934), pp. 403–431; Clement Eaton, "The Humor of the Southern Yeoman," *Sewanee Review*, 49 (1941), 173–183; Frank L. and Harriet C. Owsley, "The Economic Basis of Society in the Late Ante-Bellum South," *Journal of Southern History*, 6 (1940), 24–45; "The Economic Structure of Rural Tennessee," *Journal of Southern History*, 8 (1942), 161–182; Robert R. Russel, "The Effects of Slavery Upon Non-slaveholders in the Ante-Bellum South," *Agricultural History*, 15 (1941), 112–126; and Bell I. Wiley, *The Life of Johnny Reb: The Common Soldier of the Confederacy* (New York, 1943). Owsley's research culminated in his *Plain Folk of the Old South* (Baton Rouge, La., 1949), an invaluable study of its subject.

would be to mistake their nature and function, impoverish their meaning, and praise them for demonstrably wrong reasons. Measured against the realities of the Southern farmer's lot, "Shingles for the Lord," "A Bear Hunt," and the others hardly meet the test of strict historical or sociological accuracy. Indeed, Faulkner's frequent divergence from that standard helps point up the ideality of his fictional Country.

In economic terms, for example, the life of Faulkner's Country does not reflect conditions prevailing during the period in which these stories are set—the 'thirties and early 'forties, when President Roosevelt declared the rural South "the nation's number one economic problem."[5] There is no agricultural depression in Frenchman's Bend, no grinding poverty, malnutrition, or unemployment, no drought, soil exhaustion, or crop failure, no absentee ownership or mortgaging of land, and almost no labor migrancy or tenant farming—Abner Snopes, the wandering sharecropper of "Barn Burning," being the lone exception.

Technological change and political responses to it have not affected the traditional economy of Faulkner's Country. The yeomen have no tractors, mechanical seeders, or chemical fertilizers, and they want no part of the farm relief programs sponsored by the New Deal (29, 55–56). The men of Frenchman's Bend continue to cultivate their ancestors' land with the same kinds of hand tools used there for generations, and they foresee no change in their manner of work. Since the Country seems immune to economic pressures, the members of the younger generation, unlike their actual prototypes, need plan no flight to the city. Personal roots run deep and hold firm in Frenchman's Bend. The Grier and McCallum children, for example, expect to till the soil of the Country contentedly for the rest of

5. "Barn Burning," the first story in section I, falls outside these chronological bounds. A passing reference to Abner Snopes's wounding by "a Confederate provost's man's musket ball . . . thirty years ago" (p. 5) places the events of this story in the 1890s. But the date is of no importance, except to suggest that the pattern of life in the Country is essentially unchanging. "Barn Burning" could as easily have been set forty years later; the landscape and agrarian economy would have been unaltered, and all the characters would have behaved, spoken, and thought in exactly the same way.

their lives. "There was the land," muses Orestes Grier's nine-year-old son after his brother's death in "Shall Not Perish";

the seventy acres which were our bread and fire and keep, which had outlasted the Griers before us because they had done right by it, and had outlasted Pete because while he was here he had done his part to help and would outlast Mother and Father and me if we did ours. (102)

Thus, even in Southern agriculture's most disastrous decades, the land of Frenchman's Bend is a reassuring symbol of permanence in change. Farming their ancestors' land—and raising their children to do likewise—gives Faulkner's yeomen a sense of familial solidarity, temporal continuity, and purposeful direction.

In social terms, as well as economic, the life of the Country differs radically from that of the region these stories ostensibly portray. Even in his own time, as Faulkner well knew, patterns of behavior in the Mississippi back country were not far removed from their frontier beginnings. But there is in Frenchman's Bend none of the religious hysteria or tendency to violence that W. J. Cash associates with the frontier inheritance of the Southern folk. The yeoman's worship, as presented in "Shingles for the Lord," is restrained and dignified (28–29), and no native of the Country ever maims or kills another. In "A Bear Hunt," for example, Luke Provine loses his temper over a practical joke and attacks V. K. Ratliff; but several bystanders promptly intervene, separate the combatants, and give each a drink to settle his temper (76). Even the rapacious Snopeses, who bring moral and social anarchy to Frenchman's Bend in *The Hamlet*, are checked in these stories and their energies even directed, in two cases, from self-aggrandizement to the communal good. When he plans to set fire to the de Spain barn, Abner Snopes is opposed by his own son ("Barn Burning," 22–23); and, in "Shingles for the Lord," another Snopes agrees to donate his precious time and labor to the rebuilding of the local church, though he is, not surprisingly, the last to volunteer (41).

The taming of Luke Provine and the Snopeses shows that violence, physical or moral, has no place in the Country. In this respect, the socially harmonious world of these stories diverges not only from historical truth, but also from the Frenchman's Bend depicted in *As I Lay Dying* (1930), *Sanctuary* (1931), and *The Hamlet* (1940), where mutual distrust and savage conflict are usually the first laws of life. As the "sole owner and proprietor" of Yoknapatawpha County, Faulkner reserved the right to change a character's personality from book to book, as the exigencies of a particular fictional situation might demand. In section I of the *Collected Stories*, he takes the same liberty with all of Frenchman's Bend, transforming it from a world of violence to a realm of communal order.

Outwardly peaceful, the Country is also free of underlying class antagonism and racial tension. Consequently, its inhabitants—unlike their actual prototypes—would be immune to the lure of political demagoguery. Major de Spain, the resident aristocrat of the Country, is respected by the plain folk, but never feared or envied. "He's a man" is Ratliff's simple tribute to the Major (67). De Spain earns the yeomen's respect by fulfilling the traditional responsibilities of his station. His home is as "big as a courthouse" (10), and the Major is a quiet champion of social justice in the community he leads. His role is most fully dramatized in "A Bear Hunt," where the Major aids those in need (64), mediates in disputes and tries to keep the peace (67–68), and invites his neighbors to share his good fortune by joining in his annual hunt, with its "free eating and whisky" (68). Though he is an aristocrat, de Spain is unwilling to set himself above the wisdom of the community. When, in "Barn Burning," the local justice of the peace greatly reduces the Major's already modest claim for damages against Abner Snopes, de Spain accepts the verdict without a word of protest, for his opponent is a poor man (18–19).

As this episode suggests, relations between the classes in Frenchman's Bend are human rather than impersonally economic or conventional. In "A Bear Hunt," the Major joins the yeomen in the fraternal rituals of the camp and poker table without a hint of reserve or condescension. Conversely, the plain folk regard the aristocrat as a person rather than as a social or economic symbol. In "Shall Not Perish," Orestes Grier's wife enters the Major's great house with no self-consciousness and gently dissuades de Spain from the suicidal despair into which the death of his son has plunged him (106–110). She, like the Major, has lost a son, and all class distinctions vanish in their common grief.

Like the classes, the races live in harmony in the Country. "There [are] Negroes among us," muses the narrator of "A Bear Hunt," "who [have] our family names" (66); and the action that follows suggests that the races' sense of kinship is more than merely nominal. In this story Negro and Indian join forces to turn the tables on Luke Provine, a prankish white man; and the white community, represented by V. K. Ratliff, heartily approves of Luke's discomfiture. Racial distinctions need not be jealously guarded in the Country; such barriers seem simply irrelevant to the enjoyment and sharing of a good joke by all the people of Frenchman's Bend.

Finally, it is noteworthy that no deaths occur in the Country itself, though there are more than a score in the rest of the *Collected Stories*. Pete Grier and the Major's son, the only characters to die in section I, are killed in the Pacific during World War II ("Shall Not Perish"). The ancestors of the McCallum family, whose activities are recalled in "The Tall Men," are in a sense not dead, for their descendants bear their names, live in their house, till their land, and think and behave in the same way those forebears had.

Clearly, then, Faulkner's Country will hardly serve as a sociologically or historically accurate "mirror" of the rural South in this century. But while it is untenable to praise the strict verisimilitude of these stories, it would be equally wrongheaded to condemn them as "unrealistic"—as naive as to complain that there are no bandits in the Forest of Arden and no milking machines in Frost's New Hampshire. Like Frost's technique,

Faulkner's obviously selective mode of presentation in these works is mythic, akin to pastoral idyll, and the stories function in the traditional manner of pastoral. The first part of the *Collected Stories* defines an ideal of communal health, wholeness, and peace against which the reader can measure the social and personal disintegration rendered in subsequent sections and throughout the Faulkner canon.

Each of the stories set in the Country focuses on a single institution or ritual as a center around which this model community organizes itself. The most important of these centers are the hunting camp ("A Bear Hunt"), the farm home and family ("The Tall Men," "Two Soldiers," "Shall Not Perish"), the rural church ("Shingles for the Lord"), and the court of law ("Barn Burning"). Taken together, the six stories offer a remarkably complete depiction of this little society and of the principal forces, public and private, secular and sacred, that bind its members together into an organic whole. Three of these works merit close analysis. "A Bear Hunt," "Shingles for the Lord," and "Barn Burning" are the most successful stories in the group and best dramatize Faulkner's central theme: the primacy of the community and man's inescapable need to respect its integrity and participate in its life.

Major de Spain's bear hunt is an annual rite, organized and conducted by the community's leader, in which representatives of all the classes, races, and generations of the Country take part. In Faulkner's other hunting stories—"The Bear" and "Race at Morning," for example—dramatic emphasis falls on the individual as he tests his personal resources in a confrontation with the wilderness. In "A Bear Hunt," however, Faulkner is not concerned with the lone hunter, but with the fraternal solidarity of the group in camp and their need to maintain that solidarity in a hostile environment.

Outside the camp lies a "wild, flat jungle," where it seems that a mysterious "dark power still dwell[s] or lurk[s], sinister, a little sardonic, like a dark and nameless beast lightly and lazily slumbering with bloody jaws" (65). Toward sundown, as this "dark power" begins to assert its dominion, the hunters return to their camp. In camp there is light to hold back the darkness. There is communal drinking and eating; wild nature has been subdued and accommodated to human use, and the hunters feast on "possum-rich bear pork—let alone the venison they had, with maybe a few coons and squirls throwed in for seasoning" (68). After the meal, hours of poker, joking, and conversation continue to knit the little fraternity together. Major de Spain, the founder and chief of this miniature society, vigorously objects whenever anyone leaves the group after sundown (73–75). His camp is an island of human warmth and security in the midst of the "sinister" wilderness and, as such, is a bulwark against the "mindless fear" (66) that wilderness arouses. The community of his own kind, then, is man's proper sphere in an alien, menacing universe; and the annual camping in the dark forest is a ritual affirmation of that fact.[6]

One of the Major's party, however, is not fully assimilated into the group and must learn to respect the imperative of communal involvement. Luke Provine's status in the Country is undefined. He never works, preferring to loaf "wherever he will be allowed, never exactly accepted by any group" and never seeking acceptance. Luke is content with his marginal position, for it leaves him free to commit "certain outrageous and spontaneous deeds," such as "letting off pistols . . . late Saturday nights" and galloping his horse "down scurrying and screaming lanes of churchgoing ladies on Sunday mornings."

The people of the Country usually smile at these pranks. Indeed, the men admire Luke's "fine frenzy" and the "driving, inarticulate zest" for living (64) that compels him to defy social

6. In the slightly revised version of "A Bear Hunt" he included in *Big Woods* (New York: Random House, 1955), Faulkner makes the traditional, even ritualistic nature of the camping more explicit. The Major de Spain of this story, the narrator tells us, has inherited his title, his leadership, and his responsibilities in the community. He is the son of the Major who founded the hunt, and the other members of his party are descendants of the original hunting group (*Big Woods*, pp. 145–147). Each year, these sons reenact their fathers' camping in the wilderness and thus affirm the living continuity of tradition, family and fraternal solidarity in the Country.

constraint. Though "never exactly accepted by any group," Luke is not rejected either. He is "a native" (63) of the region, and the Country cares for its own. Since Luke "makes no effort whatever to support his wife and three children," Major de Spain helps them and intervenes whenever Luke's high spirits get him into trouble with the law (64).

The Country, however, cannot grant complete and perpetual license to any of its inhabitants. Luke's indifference to his family's welfare suggests that he—like Flem Snopes and Thomas Sutpen, the worst of Faulkner's fictional husbands—is unwilling to assume his responsibilities within the larger human family. Moreover, Luke's anarchic energy is a potential threat to the community's stability, and finally he must pay for one of his disruptive escapades—"the Negro-picnic business." "The picnic," the narrator recalls, "was at a Negro church a few miles from town. In the midst of it" Luke and two friends,

> returning from a dance in the country, rode up with drawn pistols and freshly lit cigars; and taking the Negro men one by one, held the burning cigar ends to the popular celluloid collars of the day, leaving each victim's neck ringed with an abrupt and faint and painless ring of carbon. (64–65)

Old Ash, the Major's camp cook, was among Luke's victims on this occasion; and, even though the burning of his collar was "painless," Ash watches for his chance to turn the tables on Luke. He waits, in fact, for twenty years (79), presumably confident that since he and Luke will remain in the unchanging world of the Country their accounts will one day be squared.

Luke's unbounded self-indulgence at last gives Ash his chance and so recoils, appropriately, on Luke himself. In camp, Luke eats and drinks so much that he develops a gargantuan case of hiccups. "Durn young fool," comments Uncle Ike McCaslin, "eating and drinking himself to where he can't talk nor swallow neither" (75). Uncle Ike, the oldest of the hunters, has wisely summed up Luke's predicament. His uncontrollable hiccups bar Luke completely from the activities that bind the group together: he cannot eat or drink, cannot play poker, and cannot talk or joke with his fellows. Nor can he hunt with them; each time Luke attempts to join someone on a bear trail or deer stand he is driven away, for his noise makes hunting impossible. "Confound you boy," growls Uncle Ike, "get away from here. Do you reckon any varmint in the world is going to walk up to a hay baler?" (69).

Uncle Ike's calling Luke a machine is echoed repeatedly by the other hunters. Luke hiccups "three times to the minute," Ratliff notes, "like one of these here clock bombs"; and Luke's sputtering reminds the Major of "a motorcycle" (68). Others liken the sufferer to a "one-cyclinder gasoline engine" and a "loud-speaker down in a well" (69). Luke even describes himself as a machine. In seeking a cure, Luke has gulped so much water and air that he feels, he says, like an "artesian well" (69) or oversized "automobile tahr" (71). Luke's mechanically regular hiccups make him, of course, an object of laughter. But his describing himself as a machine implies something more serious: because his lack of self-control has led to his exclusion from the activities of others, Luke senses that his very humanity is in doubt.

Until now, Luke had been content to hover at the edge of the community, confident that it would wink at his pranks and help him, unasked, through any difficulties. This time, however, Luke has made a pariah of himself; and, in the painful extremity of his isolation, he makes an unprecedented appeal for the group's sympathy and help: "Hit ain't a man hyer has got any mercy on me, white or black" (72).

Before the pariah can be brought into the little society of the camp, two conditions must be met. First, Luke's ostracism must be absolute: he must leave camp, face the terrifying wilderness alone, and so recognize the depth of his need for his fellows' support. Second, Luke must be taught that membership in a community entails self-control and respect for the dignity and property of others, that is, he must learn that one should honor his neighbor's collar.

Both conditions are met in a single action. Ratliff completes Luke's banishment by suggesting that he go into the dark forest and ask the Indians to cure his hiccups—an absurd proposal, intended as a joke, but one that Luke is desperate enough to accept. Old Ash overhears Ratliff's suggestion and enlists the Indians in his cause. They threaten to burn Luke at the stake— just as he had used fire to embarrass Ash twenty years before— and he runs five miles back to the security of the camp. Frightened out of his hiccups, Luke can now join the group in its eating, drinking, and conversation (76–77). He is not completely chastened, however. His first impulse on returning to camp is to leap on Ratliff for sending him into the forest. But the community will not readmit Luke on his former, violent terms. Major de Spain and the other hunters promptly separate the two, give each a drink, and the fight is soon forgotten (77).

Luke will also learn that he has at last had to pay for "the Negro-picnic business." Ratliff questions Ash, congratulates him on tricking Luke in the forest, and gets his implicit permission to let the victim in on the joke and the reason for it. "I ain't skeered for him to know" (79), says Ash, confident that Luke and the miniature community of which both are part will recognize that justice has been served.

Not only the camp, but all of the Country will share in this knowledge. "A Bear Hunt" begins with a prologue, in which an anonymous speaker introduces Ratliff, the narrator of the tale proper. The bulk of the story is a dramatic monologue, spoken by Ratliff to the "boys" who meet him on his return to camp. In "tell[ing] about Lucius Provine and his hiccup" (66), Ratliff is adding to the folklore of this community with a story affirming what the Country already knows: that, since isolation is intolerable, the individual must feel himself to be part of a social whole, and that membership in a group entails self-restraint and respect for one's fellows, white or black.

Ratliff's telling the story to "the boys" is in itself a contribution to the social unity of the Country. Faulkner's most isolated characters are usually dumb or inarticulate; Benjy Compson, Popeye, Flem Snopes, and the hiccuping Luke Provine are all cases in point. In Faulkner's early New Orleans sketches and in his New Orleans novels, *Mosquitoes* and *Pylon*, the characters talk, but only to soliloquize in bizarre anti-languages of their own; and this collapse of dialogue helps to dramatize the social fragmentation of the city. In contrast, the people of the Country share a functioning language, and they can and do converse—"Shingles for the Lord," "The Tall Men," and "Two Soldiers," for example, are one-half to two-thirds dialogue. Speech is the community's vital medium: it enables the yeomen to share in one another's experiences, to work and play together, to articulate social traditions and values, to preserve the communal past, and so to knit themselves into a coherent and enduring group. Ratliff's yarn-spinning implies all this and one thing more. "A Bear Hunt" is, above all, a very funny story. In telling it, the comic raconteur will bind himself and his audience together in the fellowship of laughter.

"Shingles for the Lord" is another comic affirmation of social solidarity and of the individual's need to integrate his separate existence with the lives of others. In this story the rural church is the institutional center around which the little world of the Country organizes itself. Frenchman's Bend is a community of belief and worship, as is dramatized when the men, women, and children of the Country gather outside the church that gives coherence and direction to their lives. "We was all there now," thinks the narrator, Orestes Grier's boy, "all that belonged to that church and used it to be born and marry and die from—us and the Armstids and Tulls, and Bookwright and Quick and Snopes" (41). Like the land, the McCallum home and name, and the annual hunting camp, the church is a symbol of permanence in change, of the stable, ongoing life of the community that worships there. "That's all it was," the boy narrator says of the church into which he and all his fellows are received at birth, "jest indestructibility, endurability" (42).

Reverend Whitfield, leader of this congregation "for more than fifty years," is the spiritual counterpart of Major de Spain, the secular head of the Country. Whitfield reminds the narrator of "the old strong Archangel Michael" (49), traditionally, the weigher of men's souls. Tall and stern, the minister even has the aura of the Old Testament Jehovah about him. His forehead resembles a rugged "cliff" (29), and his voice "thunder[s] . . . like a cloudburst." Like Major de Spain, Whitfield is a unifying force in his community, a force to which all the yeomen accord the supreme tributes of loyalty, respect, and obedience.

Whitfield's God labors mightily in man's behalf. "I made them," the minister imagines God saying; "I don't know why. But since I did . . . I'll roll up my sleeves and drag them into glory whether they will or no!" (28). Such a toiling God will exact man's work in return, and in "Shingles for the Lord" Whitfield enforces that demand by insisting that the men of the congregation repair the church roof. As the title of the story implies, this labor is to be a collective act of worship in which the participants will affirm the faith and sense of duty to God that bind them together. Whitfield consecrates the work as he asks divine blessing on it: "Lord . . . make them good straight shingles to lay smooth, and let them split out easy; they're for you" (29).

Three of the yeomen—Orestes Grier, Solon Quick, and Homer Bookwright—are to begin work on the roof. Their classical Greek names at first seem only comic devices meant to reduce the characters' stature. 'Res Grier, for example, is a blundering buffoon rather than a tragic penitent. Solon Quick, as his surname implies, is less the wise lawgiver than the sharp trader. And Homer Bookwright is sadly lacking in the eloquence his full name suggests: in the whole story, he utters only ten monosyllabic words. The Greek names, however, serve a more serious and important purpose, for they point to a political concept and a social ethic, both far older than Whitfield's Christianity, as norms against which to measure the characters' behavior. Implicit in "Shingles for the Lord"—and throughout section I of the Collected Stories—are the idea of the classical Greek city-state or polis and the Greek view of citizenship, its benefits, and its responsibilities.

Faulkner's library did not include Plato's *Republic* or *Laws* or Aristotle's *Politics*; but he was a devoted reader of Greek tragedy, from which he could have derived the concept of the polis. One suspects, moreover, that Faulkner was acquainted with the *Politics*, for the Country conforms in several important respects to Aristotle's prescription for the ideal city-state. First, Frenchman's Bend is large enough to be economically self-sufficient and politically autonomous. On the other hand, the community is small enough that all its inhabitants can know one another by sight and can participate in public affairs. Fewer than two hundred people live in the area (114), and the characters in each of these stories have known one another for years. The endurance of the Grier and McCallum clans in the Country shows that the well-regulated family is the basic social unit for Faulkner as well as Aristotle; and the whole polis, like Whitfield's congregation, is composed of such families living and acting in concert. Finally, the population of the Country, like that of the ideal polis, is homogeneous—in language, religion, occupation, interests, manners, and customs; and this homogeneity is the basis for a spirit of friendly partnership in work and play alike.

As in the Aristotelian city-state, participation in public affairs is a duty the citizen of Frenchman's Bend owes to his community and to himself as well, for through such social involvement he will develop his personal capacities, train himself in virtue, and so complete his nature. The member of the polis, therefore, must subordinate his purely selfish interests to active service of the larger communal good. In "Shingles for the Lord" Solon Quick makes this imperative explicit when he twice chides Orestes Grier for putting his supposedly "urgent private affairs" (33) ahead of his promise to work on the church roof.

Helping to repair this roof, then, is a twofold responsibility: a believer's sacred duty to his God, and a citizen's secular obligation to his community. Orestes Grier, however, is two hours late on the appointed work day and so fails both God and polis. Reverend Whitfield upbraids Grier for the first lapse: "You have known for a month now that you had promised this one day out of a whole summer toward putting a roof on the house of God" (28). And Solon rebukes him for the second: "Well, men," 'Res says, "let's get started. We're already late." "Me and Homer ain't," Solon counters; "we was here" (29).

To make amends for his irresponsibility, 'Res reluctantly agrees to sell Solon a fine hunting dog the latter has long wanted. As part of the bargain Solon is to contribute another half-day's work on the roof in Grier's stead. The transaction is openly proposed, debated, and finally sealed, with Homer Bookwright in effect acting as witness. Secretly, however, 'Res Grier is still putting his private interests ahead of any public obligations or agreements. Despite his bargain, he plans to keep the dog and, more important, to heal his wounded pride by embarrassing Solon. 'Res steals back to the church after sunset and resumes work on the roof. If he can finish the job before morning, Solon will be unable to earn the dog and Grier will have outmaneuvered him. 'Res has been censured for his tardiness and now wants to transfer that humiliation to Solon: "I don't want [Solon] jest to find out at sunup tomorrow that he is too late," 'Res gloats; "I want him to find out then that even when he laid down to sleep he was already too late" (37–38). Grier has by now completely lost sight of the proper religious and social meanings of the work and reduced it to an act of private vengeance carried out under the cover of darkness.

But the God of Frenchman's Bend apparently does not smile on broken agreements or personal vendettas. Working furiously on the roof, Grier accidentally lets his lantern fall down into the church; the building explodes in flames and quickly burns to the ground. Whitfield and his flock gather at the scene and at once begin planning to erect a new church. Grier, however, will be allowed no role in this undertaking. Branding 'Res an "arsonist," Whitfield reads him out of the congregation and the community: "If there is any pursuit in which you can engage without carrying flood and fire and destruction and death behind you, do it. But not one hand shall you lay to this new house until you have proved to us that you are to be trusted again with the powers and capacities of a man" (41). Like the classical figure of vengeance and repentance whose name he bears, Orestes Grier must suffer in exile.

Excluded from society, 'Res attempts to redefine his banishment into a willed act of withdrawal: "I been publicly notified that I ain't fitten to associate with white folks," he announces to no one in particular; "so I publicly notify them same white folks . . . not to try to associate with me . . ." (42). Reaching home, 'Res tries to complete his isolation by banishing his family from the bedroom. But his wife and son quietly stand by him. She hands 'Res a hot toddy and the giving and receiving of the drink, as in "A Bear Hunt," signals the impending reconciliation of the pariah to the group. Secure in his home, 'Res "draw[s] a long, shuddering breath" and vows to resume his life in the larger community outside: "I Godfrey, if [Whitfield] and all of them put together think they can keep me from working on my own church like ary other man, he better be a good man to try it" (43).

"Shingles for the Lord" and "A Bear Hunt" are examples of the traditionally patterned comedy that can be rooted in a coherent, stable culture. In both stories the foolish deviator from communal norms of good behavior and good sense is mocked, suitably chastised, and so prepared for reassimilation into the ongoing, unified life of the group. In "Barn Burning," however, matters take a potentially disastrous turn, for the outsider not only refuses to acknowledge any personal need for social ties, he dedicates himself to their annihilation. The title of the story announces the gravity of the situation. Burning another's barn in Frenchman's Bend is more than an offense against law and private property. In the agrarian world of the Country, it is a crime against the harmonious relationship of yeoman and land on which the whole life of the community is based.

In this story the barn-burning villain, Abner Snopes, is the personification of anarchic energy. Like the comic pariahs in "Shingles for the Lord" and "A Bear Hunt," Snopes is repeatedly associated with fire. His commitment to destructive fire, however, is far more deliberate and intense than 'Res Grier's or Luke Provine's. "The element of fire [speaks] to some deep mainspring of his . . . being," the narrator tells us, "as the element of steel or of powder [speaks] to other men, as the one weapon for the preservation of integrity, else breath were not worth the breathing. . . ." Snopes's very "integrity," his deepest sense of himself, requires that he wage fiery war against any man or institution that challenges his "wolflike independence" or tries to impose limits on his "ravening ferocity" of will. For Abner Snopes, living is perpetual conflict in which each man must struggle to "beat" every other (7–8).

The military allusion to "steel" and "powder" quoted above is partly ironic, and the irony is underscored by Snopes's first name. In *Absalom, Absalom!* (1936) Faulkner had evoked the Biblical story of David and his sons as an extended analogue to the history of the Sutpen family. In writing "Barn Burning" (1939) the author doubtless recalled the account of the Israelite Abner given in the same source (I–II Samuel).[7] The Biblical Abner was a leader of his people—a valiant general, a reformed rebel, David's valued ally; in short, he was all that his modern namesake is not. Abner Snopes was once a soldier, a Confederate irregular; but his supposed service to his embattled homeland was to him only an opportunity to steal horses "from all men, blue or gray" (7):

> He had gone to that war a private in the fine old European sense, wearing no uniform, admitting the authority of and giving fidelity to no man or army or flag, going to war . . . for booty—it meant nothing and less than nothing to him if it were enemy booty or his own. (24–25)

7. Faulkner probably supplemented the biblical account of Abner with that given in the *Antiquities* of the first-century Jewish historian, Flavius Josephus. There is "a Josephus" in John Sartoris's library (*The Unvanquished*, New York, 1938, p. 18), and Faulkner kept an 1856 edition shelved next to his Bible at Rowan Oak. Faulkner's copy is signed and dated 1933; see Joseph L. Blotner, *Faulkner's Library: A Catalogue* (Charlottesville, Va., 1964), p. 11.

Snopes's apolitical cynicism is one aspect of his uncompromising refusal of allegiance to anything or anyone outside himself. He is not a native of Frenchman's Bend. Completely rootless, he has dragged his wife and children to more than thirteen different houses in ten years (6), and he is coldly indifferent to the coherence and welfare of the family unit. Snopes's dependents sleep "scattered without order or claim up and down the two rooms" (14) of their shack. Abner addresses his wife and children only to give orders or stifle dissent, reveals no interest whatever in them as persons, and never calls any of his four children by name. In contrast to the shared labor of the Grier and McCallum families, each Snopes works apart from the others (13–14). Meals are silent, joyless consumptions of "cold food" (8, 14, 20). The father rules only through force and fear. Abner's group, in short, is a fragmented mock-family in which husband and wife, parent and child, brother and sister are invariably at odds.

Snopes feels no more concern for the larger human family than he shows for his own. In the Country, speech is the community's sustaining medium, the basic means by which the individual can establish and develop social ties. But the barn burner rarely uses his "cold, dead voice" (21) outside his immediate family, except to make an occasional comment "to no one in particular" (20) or to utter "something unprintable and vile, addressed to no one" (5).

In Faulkner's world the detached, isolated individual finally loses his humanity, and Abner Snopes brings that fate upon himself. He seems to be "without face or depth—a shape black, flat, and bloodless" (8), and there are further aspects to his dehumanization. In the first book of the *Politics*, Aristotle declares that the "citiless man"—the person unwilling to identify himself with a community—must be something more or less than human, either a god or a lower animal. In "Barn Burning" Faulkner seems to carry these ideas a step farther: his asocial Snopes is on the one hand a devil, and on the other a machine. The hints of diabolism in Abner's nature and appearance are unobtrusive, but clear: he is obsessed with fire; like Hawthorne's demonic villains, he dresses in black and skulks about at night seeking vengeance; his hand resembles "a curled claw" (11); he seems to cast no shadow (10).[8] On the other hand, recurrent images of metallic rigidity and stiff movement reduce the barn burner to a robot. "In the iron folds of [his] frockcoat," for example, Abner seems to be "cut from tin"; his voice is "harsh like tin and without heat like tin" (8). Fire appeals to the "deep mainspring of his . . . being" (7); his stride is "stiff," "undeviating," "clocklike," "machinelike" (10–11).

Radically isolated and therefore dehumanized, Abner Snopes can assert his existence only by anarchic acts of violence—by the compulsive barn burnings that inevitably drive him deeper into exile. Against this monstrous individualist Faulkner sets Abner's new landlord and intended victim, Major de Spain, symbol of social responsibility in the Country. Descriptive details underscore the contrast between the two. While Snopes is repeatedly associated with black, for example, de Spain is "linen-clad" (12); his house is white, and he is five times referred to as "the white man" (23). The Major's swift, fluid movements (12–13, 15–16, 24) point up the robotlike stiffness of Abner Snopes. The latter's face and voice are cold and dead; de Spain's are always animated by emotion (12, 15–16), and the warmth of the Major's home (11) contrasts with the "cold hearth" (22) around which Snopes's mock-family assembles. The cumulative effect of these details is to juxtapose a living human being with a monster who is at once devil and machine.

In Faulkner's stories, social involvement is essential to a character's full humanity, and the chief difference between Abner and his landlord lies in their attitudes toward the community and the individual's duties to it. During the Civil War, de Spain served his homeland as a military leader, while Snopes

---

8. The diabolical side of Abner Snopes is examined by William Bysshe Stein in "Faulkner's Devil," *Modern Language Notes*, 76 (1961), 731–732; and by Charles Mitchell in "The Wounded Will of Faulkner's Barn Burner," *Modern Fiction Studies*, 11 (1965–1966), 185–189.

was a predatory opportunist loyal only to himself. As Luke Provine learns in "A Bear Hunt," membership in a community entails self-restraint and respect for others' rights, as those rights are defined by custom and law. Major de Spain abides by this principle. His home is as "big as a courthouse" (10), and he demonstrates his respect for law when he quietly accepts a local court's reduction of his already modest claim for damages against Abner Snopes (18–19). The latter, of course, recognizes no law but the anarchic impulses of his own will and no justice but the satisfaction of those impulses at another's expense.[9]

As outlined above, the conflict between Snopes and de Spain seems morally schematic, as abstract as the struggle between a "vice" and a "virtue" in a medieval morality play.[10] Faulkner

9. Lionel Trilling suggests that "Snopes has a kind of ultimate justice on his side when he says of Major de Spain's house that its whiteness is the sweat of the men, black and white, who have worked the Major's land" (*The Experience of Literature*, New York, 1967, p. 748). The passage referred to, however, tends in context to undercut such an interpretation. Looking at the de Spain house, Snopes comments, "Pretty and white, ain't it? . . . That's sweat. Nigger sweat. Maybe it ain't white enough yet to suit him. Maybe he wants to mix some white sweat with it" (12). But in the very next scene Abner Snopes is resting in a chair while his wife and children toil. In fact, he does no work at all, except to bark orders at his dependents. If Major de Spain does exact "white sweat" of his tenants, none of it will be Abner's. The charge of exploiting others' labor rebounds on Snopes himself. Abner's implied sympathy for the Negro in the passage quoted above is equally hypocritical. Two incidents dramatize his real attitude toward the black man. First, probably intending an insult, he sends a Negro to pay a small debt he owes another white man (4). Second, he brushes aside de Spain's butler with a contemptuous "Get out of my way, nigger" (11). Abner Snopes, then, cannot be viewed as a spokesman for the oppressed; he is an oppressor, and he identifies himself with no social class at all. The "they" he feels he must "beat" (8) are all mankind, rich and poor, white and black alike. Finally, whatever one may think of Southern landlords and the sharecropping system, there is no evidence in "Barn Burning" that Major de Spain exploits or even condescends to anyone, Abner Snopes included.

10. Elmo Howell interprets the Snopes / de Spain conflict in the allegorical terms first proposed by George Marion O'Donnell in his seminal essay on Faulkner's novels: in Howell's view, the Major represents "traditional morality," while Abner stands for "amoral modernism" (see "Colonel Sartoris Snopes and Faulkner's Aristocrats," *Carolina Quarterly*, 11, 1959, 13–19). Phyllis Franklin concedes the general validity of this interpretation, but argues effectively that the central theme of "Barn Burning" is the ethical maturation of its protagonist, Sarty Snopes ("Sarty Snopes and 'Barn Burning,'" *Mississippi Quarterly*, 21, 1968, 189–193).

gives this conflict psychological immediacy and emotional power, however, by dramatizing it within the troubled mind of a third character—Abner's ten-year-old son Sarty, who is the Jamesian "central consciousness" of the story. Caught between his father and de Spain, the boy is "pulled two ways like between two teams of horses" (17), and his dilemma is epitomized in his full name: Colonel Sartoris Snopes.[11] He is attracted on the one hand to the ideal of principled conduct and civic responsibility suggested by his first name and dramatically embodied in Major de Spain. But on the other hand Sarty cannot ignore "the old fierce pull of blood" (3) that binds him to the father he longs to admire and love.

The story traces the boy's moral growth, as he gradually moves from passive grieving over his father's anarchic acts to an active repudiation of violence, a process which culminates in Sarty's warning Major de Spain that Abner Snopes is about to set fire to his barn. Sarty's climactic moment of choice is subtly prepared for and its meaning implied by two earlier scenes, both set in courts held in rural stores by justices of the peace. In "Barn Burning" the court of law serves the same purpose as the camp in "A Bear Hunt" and the church in "Shingles for the Lord": it is an institutional synecdoche for the entire community of the Country. In both episodes Sarty watches as the community assembles, confronts his father, and tries to protect itself from the outlaw and at the same time to deal fairly with him. Sarty's growth is summed up in his differing responses to each trial scene and in the attendant imagery that helps to render his changing conception of himself, his situation, and his responsibilities.

11. Faulkner nowhere explains the circumstances of the boy's naming, but one infers from "Barn Burning" that the name Abner Snopes has given his younger son may be one of his many gestures of defiance. He apparently takes special pleasure in ordering Sarty about, as if in so doing he can invert the social order and revenge himself on the ruling class for one of whom his son is named. If a desire for vicarious and therefore unpunishable vengeance accounts for Sarty's naming, this is a petty gesture on the father's part and, still worse, is another example of Abner's tendency to use his dependents as means to his own selfish ends.

In the first courtroom episode (3–5) Abner Snopes is questioned about his part in a recent barn burning. He refuses to speak and his victim, Mr. Harris, suggests that Sarty be interrogated. The justice of the peace, however, is reluctant to compel a son to testify against his father, and Harris withdraws his request. It is clear to all present that Snopes is guilty, but the court will not condemn the outlaw without adequate proof. The case is dismissed and the verdict silently accepted by the assembled yeomen. The community thus acknowledges Abner's familial and legal rights, a recognition he never grants to others.

Throughout this scene Sarty is isolated, confused, and passive. At first he sits by himself "at the back of the crowded room" (3), then walks alone up "a lane of grim faces" (4) gathered for the hearing. Emotionally perplexed, Sarty is unable to sort out the inchoate muddle of sensations, thoughts, and feelings that stream through his mind: "Voices [come] to him . . . through the smell of cheese and sealed meat, the fear and despair and the old grief of blood." Determined to remain loyal to this "blood," the boy perceives his surroundings as if through a distorting "red haze" (5). He does not *listen* consciously to the proceedings; passive and distracted, Sarty only "hears" random fragments of sound that compose no pattern for him (3–5). He cannot "see that the Justice's face [is] kindly nor discern that his voice [is] troubled" (4) when Harris suggests that Sarty be questioned. The boy's passivity is repeatedly emphasized: he speaks only when addressed and moves only when bidden (4). Sarty's feeling of helpless isolation in this first scene is crystallized in his sense of weightlessness and immobility: as he approaches the justice, "he [feels] no floor under his bare feet . . . . it [is] as if he [has] swung outward at the end of a grape vine, over a ravine, and at the top of the swing [has] been caught in a prolonged instant of mesmerized gravity, weightless in time" (4–5).

Soon after this first courtroom episode Abner tells Sarty that he is "getting to be a man" (8), and the statement ironically proves prophetic. Sarty's experience in court has made him acutely aware of

the terrible handicap of being young, the light weight of his few years, just heavy enough to prevent his soaring free of the world as it seemed to be ordered but not heavy enough to keep him footed solid in it, to resist it and try to change the course of its events. (9)

By the time of the second scene in court, however, Sarty has begun to think of himself as an autonomous individual with the power to speak and act, rather than as a passive, "weightless" victim of external forces.

In this scene (17–19) Abner Snopes confronts Major de Spain, whose rug he has wilfully destroyed; and Sarty is no longer the confused, quiescent child. Now he asserts himself and speaks up; his mind is alert and his senses clear. His father orders Sarty to return to their wagon, but the boy disobeys him for the first time and "retreat[s] to the rear of the room, crowded as that other had been, but not to sit down this time, instead, to stand pressing among the motionless bodies, listening to the voices" (18). The faces of these onlookers no longer seem "grim" to Sarty; indeed, in standing among them he has separated himself from his father and implicitly aligned himself with the community in its quest for justice.

In this second trial scene the community again deals leniently with the pariah, but again he remains unreconciled to it. When Abner prepares that night to set fire to the de Spain barn, Sarty's duty is clear to him: he must exchange the observer's role for the participant's. The boy tears himself from his mother's grasp, runs to the de Spain house, shouts a warning, and so affirms his moral maturation and autonomy.

Michael Millgate has proposed that "Barn Burning," the first of the Collected Stories, be viewed as a thematic overture to the volume as a whole, and there is merit in the suggestion.[12] The

12. The Achievement of William Faulkner (New York, 1966), p. 270.

story confronts its protagonist with the social and moral alternatives that run through the entire book—communal order and anarchic violence—and dramatizes the proper choice between them. The reader senses that this choice is somehow inevitable in the organic society of the Country, where the communal spirit is palpable and strong enough to lead a mere boy to repudiate his father and his immediate family for the sake of a larger communal ideal of justice and peace.

The social and personal disintegration rendered in subsequent parts of the *Collected Stories* is the more vivid and appalling when contrasted with the organic union of self and community defined in the volume's opening section. Families suffer compromise or collapse, for example, in "Centaur in Brass," "The Brooch," "Golden Land," and "Mountain Victory." Class and racial tensions explode into violence in "A Rose for Emily," "Elly," "Dry September," and "That Evening Sun." Custom and religion become divisive forces in "That Will Be Fine" and "Uncle Willy." The normative function of Faulkner's Country extends far beyond his *Collected Stories*, however. To juxtapose the ordered society of Frenchman's Bend with the anarchic worlds of *Sanctuary*, *Light in August*, and *The Sound and the Fury* is to heighten our awareness of the terrifying consequences that attend destruction of the communal spirit throughout Faulkner's works. Thus Faulkner's Country functions in the traditional manner of pastoral—to define an ideal vantage point from which to measure the corrupt realities of a fallen world, and to evoke a condition of social and personal fulfillment toward which men of moral imagination may strive.

PHILIP MOMBERGER
*University of West Florida*

# SANCTUARY: YOKNAPATAWPHA'S
# WASTE LAND

Critics have always been uneasy in the presence of William
Faulkner's *Sanctuary*, not only because it was from the first a
popular novel, but also because of Faulkner's statements in his
1932 Introduction to the Modern Library edition that seemed to
confirm that he wrote the book as a pot boiler. By this time the
story of the novel's origin and revision is familiar. Faulkner
wrote a version quickly in 1929, in the wake of his production of
*The Sound and the Fury*, and the publisher ("Good God, I
can't publish this. We'd both be in jail."[1]) put the manuscript
aside, and set it up in type only after publishing *As I Lay Dying*
(1930). By this time Faulkner was embarrassed by *Sanctuary*
and revised it extensively in galley proof, largely at his own
expense. *Sanctuary* appeared in 1931, became a best seller
(Faulkner's first), and was selected for the Modern Library
series in 1932. Faulkner's Introduction opens: "This book was
written three years ago. To me it is a cheap idea, because it was
deliberately conceived to make money."[2] This statement was the
origin of most of the early criticism of the novel, but by now
most critics have noted that Faulkner, even in that Modern Library Introduction, made clear that his derogatory comments
applied to the first version of the novel, and that he went on to
claim that he had made a "fair job" of the revision. Moreover,
the Introduction has something of the air of a spoof or tall tale,
a deliberate exaggeration of base motives merely to shock. Faulkner had a hard time living down those remarks when he confronted students of his work in the latter part of his life, but

1. James B. Meriwether, ed., *William Faulkner: Essays, Speeches, and
Public Letters* (New York, 1965), p. 177.
2. Ibid., p. 176.

he was always careful to place emphasis on the revision of the work, and insisted that he did the "best he could" in the revision.[3] During this period Faulkner was producing his greatest works, and his best should have been very good indeed.

Studies have been made of the two versions of *Sanctuary* confirming that Faulkner did indeed improve the novel immeasurably in the revision.[4] The novel now opens in a startling confrontation between Horace Benbow and Popeye near the Old Frenchman's Place; it once opened with Benbow's visit to Lee Goodwin in prison, after Popeye's murder of Tommy. Horace Benbow's paralyzed sensibility, ineffectuality, and despair now suffuse and color the novel; earlier Benbow was its central and controlling focus. Popeye's shocking rape (by corn cob) of Temple Drake and its consequences and implications, both local and cosmic, are now the novel's center of interest; this center was once blurred in the shadows of Benbow's spreading intelligence. The novel now sketches, in the last chapter, a curious summary of Popeye's history and background; in the earlier version there was no past history given for Popeye. This list of major changes is sufficient to suggest the radical surgery performed by Faulkner on his novel. It also reveals that Faulkner's concern was not what he called the "cheap idea" of the novel, but rather the strategies and techniques of its embodiment. The shocking material and subject remained intact, and perhaps were brought into clearer focus. The process of revision, in fact, casts into considerable doubt that Faulkner ever thought the idea was really "cheap." He probably simply saw the phrase as an arresting, even startling, yet still self-deprecating way of opening an essentially superfluous Introduction to a literary work which must, he knew, ultimately speak for itself.

As any student of Faulkner's entire work quickly sees, *Sanc-*

3. See, for example, Frederick L. Glynn and Joseph L. Blotner, *Faulkner in the University* (Charlottesville, Va., 1959), pp. 90–91.
4. See Linton Massey, "Notes on the Unrevised Galleys of Faulkner's *Sanctuary*," *Studies in Bibliography*, 8 (1956), 195–208; and Michael Millgate, *The Achievement of William Faulkner* (New York, 1966), pp. 113–123.

*tuary* has strong links with *Sartoris* (1929) in reintroducing such characters as Horace Benbow, his sister Narcissa, and Aunt Jenny. It also, like other Faulkner novels of this period, foreshadows the later work—in, for example, its presentation of a number of people and places (the Snopeses, the Old Frenchman's Place) that figure prominently in later works such as *The Hamlet*. And indeed, Faulkner was so haunted by the characters and their fate that he wrote what can only be described as a sequel, *Requiem for a Nun* (1951). This novel, written in the form of a play, is so bad that it further damaged the reputation of *Sanctuary*. The motion picture called *Sanctuary* (1961, directed by Tony Richardson) was a pretentious and disastrous mishmash of the two books, but emphasized the worst faults of *Requiem for a Nun*. The waters were further muddied by a widely circulated paperback volume in which both novels appeared.

Faulkner has been unkinder to *Sanctuary* than to any of his other productions; his flip Introduction and weak sequel have deflected critical attention from the simple excellence of the novel that he revised into being. This essay is meant to be something of a rescue operation. There have, of course, been other generally favorable treatments of *Sanctuary* recently, but in all of them there has sounded a tone of condescension, as though there was a critical consensus that the novel, whatever its merits and qualities, did not finally measure up and—to be sure—exhibited some obvious defects. In an attempt to counteract these views, this essay will focus on the novel as given us, not on the earlier version and not on its relation to earlier and later Faulkner works. Indeed, the time has come to disconnect *Sanctuary* from *Sartoris* and *Requiem for a Nun*, and to place it in its genuine context in Faulkner's work: it belongs with *The Sound and the Fury, As I Lay Dying, Light in August*, and *Absalom, Absalom!* as one of the five important works of Faulkner's finest period of creativity. If Faulkner's work of this period tends to present a discernible thematic pattern, a "figure in the carpet," then *Sanctuary* provides an important part of the figure and design.

To omit *Sanctuary* is to omit a significant detail of design. To
place *Sanctuary* with these works is to place it in its proper
company, not only to appreciate its virtues, but also to comprehend its meaning. It was, after all, something of this sort that
Faulkner was trying obliquely to tell us when he wrote in his
ill-starred Introduction that in revising *Sanctuary* he had tried
"to make out of it something which would not shame *The Sound
and the Fury* and *As I Lay Dying*."[5]

In the commentary that follows, an attempt will be made to
come to terms with the critical issues that have been raised about
*Sanctuary*, particularly by those critics who have offered it faint
praise while denying it its rightful place. But at the same time
the analysis is meant to be comprehensive and the interpretation
designed to stand on its own.

I

In *The Novels of William Faulkner*, Olga Vickery groups *The
Sound and the Fury, As I Lay Dying, Light in August*, and
*Absalom, Absalom!* for treatment under the title, "The Achievement of Form." She separates *Sanctuary* for treatment under a
later section, "The Pursuit of Theme," in a chapter combining
it with *Requiem for a Nun*. In effect, her order of treatment
represents her value judgment. And she opens her discussion of
*Sanctuary* by referring to the "bizarre and exaggerated brutality"
of its events.[6] In his book (*William Faulkner*), Irving Howe
writes of *Sanctuary*: "Faulkner's occasional clumsiness in handling shock and his failure to provide dimension for his characters, trouble the shape of the book."[7] In *The Achievement of
William Faulkner*, Michael Millgate refers to distracting passages in *Sanctuary* that appear "mechanically contrived," to a
"certain overstrenuousness" and "extraordinary emphasis on de-

5. James B. Meriwether, ed., *William Faulkner: Essays, Speeches, and
Public Letters*, p. 178.
6. Olga W. Vickery, *The Novels of William Faulkner: A Critical Interpretation* (Baton Rouge, La., 1959), p. 103.
7. Irving Howe, *William Faulkner* (New York, 1952), p. 197.

scriptions of the characters' eyes," and to "a slightly arbitrary extravagance about the imagery" throughout the book.[8]

Remarks of this kind, expressing puzzlement and critical reservation, can be found scattered throughout Faulkner's best commentators when they come to *Sanctuary*. And there can be no doubt that these remarks and asides represent an attempt to get at something important and jarring in the novel, and it is that something that should be dealt with at the outset. It is encountered on the opening pages of the work.

Horace Benbow bends over a stream to get a drink of water. "Somewhere, hidden and secret yet nearby, a bird sang three notes and ceased" (3).[9] As he rises, he sees Popeye's straw hat reflected in the water. He looks across the stream at Popeye: "His face had a queer, bloodless color, as though seen by electric light . . . he had that vicious depthless quality of stamped tin" (4). Again, "the bird sang . . . three bars in monotonous repetition" (4). As the encounter deepens in sinister overtones, the two men freeze. "They squatted so, facing one another across the spring, for two hours" (5). Occasionally the bird sounds its single notes, and occasionally the sound of a passing automobile is heard, but still the men squat. Popeye's hands are "little, doll-like hands," and his face like the "face of a wax doll set too near a hot fire and forgotten" (5). His eyes "looked like rubber knobs," and seemed to have the "whorled smudge of the thumb on them" (5–6). When finally the two men proceed on their way, Popeye in command and in the lead, his "tight suit and stiff hat all angles," he looks like "a modernistic lampstand" (6). And they make their way to the Old Frenchman's Place: "A moment later, above a black, jagged mass of trees, the house lifted its stark square bulk against the failing sky" (7).

In short, the two men walk out of this world into the world of the novel; out of a realistic world into a world bizarre and sur-

8. Michael Millgate, *Achievement*, pp. 121–122.
9. Page numbers in the text refer to the Modern Library edition of *Sanctuary* (New York: Random House). The current edition is published without Faulkner's 1932 introduction.

realistic. Indeed, they were already in an unrealistic world as they squatted for two hours by that stream. Two hours? Could real people walk after such a stint of squatting? The critical question that these opening pages fling out is whether Faulkner was trying for reality and misfiring, or whether he was trying for something else—a trans-real quality, an absurd and nightmarish quality—and actually succeeding superbly well.

The world that Faulkner is creating for his novel in this opening chapter is compounded of many elements, drawn from a variety of sources. Perhaps the most obvious are gangster and detective books and movies. Faulkner grew fond of using such material for serious fiction (as in *Knight's Gambit* and *Intruder in the Dust* and elsewhere). Benbow, following Popeye in the opening scene, sees "the continuous jerking of the hat from side to side as Popeye looked about with a sort of vicious cringing. The hat just reached Benbow's chin" (7). There is here, in this cinematic-like scene, as frequently elsewhere in the novel, a curious mixture of the sinister and the ridiculous, of the grim and the absurd, of the ominous and the funny. But there are, too, other sources and models for Faulkner, and perhaps the one most clearly delineated is the comic strip. As a matter of fact, it is difficult to read the first chapter of *Sanctuary* without seeing the action in a series of frames with occasional balloons containing appropriate dialogue.

Several frames might well be devoted to Horace Benbow and Popeye at the spring. Even the bird, with its three distinct notes, could be portrayed in a frame. Popeye himself is described in the one-dimensional terms of a comic strip character, and his rubber knob eyes could even, in a close-up, show the thumb whorls. The two-hour squat face to face across the spring, which in reality would be paralyzing, could probably achieve its only natural visual representation in a comic strip. The walk from the spring to the Old Frenchman's Place has the mechanical quality easily adaptable to the frame of a comic strip. And it is difficult not to visualize the house itself as it looms mysteriously up against a "failing sky" in a frame all by itself.

All this is not to say that Faulkner was competing with comic strips as a form, but merely that he was striving for a deliberate distortion of reality not unlike the distortion of the comic strip world. He is drawing the reader into a world where his usual sense of normality and of cause and effect will be jarred and upset, where incongruities will abound, and where the sinister and the absurd will intermingle and meld one into another with imperceptible shifting. In such a world it is pointless to object to one-dimensional characters: it is just such characters that help create and establish the world to begin with.

If the bird with its single distinct notes in the first chapter of *Sanctuary* happens to suggest the nightingale of T. S. Eliot's *The Waste Land*, which sings " 'jug jug' to dirty ears," it might just be a part of Faulkner's intention. It is only the first of a number of echoes of the famous poem in the novel. Faulkner's natural setting has none of the innocence usually associated with the natural scene. On the contrary, Popeye's presence, with all his mechanistic qualities, is profoundly subverting. And even the bird sings his three bars "in monotonous repetition: a sound meaningless and profound out of suspirant and peaceful following silence which seemed to isolate the spot, and out of which a moment later came the sound of an automobile passing along a road and dying away" (4). "Twit twit twit / jug jug jug jug jug jug / So rudely forc'd."[10] Eliot's nightingale, Philomel, sang of her rape; Faulkner's "fishingbird" perhaps prophesies one.

There is much in the landscape around the Old Frenchman's Place to evoke Eliot's poem. When, further along in the novel, Temple Drake appears on the scene, one of the characters that unnerves her and finally begins to haunt her is the old blind man. Early in her appearance, in her attempt to escape his "sight," she runs off a porch and ends up "on hands and knees in a litter of ashes and tin cans and bleached bones" (42). But she is soon to discover that this "sanctuary" offers no place to hide, and especially no place to hide from the seeming omni-

10. T. S. Eliot, "The Waste Land," *The Complete Poems and Plays* (New York: Harcourt, Brace and Co., 1952), p. 43.

presence of the old blind man. With his tapping cane, he seems to be following her, and she flees. Cornered in her flight, she darts about erratically in the rooms of the house. At one point on hearing the approach of his "dry tapping," she rushes to the kitchen and clutches the box holding Ruby's baby and tries to pray—in a kind of grotesque rendering of a Madonna and child scene: ". . . she could not think of a single designation for the heavenly father, so she began to say 'My father's a judge; my father's a judge'" (50).

In the violent rape scene that lies quietly like a time bomb at the heart of *Sanctuary*, Temple finds herself cornered in a crib of the barn, confronting a crouching rat, prevented from escape by Tommy guarding the barn door. The men of the Old Frenchman's Place circle restlessly about the barn, as images blur and recur. But one image that reappears and expands is that of the old blind man sitting on the porch, "his face lifted into the sun" (89). Indeed, Faulkner's deliberate blurring of the sequence of events seems intended in part to let the old man's presence dominate the scene in which he does not actively participate. Popeye drops from above into the crib with Temple, and begins his perverted assault with the corn cob (the reader, of course, does not discover precisely what is going on until later). Temple's response to her rape is directed to the old blind man who exists for her only as a kind of presiding image and deity: ". . . she began to say Something is going to happen to me. She was saying it to the old man with the yellow clots for eyes. 'Something is happening to me!' she screamed at him, sitting in his chair in the sunlight, his hands crossed on the top of the stick. 'I told you it was!' she screamed, voiding the words like hot silent bubbles into the bright silence about them until he turned his head and the two phlegm-clots above her where she lay tossing and thrashing on the rough, sunny boards. 'I told you! I told you all the time!'" (99).

It is left to Horace Benbow, in recalling for his sister his experiences at the Old Frenchman's Place, to raise the old blind man to the mythic level of a seer-prophet: "And that blind man, that old man sitting there at the table, waiting for somebody to feed him, with that immobility of blind people, like it was the backs of their eyeballs you looked at while they were hearing music you couldn't hear; that Goodwin led out of the room and completely off the earth, as far as I know. I never saw him again. I never knew who he was, who he was kin to. Maybe not to anybody. Maybe that old Frenchman that built the house a hundred years ago didn't want him either and just left him there when he died or moved away" (105). Mysterious in origin, omnipresent, seeing nothing yet seeing all, suffering for self and others, the old blind man is clearly related in function to Eliot's Tiresias.

At the heart of *The Waste Land*, in the middle of "The Fire Sermon," Tiresias becomes the presiding voice of the poem: "I Tiresias, though blind, throbbing between two lives, / Old man with wrinkled female breasts, can see / At the violet hour, the evening hour that strives / Homeward, and brings the sailor home from sea." What Eliot's Tiresias sees through his transcendent blindness is the tired seduction of the typist by the "young man carbuncular." But of course, Tiresias does more than see: "And I Tiresias have foresuffered all / Enacted on this same divan or bed; I who have sat by Thebes below the wall / And walked among the lowest of the dead."[11] Tiresias is a participant in the young man's assault on the bored typist, but in his male-female identity he obscurely plays both roles, suffers for both seducer and seduced. In his notorious footnotes, Eliot tells us: "What Tiresias *sees*, in fact, is the substance of the poem."[12] Is what the old blind man *sees* in Popeye's "rape" of Temple the meaning of *Sanctuary*? The reader's attention is deflected by the sensationalism of the corn cob, which he will witness later in the courtroom. But perhaps the old man senses the presence of twisted passions that destroy, in contrast to the life-giving sun to which he turns. And of course it is to him that Temple turns as a kind of confessor in the middle of the viola-

11. Ibid., pp. 43–44.
12. Ibid., p. 52.

tion of her body (temple); it is his image she conjures up when in need of someone to share her outrage, however confused it might be with unconscious pleasure.

In drawing on the resources of high culture and low, of modern poetry and comic strips, and in creating a world of highly stylized characters and elements, Faulkner made *Sanctuary* probably his most contemporary book. Like the "realism" of recent American fiction, *Sanctuary*'s stylized realism is a strange mixture of the actual and the semi-allegorical, the everyday and the extraordinary—all artfully contrived to convey a more acute sense of the way things *really* are than traditional realism can. And the way things really are is rather horrible. We have become accustomed to talking about our own time as so intrinsically awful and reality so unbearable that we have granted the novelist the privilege of abandoning traditional realistic techniques and of adopting more stylized as well as more shocking methods and strategies. In "The Fiction Writer and His Country," Flannery O'Connor has provided a rationale for these new techniques: ". . . you have to make your vision apparent by shock—to the hard of hearing you shout, and for the almost blind you draw large and startling figures."[13] Faulkner anticipated and foreshadowed these techniques in *Sanctuary*, and achieved in the process a higher or transcendent or an essential reality. What Faulkner did in *Sanctuary* connects in many fascinating ways with what Flannery O'Connor does in *Wise Blood*, Joseph Heller in *Catch-22*, Thomas Pynchon in *V.*, Ken Kesey in *One Flew over the Cuckoo's Nest*, Kurt Vonnegut, Jr., in *Cat's Cradle*, or Jerzy Kosinski in *The Painted Bird*. All of these novelists at various points violate our sense of reality, but at these very points they all, too, give us a transcendent sense of the world that is so real that it is painful, when it is not hilarious. Often it is both, simultaneously. Comedy and humor

13. Flannery O'Connor, "The Fiction Writer and His Country," *The Living Novel: A Symposium*, ed. Granville Hicks (New York, 1957; rpt. New York, 1962), p. 163.

play no small part in these recent works, and they play a similar important part in *Sanctuary*.

## II

The comedy of *Sanctuary* not only evokes the reader's laughter, but also startles him—because of its context of violence, brutality, degradation. Perhaps because he is startled, the reader is discomfited by the humor, shamed in the vague realization that he is laughing where he should be serious, is giggling where he should be sympathetic, is amused where he should be repelled. If this novel is, as some critics have claimed, Faulkner's darkest, why should the reader get a kick out of reading it? Didn't, indeed, Faulkner make a mistake by inserting comedy in an essentially serious work, thereby diminishing its impact? Lawrance Thompson (in *William Faulkner: An Introduction and Interpretation*) may serve as a typical example of critical reaction. He cites examples of Faulkner's comic scenes and then comments: "Such entertaining lapses into burlesque do obviously constitute artistic faults; but they at least heighten the reader's awareness that Faulkner is consistently employing variants on the comic and satiric mode, as a means of keeping his moral indignation under artistic control."[14] Thompson's charge that Faulkner's satire descends too frequently to burlesque may be admitted—or rather, it may be admitted that much of Faulkner's comedy is a form of burlesque: whether burlesque is a "lapse" from satire is a question that does not seem as critically relevant to *Sanctuary* as the simple question whether the comic scenes, satire or burlesque, destroy the book's serious tone and meaning.

In short, are the comic scenes simply a mistake, a means for Faulkner of keeping his "moral indignation under artistic control" (as Thompson suggests), or do they serve some other purpose? As a matter of fact, *Sanctuary* is not divided neatly into

14. Lawrance Thompson, *William Faulkner: An Introduction and Interpretation* (New York, 1963), p. 114.

serious and comic scenes, but almost all the episodes are some curious mixture of the two elements. That opening scene is shot through with comic detail, and the very movement of the action hovers precariously on the thin line separating the humorous and the serious. Other scenes, like the confusing and multiple and continuous pursuit of Temple through the night at the Old Frenchman's Place, are implicit with comedy, and there are even comic overtones, however muted, to the novel's central event of horror—Popeye's use of a corn cob to rape Temple (some of these are suggested when Temple tells the story of the rape to Horace Benbow, "with actual pride, a sort of naive and impersonal vanity"). Thus the so-called comic scenes do not represent the introduction of elements generally foreign to the novel. Considered in their context, they appear to be in their natural setting, and represent the surfacing and coming into central focus of an element that runs through all the novel. Indeed, the comedy and horror are so closely intertwined in *Sanctuary* that no single scene is so "pure" as not to posit, at some depth or level, the opposite of its main emotional coloring and impact: the comic has substrata of horror, and the horror has its substrata of the comic. Perhaps somewhere in this mixed structure lies the novel's ultimate meaning.

The comic scenes that have attracted the most critical attention are those in chapters 21 and 25, the first telling the story of Virgil and Fonzo Snopes's puzzled stay at Miss Reba's house in Memphis, the other describing Red's funeral at the roadhouse followed by a small gathering (including the small boy, Uncle Bud) at Miss Reba's to mourn Red's death. In concentrating on these scenes, critics have sometimes forgotten their setting. Fitted neatly in between them, in the long chapter 23, appear the scenes that give the most graphic and repellent descriptions of the corn cob rape (as narrated by Temple to Horace Benbow), and the scenes of intensest nausea experienced by Horace in reaction to what he has witnessed and heard. Thus, two comic highlights are intersected by the novel's grimmest elements, reminders of the terrible event that lies at the center of the novel's action, and they are followed swiftly by the trial and conviction of Lee Goodwin and his lynching by burning (chapters 26-29). It is hard to believe that this structuring was careless on Faulkner's part. Indeed, the back-to-back juxtaposition of the comedy and horror is so striking and deliberate that Faulkner must have been counting on some kind of fused effect.

Virgil and Fonzo rent rooms at a place they take to be a hotel but which turns out to be Miss Reba's. As they lie in bed hearing the mechanical piano and the numerous voices, they speculate on what is going on. First they think Miss Reba must have a big family; then they decide it is a party. Later they wonder what business she is in, and, when they find a woman's undergarment around the wash stand, they decide she is a dressmaker. They count themselves lucky to find a brothel nearby, but Virgil is cautious of the value: "Aint nothing worth three dollars you caint tote off with you" (190). The reader is likely to find all this amusing until he recalls that this is the same house that houses Temple as prisoner, and until he remembers that the sexual itch or compulsion moving Virgil and Fonzo is the same that, in a perverted form, drove Popeye to his rape of Temple. And the chapter closes with the entrance of the repulsive "Cla'ence" Snopes who leads his country kinsmen to a Negro brothel, where they see "a room filled with coffee-colored women in bright dresses, with ornate hair and golden smiles" (192).

Following on the heels of this sexual comedy (with its sinister undertones) comes the full force of the book's sexual horror. Horace Benbow seeks Temple out at Miss Reba's (he has bought the information from Cla'ence Snopes) and gets the full account of her rape in her own irrational narrative (which in its whimsy has its comic undertones). Horace Benbow is profoundly shocked by what he hears: "He thought of her [Temple], Popeye, the woman [Ruby], the child, Goodwin, all put into a single chamber, bare, lethal, immediate and profound: a single blotting instant between the indignation and the surprise" (213-214). But even this vision of "cauterising" all the principal actors in the drama "out of the old and tragic flank of the world" does not leave Horace in peace. He has been shaken to the roots of his soul, and he suddenly identifies the "voice of the night" as "the friction of the earth on its axis" (215)—a vision that affirms the inevitability of man's—and woman's—sexuality. He is forced finally to confront his own deep-down terror at his stepdaughter's sexuality as he identifies her with Temple at the moment of the rape, hears the corn shucks sounding beneath her thighs, and rushes in panic, nausea, and dread into the bathroom to collapse and vomit. This may be for Horace his lowest moment, his moment of clearest self-knowledge, and the moment when his defeat by the "evil" he battles is determined. If his stepdaughter is Temple, can he be—can he contain—Popeye? Is the murderer of Tommy within? How sensitive can a sensitive man be and still function in the world? Finally all he hears is the "furious uproar of the shucks" (216).

If the Snopes sexual comedy offers ironic contrast to the horror of the novel's central sexual violence, so the murder of Red and his surrealistic funeral offer ironic contrast to the novel's other murders and their violent consequences. Red's murder, committed off stage, results in nothing more than a grotesque funeral orgy during which, at one point, the body rolls out of the coffin on to the floor, where the bullet hole through his forehead lies exposed to view. The sentimentality, drunkenness, and desire for pleasure and sensation all flow together to form a picture both bizarre and refracted—as though seen through a rain-sheeted window.

In contrast, the earlier murder of the "feeb" Tommy sets in motion the major action of the novel. But the action set in motion is as bizarre in a way as Red's funeral, and as far removed from genuine justice as the funeral from genuine piety. The final consequence, inasmuch as any consequence in Faulkner's universe can be "final," is another murder, that of Lee Goodwin by a lynch mob. Although Lee Goodwin is innocent of any crime, having neither raped Temple nor killed Tommy, his death gives the townspeople great psychic satisfaction: he is their scapegoat for their own furtive desires to rape Temple and commit violence ("I saw her. She was some baby. Jeez. I wouldn't have used no cob" [287]).

Sexuality and death thus offer Faulkner both his comic and serious themes in *Sanctuary*. Looked at one way, they are comic; looked at another way, they are grotesque and horrible. By bringing the two perspectives so close together, Faulkner was implying something about the nature of human experience itself: that it absurdly contains, at one and the same time, the comic alongside the tragic—humor in the horror.

### III

Cleanth Brooks, in *William Faulkner: The Yoknapatawpha Country*, states flatly that "*Sanctuary* is clearly Faulkner's bitterest novel."[15] Why he thinks this is so he does not make entirely clear. But even more puzzling is why he does not analyze this novel in the moral frame with which he opens his work, claiming that there are two moral standards in Faulkner's world (as in his southern heritage)—a sense of community and a "still vital religion with its cult, creed, and basic norms of conduct."[16] Of all Faulkner's novels, *Sanctuary* should have presented Brooks the greatest challenge to his thesis, but he evades the challenge. Perhaps the reason is that *Sanctuary*'s intense bitterness lies in its insight into the hypocrisy and hollowness of both the religion and the community presented in the novel.

The very title of this novel, *Sanctuary*, has traditional religious connotations. But as one reads into the novel, he discovers that those connotations are ironic. No one finds genuine sanctuary in the novel, but what little shelter is discovered is found *in spite of* community and religion. The house symbolism is intricate and rich, beginning with the Old Frenchman's Place, including Miss Reba's establishment in Memphis, and running

15. Cleanth Brooks, *William Faulkner: The Yoknapatawpha Country* (New Haven, 1963), p. 127.
16. Ibid., p. 1.

through a variety of institutions and places in Jefferson. It is one of the novel's major ironies that the two places that offer more comfort and shelter, more genuine human communion, than any other are the whore house in Memphis and the jail in Jefferson. One of these is outside the pale of community and religion, the other created to impose punishment on their enemies.

*Sanctuary* presents one of Faulkner's bleakest accounts of southern religion. Its debased state is summed up best, perhaps, in the symbolism of the heaven-tree (the ailanthus) that stands next to the jail: "The last trumpet-shaped bloom had fallen from the heaven-tree at the corner of the jail yard. They lay thick, viscid underfoot, sweet and oversweet in the nostrils with a sweetness surfeitive and moribund, and at night now the ragged shadow of full-fledged leaves pulsed upon the barred window in shabby rise and fall" (122). This repulsive tree represents the full, dark fruition of a religion that finds its contemporary meaning in the institution of the jail. Like the tree's fallen blooms, the church has become "oversweet" with a "sweetness surfeitive and moribund." There is nothing left but the stench of sentiment and dead dogmas. It is no wonder that in this strange community, the jail offers greater sanctuary than the church. As Horace reports to Miss Jenny: "This morning the Baptist minister took him [Lee Goodwin] for a text. Not only as a murderer, but as an adulterer; a polluter of the free Democratico-Protestant atmosphere of Yoknapatawpha county. I gathered that his idea was that Goodwin and the woman should both be burned as a sole example to that child; the child to be reared and taught the English language for the sole end of being taught that it was begot in sin by two people who suffered by fire for having begot it" (123–124).

In Jefferson, it is difficult to separate religion and community, as the community justifies its terrible anti-human behavior in the name of the religion. Ruby and her baby are confronted with the need for sanctuary in Jefferson, as they await the trial of Lee Goodwin, her man and the baby's father. It is the good "church ladies" of the town who pressure the hotel proprietor to evict the mother and child. Horace Benbow asks, "You mean to say you let the Baptist church dictate who your guests will be?" (175). As the proprietor makes excuses, Horace asks where Ruby and her baby have gone. The proprietor does not know, but he says, "I reckon somebody took her in, though." "Yes," Horace replies, "Christians. Christians" (175). Indeed, nobody has taken the woman in—and, on the contrary, the townspeople have seen it as their Christian duty to run her out of town. Horace's sister, Narcissa, proves the most "Christian" of all in betraying her brother to force him to stop supporting Ruby and defending Goodwin (she gives the district attorney, in charge of prosecuting Goodwin, enough information to find Temple and use her to destroy Horace Benbow's case at the trial). Ruby's sanctuary does, finally, turn out to be on the edge of town, in an old shack occupied by "an old half-crazed white woman who was believed to manufacture spells for Negroes" (193). It is a strange place: "All night a dim light burned in the crazy depths of the house . . ." (193). At almost any hour of the day, Negroes could be seen entering or leaving. Although Faulkner leaves this sanctuary in considerable shadow, it appears that the old woman and her establishment represent a vitality that has run out entirely from the institutional Christianity in the community. In some ways, the half-mad woman appears to represent in the novel something of the same nature represented by Madame Sosostris, the "famous clairvoyante" with the "wicked pack of cards"[17] (with which she prophesies the poem) in Eliot's *The Waste Land*. Both figures represent an energy, integrity, and earnestness (however superstitious) that have disappeared from religious belief.

IV

The concluding chapter of *Sanctuary* presents Popeye's background, describes his hanging for a murder he did not commit, and shows, finally, Temple and her father in Paris, bored, de-

17. T. S. Eliot, "The Waste Land," p. 38.

tached, restless. The action of the novel has in a sense already been completed. Lee Goodwin has been lynched by the self-righteous and "Christian" community for a crime he did not commit, and Horace Benbow has returned to the home and wife that, at the opening of the novel, he was trying to escape. He has been soundly defeated in his efforts to cope with an evil he does not fully understand by a community bent on maintaining its myths of innocence and respectability. Horace's return home appears to be a capitulation to those myths, an acknowledgement of defeat and loss of self, and a return to the spiritual and moral paralysis from which he had feebly tried to escape. He has perhaps gained the self-knowledge of his futile psychic involvement with his stepdaughter, Little Belle, and recognizes that he must reconcile himself to her loss of sexual innocence.

In trying to come to terms with *Sanctuary*'s last chapter, critics have found themselves either baffled or disapproving. Irving Howe, for example, writes: "Only in the last chapter, a perfunctory summary of Popeye's early life, does Faulkner stumble."[18] Allen Tate, in an Introduction to a paperback edition of *Sanctuary*, writes: "Awkward as the conclusion may be, and anti-climactic as the mere expository account of Popeye and Temple is at the end, it is difficult to imagine a resolution to the violence at the center of the novel. There is nothing to be resolved."[19]

Much of the difficulty with the conclusion springs from the difficulty with coming to terms with the character of Popeye throughout the novel. He is one of the most vivid and memorable of all Faulkner's characters, a creature of horror who seems to be something of a cross between T. S. Eliot's hollow man (headpiece filled with straw) and Sweeney (but because he is impotent, not "Sweeney Erect")—with something thrown in too of *The Waste Land*'s fisherking, sexually crippled in a dry and burnt out land. But more than these or any combination of

18. Irving Howe, *William Faulkner*, p. 197.
19. Allen Tate, "Introduction," *Sanctuary*, by William Faulkner (New York: New American Library—Signet, 1968), pp. xii–xiii.

them, Popeye is himself and unique. It is usual for the critics of *Sanctuary* to make some such remark as this by Dorothy Tuck (in *Crowell's Handbook of Faulkner*): "Popeye is a figure of pure evil."[20] What does such a description mean?

Faulkner sheds some light on Popeye in some of the conversations recorded on his work. In *Faulkner in the University*: "Q. In *Sanctuary*, Mr. Faulkner, is the character of Popeye emblematic of evil in a materialistic society? What would he stand for? A. No, he was to me another lost human being. He became a symbol of evil in modern society only by coincidence but I was still writing about people, not about ideas, not about symbols."[21] In *Faulkner at West Point*: "Q. Sir . . . Did you see or do you see Popeye and Joe Christmas as being similar people? A. Not at all. Popeye was the monster. . . . Q. Sir, did Popeye have the same problem of not having a society to belong to? A. Now I don't understand Popeye. He, to me, was a monster. He was just there."[22]

If we, with Faulkner, see Popeye as "another lost human being," or as a "monster," it is difficult at the same time to label him "a figure of pure evil." Such a label, if it means anything, means that he is some kind of satanic villain, deeply motivated and fiercely committed to do evil. Such, of course, is simply not the case. As readers and critics, we have yearned to heap blame on Popeye for all the terrible events of *Sanctuary*, and we have been upset in finding out that his frail figure will not bear the weight of our wrath. Indeed, Faulkner planned it that way as a trick on his audience, a trick designed to bring self awareness and insight.

Did Faulkner fumble in summarizing Popeye's background in the last chapter of *Sanctuary*? There is a little-known account of *Sanctuary's* conclusion by the Englishman Jonathan Cape,

20. Dorothy Tuck, *Crowell's Handbook of Faulkner* (New York, 1964), p. 41.
21. *Faulkner in the University*, p. 74.
22. Joseph L. Fant and Robert Ashley. *Faulkner at West Point* (New York, 1964), p. 83.

one of Faulkner's publishers, in J. Maclaren-Ross's *Memoirs of the Forties*:

Our New York branch did *Sanctuary*, though Chatto and Windus brought it out over here because they'd a contract as his British publishers. Faulkner wrote it while he was working as a night-watchman, and when I'd read the typescript I said to him "This is all very well, but I'd like to know more about Popeye's background, where he came from and so on, also why he's impotent like this." And Faulkner said: "Why it's all there in the first chapter, all about his parents and childhood." Well I looked back through the first chapter but damned if I could find anything like that except that Popeye was scared of birds, so then Faulkner himself had a look. "By God," he said, "If I haven't forgotten to write it after all!". . . He went off back to his watchman's shack and over a jug of corn liquor got out the missing chapter. But by that time the book was being printed, and we couldn't fit it in at the beginning, so Faulkner said: "Let's put it in last and the hell with them." So that's how the book comes to be constructed like that. Faulkner was most apologetic about it, couldn't think how it had come to slip his mind.[23]

This is a fascinating account, but perhaps betrayed by its glibness. It does not square with what Faulkner has said about improving his work in revising *Sanctuary*, nor with what we know about the revision from the preservation of the original proofs. But most important of all, this account presents Faulkner as an ordinary novelist simply concerned about sticking in information about a character's background. We know from Faulkner's other great novels that he simply did not work that way. We can, I think, only assume that in this episode, Faulkner was spoofing Jonathan Cape, or that Cape is misremembering or embroidering an event of the past.

23. J. Maclaren-Ross, *Memoirs of the Forties* (London, 1965), p. 19.

Popeye's background, had it been given early in the novel, would change entirely the way we read *Sanctuary*. There can be no doubt that Faulkner was fully aware of this simple fact. As the novel is now structured, Popeye is the first character to appear in the novel, and he is a sinister presence throughout, his rubber-knob eyes haunting the appalling action as it unfolds (not unlike the eyes of Dr. T. J. Eckleburg haunting *The Great Gatsby*, but of course to different effect). It is Popeye who has committed the rape with a corn cob, who has killed Tommy, who kills Red—who, in short, sets all the events in motion that bring a train of disasters in their wake which disrupts the community and destroys the innocent. Just as we have inflated his image to bear the weight of all his guilt, perhaps even smug in our satisfaction in having a scapegoat to blame for all the novel's evil, we discover in the novel's last chapter that he is indeed a hollow man made of stamped tin and rubber eyes, that he is indeed simply "another lost human being," that he is indeed a "monster." He had no hair until he was five years old, and the doctor told his mother that alcohol would kill him: "And he will never be a man, properly speaking. With care, he will live some time longer. But he will never be any older than he is now" (300). We discover, perhaps to our horror, that we have been heaping our hatred on a child-man, devoid of the normal attributes of a human being, a monster more to be pitied than blamed, a creature simply unworthy of the grandiose role of evil-doer that we want to assign him. His birth on Christmas day perhaps brings to mind, ironically, W. B. Yeats's "The Second Coming": "And what rough beast, its hour come round at last, / Slouches towards Bethlehem to be born?"[24]

In placing Popeye's background in the last chapter of *Sanctuary* for its most resonant effect, Faulkner was following a method he was to follow in all his great fiction. Faulkner's novels tend to flow backward in time at the same time that they move closer to the present. For example, in *Light in August* we do not learn

24. W. B. Yeats, "The Second Coming," *Collected Poems* (New York: The Macmillan Co., 1947), p. 215.

of the ambiguity of Joe Christmas's birth until deep into the last half of the novel. In *Absalom, Absalom!* we do not learn of Thomas Sutpen's crucial boyhood experience until long after he has appalled us by his behavior. As I have written in *Quests Surd and Absurd*: "In a sense . . . each one of Faulkner's novels represents a descent into the vortex of time, a vortex created by an event that disturbs, upsets, alarms, or frightens the family or community. In moving frantically back and forth in the search for the causes and consequences of this key and singular event, Faulkner creates the structure of his novels: a whirlpool or circular structure suggesting that the secret of time (or life) is not to be found in the simple, straight chronology of one event following another, but rather in hidden corners . . . of the past, with only remote or oblique or subterranean . . . connections with the event of the present being probed."[25]

Popeye is executed in Birmingham for a crime he did not commit, and he appears to be without ordinary human feelings, indifferent to his life or death. Temple and her father sit in the Luxembourg Gardens in Paris, hearing the music of Massenet, Scriabin, and Berlioz. Temple yawns, and gazes in her compact at a face that is "sullen and discontented and sad": "She closed the compact and from beneath her smart new hat she seemed to follow with her eyes the waves of music, to dissolve into the dying brasses, across the pool and the opposite semi-circles of trees where at sombre intervals the dead tranquil queens in stained marble mused, and on into the sky lying prone and vanquished in the embrace of the season of rain and death" (309). These last, quickly sketched scenes are some of the bleakest in *Sanctuary*, not unlike some of the scenes of sophisticated decadence in *The Waste Land*. Just at the time that we come to some kind of dim understanding of Popeye, he is extinguished in circumstances irrelevant to his deeds and to any definition of justice. Temple, originator of much of the novel's violence and brutality and inhumanity, walks the earth

25. James E. Miller, Jr., "William Faulkner: Descent into the Vortex," *Quests Surd and Absurd* (Chicago, 1967), p. 53.

bored with the uneventfulness of her life, prepared for the next, new sensation. The very sky itself, "lying prone and vanquished," appears to proclaim the withdrawal of any God of justice or deity of concern. The season of *Sanctuary* is, indeed, the season of "rain and death."

JAMES E. MILLER, JR.
*University of Chicago*

# DJUNA BARNES AND SURREALISM: "BACKWARD GRIEF"

Djuna Barnes reached her eightieth birthday on June 12, 1972. The legend is still extending. Bits and pieces from the brilliant years in Paris, the 20s and the 30s of the expatriate luminaries, continue to drift in. Janet Flanner recalls Djuna Barnes of those enchanted days, "the most important woman writer we had in Paris." T. S. Eliot had read a Barnes play in manuscript, and reported that "it contained the most splendid, archaic language he had ever had the pleasure of reading, but that, frankly, he couldn't make head or tail of its drama." Miss Flanner, a close friend, read it, and confessed the same. "With withering scorn, she said, 'I never expected to find that you were as stupid as Tom Eliot.' I thanked her for the only compliment she had ever given me."[1]

The legend projects the image of a virtuoso. Wherever Djuna Barnes is read today in the American academic community, the image perseveres. A young woman of amazing inventiveness and independence came down the river from Cornwall-on-Hudson. She studied painting and design at the Pratt Institute. In 1919 and 1920, she was exploring and as often dictating the modes of the Village intellectuals, acting in early pieces of O'Neill at the Provincetown, and producing plays of her own on double bills with O'Neill and Millay.[2] Then she went to Paris and London. She associated with the Stein *cercle* on the Rue de

1. "That Was Paris," *The New Yorker*, March 11, 1972, p. 35. Perhaps the play may have been a draft of something akin to *The Antiphon*, published in 1958, notable for its archaic language.
2. See Helen Deutsch and Stella Hanau, *The Provincetown: A Story of a Theatre* (New York, 1931), Appendix B, programs for October 31 and December 5, 1919, and for March 26, 1920, listing plays of Djuna Barnes, Eugene O'Neill, and Edna St. Vincent Millay.

Fleurus; she knew Eliot in the praesidium of the waste land. After her work with the Provincetown, she turned to fiction. Ford Madox Ford published her stories in his *Transatlantic Review*. She produced her first novel *Ryder* (1928) illustrated with her own drawings. She wrote poetry. With her aloof good looks, her superb confidence and wit she captured the *avant garde*. All of this foray culminated in *Nightwood* (1937), read by intellectuals in Rome, Paris, London, New York. Then, once again in the Village, she chose a strict seclusion, published an occasional poem, and completed her long verse play, *The Antiphon* (1958). Her correspondence is known to have been voluminous. The obdurate solitude suggests that little or none of it will be made public, or preserved.

The legend is exotic, rather in conformity with her "Portrait of Alice" which she lent with other paintings and drawings to Peggy Guggenheim for an exhibition in 1943. The image at the center is seemingly inscrutable. Was the legend made as a studiously conceived mystery, like the self-made mystery of Garbo in seclusion? Willed or not, in America the mystery holds. In Europe Djuna Barnes is read again, especially in Germany where new claims for the splendor of the fiction are currently made, and where presumably new poems are shortly to be published.[3] One supposes that in Europe the legend was always of minor consequence and that she is read, minus the mystery, for what she said and how she said it. But then we Americans have a particular penchant for mythicizing our writers and for using aesthetic content as documentation for biography.

The prevailing approach to *Nightwood* on American campuses, the one work of Djuna Barnes which has become a minor

3. Perhaps it is of interest to note here that the post-World War II Germans were translating and publishing Bruno Traven before he was known in the United States beyond very slight notice. Concerning the new German venture with the works of Djuna Barnes, see *The New York Times*, May 24, 1971, p. 24. The article presents an interview with the author. An approaching birthday is noted. The birthdate reflected in the opening of this essay is the one given in *Who's Who in America*.

classic, is anyone's guess. No doubt it is taken as a lineal inheritor of Poe, or regarded as the work of an American Joyce.[4] But this is to assume likenesses which do not exist. Poe and Joyce are not prototypes. And if they are not, what then? Perhaps one simply takes T. S. Eliot's judgment in his enthusiastic introduction to *Nightwood*: he found "a quality of horror and doom very nearly related to that of Elizabethan tragedy." "It seems to me," he wrote, "that all of us, so far as we attach ourselves to created objects and surrender our wills to temporal ends, are eaten by the same worm."[5] This is the Eliot of Ezekiel's valley of dry bones. Devoted to temporal ends, we all need to be eaten by the three white leopards under the juniper tree! Eliot read in his own terms. He endowed the legend; but he must have assumed that the book was impenetrable with respect to logical structure, and impressive with a nightmarish blur of a journey through the terror of the human span. Today Djuna Barnes appears in courses in American literature of the twentieth century. The legend is there; and unless, in this day of the new feminism, young women students wish to advance Djuna Barnes as another proof for the equation of the sexes in creative talent, the legend must certainly predominate: this woman of mystery felt the spell of Poe's hypnagogic state, or answered the fantasies of the Blooms with her own descents into the night, or intended a vision, in the manner of Eliot, of the perilous passage to redemption.

The comment of this essay is intended to suggest some thresholds for a new reading of Djuna Barnes. Responsible critical explication in America is long overdue. The legend should be put aside, whether or not it was self-impelled. Certainly Djuna Barnes is not at any point in her work a devotée of automatic writing. She had something of radical import to say; and

4. The equivalence with Joyce was advanced insistently by the late Edwin Muir, friend and admirer of Djuna Barnes. See *The Present Age from 1914* (*Introduction to English Literature*, V, ed. Bonamy Dobrée) (New York, 1940), 149–154. Muir places *Nightwood* in the exalted company of *Ulysses, Sons and Lovers, Mrs. Dalloway*.

5. *Selected Works of Djuna Barnes* (New York, 1962), p. 231.

she said it independently. There is no reason to suppose that she wished not to be understood, even though the terms are peculiarly hers. She wrote in an American age when Cather and Glasgow, even in their finest subtleties, intended to be understood, and when Dreiser and Dos Passos purposed in their tracings of American society a vast fiction as clear as a blue-print. In the 60s a slight trickle of a new and liberated attention to Djuna Barnes began to appear.[6] Perhaps we at last begin to read her with full attention to the nature of her art.

Kenneth Burke recently made a fresh start with *Nightwood*, contending that the book "aims at . . . a kind of 'transcendence downward.' . . ." He finds an intention to make the plot absolute, in a series of "[Biblical] Lamentations, much as though this were the primal story of all mankind."[7] One is not persuaded that Burke admires the book. But his rigor with the content is a good augury. He is concerned with the Scriptural mode of the work. Had he comprehended the preceding novel *Ryder*, he would have noticed the Scriptural mode in its beginnings. It would be mad to say that Djuna Barnes intended to write a substitute Testament for humankind. What she did intend was a dismissal of Scriptural authoritarianism by deliberately crafted Scriptural frames, each playing with Biblical language, each designed to present sardonically the Law as an insufficient revelation of the nature of man, and, first for her, that of woman. Burke surveys too little. But his study proposes that Djuna Barnes was intent upon novelistic structure. We should remember that she wrote in an American era of the novel when *consciousness* was all. (O'Neill, of course, tried to use some ill-digested Freud to "expand" the American drama, without notable success.) Djuna Barnes wished to bring to the American novel the full burden of the dark of the mind, the night, the

6. See, e.g., Kenneth Burke, "Version, Con—, Per—, and In— (Thoughts on Djuna Barnes's Novel, *Nightwood*)," *The Southern Review*, 2, n.s., no. 2 (April, 1966), 329–346; and Alan Williamson, "The Divided Image: The Quest for Identity in the Works of Djuna Barnes," *Critique*, 7, no. 1 (Spring, 1964), 58–74.
7. Loc. cit., p. 335.

subconscious. She intended to be an American surrealist. Clearly she thought of herself as unique. She was unique; and today she belongs in the unique company of some of our new writers.

The doctrines of the surrealists have spread very slowly into Protestant America. T. S. Eliot noted in his introduction to *Nightwood* the perseverance of the Puritan morality, its dismissal of the images of sleep as nonfigurative in the life of the "successful" man.[8] The American future may come to evaluate the psychedelic age as prophecy. Vonnegut, Pynchon, and Hawkes, as examples from this American present, suggest the coming on of a new morality, and a new mode in an art of fiction as full exposition: the totality of the dark and the light, subconscious and conscious, the mind at the full. In the renascence of Djuna Barnes she will be read with our new novelists. The reading will not advance affinities to Poe, and, at the other end of the spectrum, to Joyce. Poe wrote his tales as symbols of the "furnishings" of one mind, his own. Djuna Barnes intended to expose the human condition, as she saw it, by fictive analogies. As for Joyce, one should simply note with André Breton, the chief French spokesman of surrealism, that Joyce is not a true surrealist. "Joyce labors to keep himself within the framework of *art*. He falls into novelistic illusion."[9] The distinction rests in the insistence of surrealism upon an exposition of universals. Thus, despite the distance between Poe and Joyce, each is intent upon art as illusion, a privacy of vision ending with the limits of each sovereign imagination. The point is that the vision does not refer, as though it were a self-contained picture from Synthetic Cubism, beyond itself. In the intent of Gertrude Stein, the deep privacy of the fiction, the poetry, the plays, there is a comparable evidence of the self-contained. All of this is to say that the work of Djuna Barnes is designed to refer beyond itself. Related to the tenets of sur-

8. Loc. cit., p. 230.
9. *Manifestoes of Surrealism*, trans. Richard Seaver and Helen R. Lane (Ann Arbor, 1969): "On Surrealism and Its Living Works" (Breton, 1953), p. 298.

realism, her work urges the need for a new morality and the need for a new scripture describing the phenomena of the human mind.

A reading with new thresholds requires a tracing of the figure in the carpet. There is a figure. It begins in the torment of mature life, and moves backward in grief to childhood, from that state of taking off beyond which, in the oppression and misguidance of false scriptures, we lost our way. It is my intention to suggest briefly the major themes in the figure. Perhaps a metaphor will hold: that we trace the dominant images in a weaving, as Procne read the scenes of the ravished Philomela in the tissue-tapestry, the wordless "letter" of her sister's grief. The verbal style of Djuna Barnes is one thing. It is intricate and, as Eliot contended, essentially poetic. But this is not poetry of a strictly private vision, of mere illusion. The script is a transparency. The letter of the grief goes abroad. At the close of *Nightwood*, Matthew O'Connor, the doctor and the listening post of the tortured, the purveyor of truth as in a reappearance of Teiresias, screams: "I say, tell the story of the world to the world!"[10] What, then, is the story?

The foreground is the doctrine of surrealism. How much Djuna Barnes knew of the formal theory of the surrealists is not at present measurable. No doubt she had read Baudelaire, the prototype. She must have agreed with Baudelaire, that a work of the imagination comes of a very real anguish, the anguish expressed, for example, in "Un Voyage á Cythère" or in "Lesbos." For this anguish is like the torment of the characters in her early stories, and like the anguish, particularly, of the lesbian Nora Flood in *Nightwood*. She must have recognized the achievement of Baudelaire beyond *l'art pour l'art* very much as Wallace Fowlie has described it: "Baudelaire went so deeply into psychoanalytic exploration that he passed beyond the per-

10. *Selected Works of Djuna Barnes* (New York, 1962), p. 359. Citations to the text of *Nightwood* appearing hereafter refer to this edition in parenthetical insertion of page numbers.

sonal reminiscence into the universal."[11] If Freud was later to teach the surrealists that man is primarily a sleeper, it was Baudelaire who had already proceeded beyond an image-ridden sleep of his own into the great dark through which all men move apart from wakefulness. The nature of the universal is named by Djuna Barnes in *Nightwood*, as Matthew O'Connor reminds Nora: "For dreams have only the pigmentation of fact" (300). The residuum from wakefulness, the insistent and presumably known reality, is no more than the color of fact. The content of the fact has been discarded.

André Breton published his *Manifesto of Surrealism* in Paris in 1924. His definition of surrealism reads: "Psychic automatism in its pure state, by which one proposes to express—verbally, by means of the written word, or in any other manner—the actual functioning of thought. Dictated by thought, in the absence of any control exercised by reason, exempt from any aesthetic or moral concern."[12] The evidence of Djuna Barnes's work shows clearly that she did not regard thought as undirected flow. Thought, to be thought, must for her be identified with an imposition of structure. Automatism, as expressed in automatic writing (very soon to be rejected by the surrealists), could not possibly have satisfied her. But Breton's description of the "normal" function of mind certainly accords with her practice in her novels. "I have no choice," Breton wrote, "but to consider it [the waking state] a phenomenon of interference. Not only does the mind display, in this state, a strange tendency to lose its bearings, but . . . it does not appear that, when the mind is functioning normally, it really responds to anything but the suggestions which come to it from the depths of that dark night to which I commend it."[13]

*Ryder* appeared four years after Breton's first manifesto. Responses to the dark assail again and again the presumed impregnability of the waking state. In this novel, which moves

11. *Age of Surrealism* (Bloomington, 1960), p. 26.
12. Op. cit., p. 26.
13. Ibid., pp. 12–13.

rapidly from an English to an American setting, there is a veiled paradigm of the thought directed to American distinctions which appears in *Nightwood*. *Ryder* gives us suggestions from the dark part of the American mind, warring against the "logic" of required family structures, of condemned "fallen" women, of blindly accepted Scriptural authority. Rising from the deep substrata of the author's mind is her furious vision of Puritan morality, and, for that matter, of all moralities named Anglo-Saxon. In *Nightwood*, as though she were remembering Breton, she commends us to the French. Dr. O'Connor again admonishes the American Nora: "The night and the day are two travels, and the French alone . . . leave testimony of the two in the dawn; we [Americans] tear up one for the sake of the other; not so the French . . . [The American] separates the two for fear of indignities, so that the mystery is cut in every cord; the design wildcats down the *charter mortalis*, and you get crime" (298–299). Whether "not so the French" is true or untrue, the insistence upon an American confusion resulting from attempts to deny the night is arresting. Surrealism began in France. When *Nightwood* appeared, the surrealists were either unknown or suspected in America. (For that matter, we may add, Freudian doctrine did not begin to penetrate American literary consciousness until a quarter of a century after it was known in continental Europe.)

A second notice of Breton in 1924 must suffice here. His statement on childhood in surrealism is so close to the thematic figuration of both *Ryder* and *Nightwood* that it might have served each as an epigraph.

The mind which plunges into Surrealism relives with glowing excitement the best part of its childhood. . . . From childhood memories . . . there emanates a sentiment of being unintegrated, and then later of *having gone astray*, which I hold to be the most fertile that exists. It is perhaps childhood that comes closest to one's "real life"; childhood beyond which man has at his disposal . . . only a few

complimentary tickets; childhood where everything nevertheless conspires to bring about the effective, risk-free
possession of oneself. Thanks to Surrealism, it seems that
opportunity knocks a second time.[14]

It is idle to press the point: the celebration of childhood is an
inheritance from romanticism. But romantic expression in its
characteristic idiom is purely sentimental and nostalgic. Breton
speaks of a later sentiment, a feeling of being unintegrated, of
having gone astray. This is a different quest. In the state of
alienation from childhood the existential element enters. For,
in Breton's terms, were it not for the sense of alienation, there
would be no surrealism. In this respect Djuna Barnes agrees
with Breton. Later comment here will present the figure of
childhood in her design, which she associates with the unknowingness of the jungle. She tells us that the tracing to the
point of beginning is "backward grief." But were it not for the
compulsion toward grief and anguish (to return to Baudelaire's
principle of a genetic anguish in all art of universal import),
there would be nothing which we could name universal in
human experience. Kenneth Burke's notice of "transcendence
downward" seems to accord with this contention. For Djuna
Barnes, in search of a new morality and a new scripture, the
"going astray" leads on the anguish. The rubrics by which we
live are false; the "logic" of the image of man is alike false.
We cannot eat of this day, this night, without the burden of
continuity in the mind, of reason and reflection. There is
nothing for us, unintegrated as we become, save to trace back,
through the dark, all that we traversed after we lost a child's
possession of the self. Our hands, it seems, are stayed against
suicide as each one of us is busy with the ritual of return, with
the attempt to understand what was lost and how he lost it.

*Ryder* is essentially a novel in the form of an extended
allegory. Its principle matter is dream, with "pigmentations of

14. Op. cit., pp. 39–40.

fact." Its use of Scriptural frames is deliberately heretical. In the initial chapter, "Jesus Mundane," the language of the New Testament is copied in a series of "teachings" and injunctions, but copied as though in a distant echo in which the style of the speech is all that lingers. Jesus addresses the enjoined of this world. The burden of the message is this: you know nothing of the human condition; you know nothing of salvation.[15] Wendell Ryder, the omnipresent impregnating male, *rider* of women and *rider* of "the monster civilization" (272) (and presumably *Wend*ell, the roamer) instructs his children in the origin and the lineage of man and woman (ch. 23). He speaks in the style of Genesis. The children hear only of endless conception, gestation, and the cycle of birth in the everlasting parturition of cries and blood. At other points in the book there are distorted echoes of the litany of praise, wherein all that lives is bidden in the Book of Common Prayer to rejoice in the Lord. These Scriptural frames represent the patency of a useless doctrine. As figures, they seem anticipated by the short story of 1923, "The Doctors." The physician-wife of a physician determines to kill herself. "There is something mournful in me because it is being." She takes as her last bed companion an itinerant Bible salesman who rings her door-bell. Having finished with her objective, death in him rather than by poison, knife, or water, she dismisses him. Weeping in supplication and still aroused, he quotes from his Bible. In the pain of desire for another encounter, he returns to the house to find black crêpe on the door.[16] Each of these Scriptural frames is compounded in the figuration of the novelist's design. The significance comes of her thought, not of some automatic flow of the mind into language: the Book of Life, the Word, tells us nothing of the nature of man, his origin, his

15. I use the text of 1928, Horace Liveright, New York. There were two printings, one in August, the second in September. To my knowledge no reprinting has yet appeared. References to the text appear hereafter in parentheses after citations.

16. *Selected Works of Djuna Barnes* (New York, 1962), pp. 54–60. Citations to the texts of the stories, all contained in this volume, will refer to this edition by parenthetically inserted numbers.

destiny, or of the dark, the sleeping part of him; and its "Law" is absurd.

As one of the progeny of Wendell Ryder (the sum of the progeny is unknown, most of it got by chance encounters), Timothy is unique: he was born of wedlock. His "legitimacy" and that of his sister Julie then requires Wendell's "instruction" in the language of a new Genesis. Assuming that Djuna Barnes takes as her target in *Ryder* the first epistle of Paul the Apostle to Timothy, we read in the Scriptural Law of the New Testament the following: "But I suffer not a woman to teach, nor to usurp authority over the man, but to be in silence. / For Adam was first formed, then Eve. / And Adam was not deceived, but the woman being deceived was in the transgression. / Notwithstanding she shall be saved in childbearing, if they continue in faith and charity and holiness with sobriety" (I Timothy 2 : 12–15). Not since Herman Melville wrote his allegory of the bondage of women in "The Tartarus of Maids" has American literature shown a comparable defiance of the Divine Sentence. But Melville's bleak assessment is reflective in the manner of a biologist. Djuna Barnes is speaking to us of the bondage which is Scriptural, and, in America, Puritanical. She is out to overthrow and grind under both the scribes of Genesis and the pontificate of the Apostle. She is out to speak of the bondage in terms of a demeaned "Christian" womanhood. Thus it is Timothy, from the loins of Wendell Ryder, who subverts the Scriptures in the presence of woman demeaned. After his adolescent strife with a whore, a supine, undifferentiating, mawkish woman, he cries out with the one male denunciation of injustice in the novel: "Curse my father and mother, their children and mine, and the people behind us, in millions and millions that have made me, Timothy, last crust to the world, a fool of a prophet without a forthcoming" (247).

The narrative line of *Ryder* displays the following story. Sophia Grieve Ryder, a native of Connecticut (later to remarry as Sophia Alexson) gives birth in 1869 to a second son, Wendell. The child was sired, in her disclosure, by Ludwig von Beethoven. In a dream she felt Beethoven "invading" her, passing into the frontside and out the backside (ch. 7). The "infusion" in this surrealistic passage should not be dismissed as singularly grotesque. If the text from the Apostle, which the author assails as Law, is compared, then we should say: there is as much "logic" in the conception of Wendell Ryder as there is in the Law of the bondage of woman dictated by the fantasies and the dreams of St. Paul. Djuna Barnes appears to contend that sexual dominance is a dictatorial mandate from the dark, the sleeping life, of every male.

The conception of Wendell occurred in England. When he reaches adolescence, he is remarkably *sportif*. Later reflections of the author give us a "Chaucerian" dream, a primal record of Wendell's early sexual prowess (ch. 10). Chaucerian rhyme and deliberate archaisms in the language suggest that, in the record of English poetry, the exploitation of woman has been the dominant theme rising from the unconscious to the conscious. Somewhat later, Wendell goes to America, taking as his bride Amelia de Grier. They are accompanied by his mother, Sophia. The three, Sophia in adjacency to another son who has an estate in the New York countryside, set up house in a log cabin at Storm-King-on-Hudson. Meanwhile Kate-Careless, a generous whore of London, "known" earlier by Wendell, has crossed the Atlantic with an English landscape painter. She has become bored with her life on a boat on Lake Erie. She deserts the painter, and arrives at Storm-King where she is at once welcomed by Sophia and installed in the house as alternate to the wife Amelia. When he chooses his own bed, Wendell divides his nocturnal agilities between the two.

If the legitimate offspring of Wendell and Amelia are preponderant, the simultaneous pregnancies of Amelia and Kate are more significant. Wendell, the musical son of Beethoven, intended the double proof. He is a music-maker; as he informs his mother Sophia (approaching her last days), he has been the exploiter of many instruments: ". . . polygamy is the only bed a man rolls out of . . . ," eternal man with his "pipe of a single

stop, [and] the core of the codpiece" (215, 219). Or, in another
sense, he has been "cooked" by the heat of many women. He
has been brought to perfection by "the superb heats of the
roasting Kate" (221). Meanwhile, Amelia, the legitimate, if
frigid, wife, and Kate, the hot wife, the alternate in the menage,
have made their peace. They agree: a child is born simultaneously of two women; cause, which is Amelia, and effect, which
is Kate (190). This is to say, as Wendell interprets the double
pregnancies and deliverances to Sophia, that "if there are two
babes, one [mother] will be the half of the other, one will
mother the body, the other give suck to the soul" (226). Reading
the message, we take Djuna Barnes to contend that woman, in
the regard of man, is both the deliverer of the soul, which is the
image of a blind continuum, and the deliverer of yet another
body to satisfy the body's lusts, pure animal vigor. Amelia delivers "soul"; Kate delivers "body."

Yet, finally, Wendell is not simply a mindless Priapus. From
him we learn that "man rides the monster civilization, but to
woman goes the shoe-cast of it, in which is the exact record of
the journey" (272). Beyond the journey he finds nothing.
Wendell admonishes one of his sons, this one got of "his plays
with a kitchen slut in Shepherd's Bush": there is "the very
uselessness of spouting," man, "forever multiplying his own
nothing by as many more as he can get, in wedlock or out . . ."
(308). What shall be said of man's uses of woman, if beyond
all uses lies nothing? Since Wendell is the dream-conceived
child of Beethoven, we should answer: this human race, delivered unto itself again and again in a Priapian rite, is a
repetition of masculine music-making, lusty, orgasmic, signifying nothing, nothing save animal instinct.

But Wendell, like all men, comes to think of death, his own
death. Dr. Matthew O'Connor, the family physician, half
charlatan and half sage, appears and reappears through the
labyrinthine night of *Ryder*. He is taking form toward the role
which he will assume in *Nightwood*, becoming in his mysteries
the *persona* of Djuna Barnes. He is the obstetrician in the cabin

on the Hudson. He becomes in the end Wendell's counsel. If for a man there is a nothing at the end of the journey, why not, Wendell reasons, suicide?[17] For though God *is*, to the cosmic energy which we name God man is nothing. O'Connor replies: ". . . [a man] never lets the effect seal the cause, he reasons it out, he leaves notes, he says it was this or that, or the other, in an endeavor to place himself on an equal footing with [the father of creation] God. It is to him death of God *and* the father." "With a woman, take whatever woman you like . . . one and all commit, in that act, their bodies to death's custom . . . because women know that there is God only, but man knows that there is God and the father" (267–268). Djuna Barnes names the difference with full seriousness. Man, the procreator, equates himself with the unknown master creator, God. He cannot accept his own death as a creator without the anguish of self-persuasion. Woman, the bearer only, knows only "death's custom." An enigma dominates; and so *Ryder* ends in enigma. If woman were freed from her eternal bondage in service to the eternal nothing, would she then be "free" in a state equal to that of man as a cocreator? The Enigma rests in biological differentiation. The new Scripture, if there is to be one, should then be a Scripture of enigma.

These are the major themes of the first novel. Djuna Barnes explores in this tortured allegory the subconscious of Protestant morality, and, as an American of unyielding tenacity, the baleful night of American Puritanism. If we accept Wendell's disclosure to his mother, a surrender of the existential burden to Catholicism in final desperation is no more than animal surrender to an arcane authority, one which presumes to make a something of the nothing. He concludes: ". . . all of [human kind] have at one moment what they would by no means crave the next; only a dog returns to his losses, and only a Catholic

17. Cf. Fowlie, op. cit., p. 24. "Surrealism at all times seemed to offer suicide as one alternative . . . Belief in suicide has been strongly counteracted by belief in the miracle of art. . . ." If Wendell is a music-maker, an "orchestrator" of women, presumably he is an artist. But it follows that every artist thinks upon his own death, beyond the expedient of suicide.

keeps for better or for worse" (220). The "backward grief" of the Protestant psyche in *Ryder* is the subconscious obsessed with the necessity of return to Adam and Eve, the first children of the race. In *Nightwood* Djuna Barnes is to explore the conscious effort of Dr. Matthew O'Connor, a confirmed Irish Catholic, to make the supreme surrender, surrender which would deny the night of suspicion, that we are no more than the animals, the dogs returning to their losses. In his search for the solace of surrender, he fails. For it is he who demands, in the end, the telling of the story of the world to the world. It will not be the story of Redemption. The tracing of the figure in the carpet has thus far refuted Eliot. Granted, the Purgatory of this life probably defines civilized man. But for Djuna Barnes the fiery passage leads to nothing. We should the better, we conclude after *Ryder*, envy the unknowing animals. Yet, there is the human estate, and the burden of the full mind, conscious and subconscious, whether or not we love and cherish it. We were born into it. We are not admonished by our author toward a surrender to Catholicism. The anguish of the "backward grief" is the proof of the human in us. Without it, as Baudelaire contended, there would be no art.

The *violence* of the night as it opposes the day of consciousness is absent in *Ryder*. "Normal" sexuality is the theme, whatever there may be of rage against the servility of woman. As allegory, the book is meditative more than dramatic. But among the early stories there are paradigms of the violence of *Nightwood*. There is the violence of "A Night Among the Horses,"[18] and that of "Spillway."[19] There is the violence of "The Rabbit" with its dark night of man the sleeper, a man who must kill, as on a signal from the jungle of the subconscious, to justify himself as a man. A poor and gentle Armenian tailor in the Bowery

18. See Flanner, loc. cit., p. 34. For this alone, Djuna Barnes gained instant fame in Paris in the mid-20s. The story is reprinted in *Selected Works*, pp. 29–35.
19. "Spillway," dealing with the theme of death born of death, a consumptive child of a consumptive and doomed mother, appears in *Selected Works*, pp. 61–70.

stitches quietly, looking in horror at the bloody carcasses in the window of the butcher shop across the street. Torn animal flesh drips like some blood-gorged display, as we think in likenesses, in a canvas of Soutine. Amietiev yearns for the love of a demeaning, acidly contemptuous Italian girl. He proves himself, nauseated with disgust at the sight of blood dripping in the opposite window, by strangling a rabbit.[20] Violence in sexuality, the clash of the subconscious with the conscious, is dominant in these small yet brilliant precursors of the first novel. *Ryder* seems deliberately restrained, intent upon a consistent but muted rage of woman. Then *Nightwood* takes form. The sexuality exposed is "abnormal." Again we confront an allegory of "backward grief." Essentially, the book is an allegory of the loss of innocence, not the innocence of Adam and Eve before the imposition of Scriptural Law, but the innocence of the jungle. The protagonists are, in this order, a Jew searching for his lost birthright, a girl dragged from a jungle unknowingness of "good" and "evil," and two lesbians, one obsessed with a Christian "mission" and the other, with the spoils of the scavenger. Dr. Matthew O'Connor of *Ryder* emerges as the fully omniscient observer. Djuna Barnes, the maker of the figure in the carpet, speaks through him.

It is one thing to say that to live intimately is to experience entanglements in the emotional lives of others. This is the language of logic and reason, the logic of the conscious, insisting upon its own "clarity," denying the dark. It is another thing to say with Djuna Barnes, speaking through O'Connor in *Nightwood*, ". . . in the end you'll all be locked together, like the poor beasts that get their antlers mixed and are found dead that way, their heads fattened with a knowledge of each other, head-on and eye to eye, until death . . ." (311). O'Connor is addressing Nora Flood. She and the second seducer of Robin Vote, Jenny Petherbridge, and Robin are the victims. The language is contralogical. It opens upon a fatal mixing of dream lives. The vision of the surrealist writer refers to somnolence, the insistence of the

20. *Selected Works*, pp. 44–53.

subconscious as it dictates this interlocking and fatal trap. An animal lust rising from the jungle commands the encounter. But sexual urgency answered, the encounter does not end in the simple resolution of parting. The mind of the human head is there. It requires the fat of knowledge, head-on and eye to eye, no matter what the certainty of anguish. Then the conscious and the subconscious are at war. The conscious never wanted the knowledge. The subconscious expands upon the anguish; the torment and the grief begin as the sleeper struggles in the wood of night to reclaim the innocence of the jungle.

Prototypes of the theme appear in the early stories, particularly in "Spillway," with its motion of the constricted stream rushing toward death, and its countermotion of the human effort to travel backward to the source of the flow. The struggle against the stream, the turning from the threshold of death to reclaim the innocence at the source, is the total existence of Julie Anspacher; and from the images which she makes to name her existence the theme of this essay, "backward grief," is taken (68). One finds another prototype in the child Julie of *Ryder*, the "total," as the novelist calls her, of "all little girls uncoiling their destiny in a close sleep" (137). These prototypes require the last disclosures of *Nightwood*. Matthew O'Connor advises Nora Flood that she is "unspinning" fate. But in his own desperation he knows that the unspinning back to childhood, where the uncoiling began, is a mandate of the subconscious, tenacity in the dark which marks all human life. Thus he concludes: ". . . death is intimacy walking backward" (331, 334).

The narrative of *Nightwood* should be traced before a conclusion is proposed. Felix Volkbein is a Jew of Vienna who inherits the pretensions of a baronetcy. His backward grief is racial, and it is the only asexual struggle in the novel. He seeks the lost birthright of the Jew. The nature of his subconscious is read through his obsession in the wood of night. He struggles to find the way back to the beginning, before the Jew was named an outcast in Christendom. In his wanderings about Europe, he arrives in Paris, and is much in the company of his friend, Dr.

Matthew O'Connor. On an evening when the two are talking
in a café, the doctor is summoned by a near-by hotel to attend a
young woman who has fainted and cannot be aroused. The patient is quickly revived, and identified. She is Robin Vote,
twenty years of age, of startling beauty and a mysterious remoteness. Soon afterward, Felix marries her and takes her to Vienna. Within the first year she bears a child, a son Guido (the
name reflecting the Italian origins of the family). Robin soon
rejects the child and her husband, and deserts the house. The
significance of "Bow Down" as the title of the first chapter is
exposed in the deference of Felix to the enigma of his lost birthright. Eventually all the characters *bow down* before the Great
Enigma of all human life, as each seeks in his dark grief the way
back to innocence. The significance of Robin's awakening in the
next chapter "La Somnambule" presents the theme of the mind's
awakening to consciousness from the jungle of sleep, the subconscious. Djuna Barnes likens the somnolent state of Robin to
the sleep of the woman in Henri Rousseau's painting, "A
Dream," with its primitive imagery of the jungle and its evoca-
tion of the primordial of the subconscious (260). In anguish
each of the characters introduced after Robin's departure from
Vienna wanders in the night toward the jungle source from
which each destiny began in its first uncoiling.

Long after his loss of Robin, Felix Volkbein remembers in a
conversation with Matthew O'Connor that his wife's eyes
showed "the long unqualified range in the iris of wild beasts who
have not yet tamed the focus down to meet the human eye." She
was "a beast turning human" (261–262). Her presence was an
authority of the subconscious. Throughout the novel she remains inarticulate in the conscious world. She speaks little; she
is spoken of, and described. Logic and reason, the plan of the
conscious mind and its action, are not of her being. She remains
primordially innocent. After wandering in Europe, she goes to
America. In New York Robin and Nora Flood meet at a circus.
They stand before the cage of a lioness whose burning yellow
eyes, as the beast stares through her bars at Robin, "flowed in

tears that never reached the surface" (276). Innocence, captured from the jungle, looks with sorrow at another innocence captive. Nora takes Robin to her country home. Later they travel in Europe and settle in Paris. Robin wanders through the streets at night. Her desertions of Nora, eternally vigilant and suffering, become more frequent. Finally she leaves Nora for Jenny Petherbridge, "the squatter," a middle-aged woman with "a continual rapacity for other people's facts . . ." (284). The persistent anguish of Nora begins as Jenny and Robin depart for America. Nora's conscious mind, long in dominance since the first meeting at the circus, flourishes in her Christian insistence upon suffering in the desire to "help" another, to save Robin from herself; her subconscious awareness, the truth of her fixation, is none other than physical longing for identification with Robin's beast-like innocence.

Before she leaves Paris for America, Nora brings her torment to the door of the Watchman of the Night, Dr. O'Connor. She discovers him dressed as a transvestite, wearing a blond wig and a woman's nightgown. The doctor's room, in its disorder, is "a cross between a *chambre à coucher* and a boxer's training camp" (295). Matthew discards the wig, sinks into bed, and in a long analysis answers Nora's request, that she be told everything he knows of the night. He describes to her the truth of her desire for Robin, the distance between her conscious Christian purpose and her subconscious longing for the primitive embodied in Robin. His revelation to his "patient" is futile. Nora is lost in her inability to accept wakefulness and sleep as of an equally urgent truth. After this dark interview, Matthew himself goes down (bows down) before the enigma of human life. His Catholicism answers nothing for him. As he finally talks with Felix Volkbein in an analysis of Nora, he is driven to admit that Nora's anguish, even in its singularity, is but one more vision of the night wood in which human beings live and struggle backward in a search for the innocence of childhood.

If there is emergence from the labyrinth of night at the close of the novel, the victory belongs to Robin Vote. She returns to

Nora's ruined estate, described earlier by the author as a property held by Nora's family for two hundred years, the house now mouldering in tangled grass and weeds (272). But it is not to Nora, the "protectress," that Robin goes. Crawling along the floor of the decaying family chapel of Nora's Christian forebears, she approaches, with the desire of a beast, Nora's dog. In the chapel she has improvised an altar before a Madonna, and laid there her votive offerings of flowers and toys. She has recaptured the child's innocence from which she was awakened by Matthew O'Connor, by Felix Volkbein, and by Nora. It is as if we heard again the words of Wendell speaking in *Ryder*: ". . . only a dog returns to his losses, and only a Catholic keeps for better or worse" (220). Lioness to Robin . . . Robin to dog: this is the beastly inarticulate in the state of original innocence, where integration is, where human children, other creatures in a jungle world, begin uncoiling their human destinies. Somewhere in life, midway or at the threshold of death, they will begin a backward grief, each attempting to unspin his fate and thread his way back through the wood of night.

Breton wrote in his *Second Manifesto of Surrealism* (1930): ". . . we are not afraid to take up arms against logic, if we refuse to swear that something in dreams is less meaningful than something we do in a state of waking. . . ."[21] So Djuna Barnes, speaking through Matthew O'Connor in *Nightwood*: ". . . they [the French] think of the two [wakefulness and sleep, day and night] as one continually . . . Bowing down from the waist, the world over they go, that they may revolve about the Great Enigma . . ." (298). When Matthew later contends against "that priceless galaxy of misinformation called the mind, harnessed to that stupendous and threadbare glomerate called the soul . . ." (350), he extends the "French" wisdom of his author, looking, at her behest, into the depths of an older culture with a profounder knowledge of *mind* and *soul*. Was it that

21. Op. cit., p. 128.

Americans were kept in relative ignorance by the stern rubrics
of Puritan "logic" and by the wider and pervasive Protestant de-
nial of the mystery, the Great Enigma, which all faithful read-
ings of Scriptural Law must reject? Did these biases prohibit in
America a knowledge of the truth of human existence, as though
we were iron-bound to Scriptural Law which was itself born of
the sleep and the dream of men? Is it foreign to Americans to
contend, with Matthew O'Connor in *Nightwood*, "To our
friends . . . we die every day, but to ourselves we die only at
the end" (308)? Gide said very much the same; so has Sartre.
Professional surrealism is not the absolute source for either of
these Frenchmen. But the angle of vision of recent French meta-
physics and French art is there. Djuna Barnes, without any
doubt, reflected most strenuously in her unique explorations the
French modes which she knew. We suppose a continued dedication on her part to French thought as she published *The Antiphon*, her long verse play, in 1958. This is a dedication to art as
antiphon, the answer from the life of the subconscious; and one
finds here, in this substantial example of her surrealist style, a
recapitulation which stretches back to Baudelaire.

> Where the martyr'd wild fowl fly the portal
> High in the honey of cathedral walls,
> There is the purchase, governance and mercy.
> Where careful sorrow and observed compline
> Sweat their gums and mastics to the hive
> Of whatsoever stall the head's heaved in—
> There is the amber. As the high plucked banks
> Of the viols rend out the unplucked strings below—
> There is the antiphon.[22]

The risk of paraphrase is great. But this poetry may be read in
this sense: the cathedral represents faith of whatever order; faith
becomes amber, honey solidified into gem; it is made by reason,
the conscious mind; but there is a music below the strings of

22. *Selected Works*, p. 214.

cathedral music, a music to "rend out" the silent strings below, the dark of the subconscious; and from below, the unvoiced dark, comes the antiphon, given a voice through the invitation of the upper voice, returning an answer to the high-plucked strings above. Art, in the sense of Baudelaire, exists to join the day and the night into a whole, the whole of the human mind. Baudelaire's principle became the credo of an art.

This essay has been written in avoidance of value judgments of Djuna Barnes. It was intended as a study of the figure in the carpet, the tapestry displaying structured themes. Much has been neglected, of first importance the poetic idiom and its relation to surrealistic practice. Her compounding of the unlike in juxtaposition, objects of essential dissimilarity compelled into adjacency, is fully in accord with surrealistic techniques. It may frequently remind us of the compulsions of Giorgio di Chirico. Eliot's contention that her work will appeal primarily to readers of poetry is upheld, of course; but the commitment of the poetry may be far other than Eliot was willing to recognize. This much is certain: Whoever studies the French affinities of American artists after the First World War will be obliged to take Djuna Barnes into serious account. Woman militant in our midst was felt in her own weight with the inception of American Transcendentalism. Woman creative as an explorer of the subconscious remains in American fiction an impressive and exceptional voyager.

JAMES BAIRD
*Connecticut College*

# THE SACRED, THE PROFANE, AND
## *THE CRYING OF LOT 49*

### I

Thomas Pynchon's first two novels (a third has been announced
at this writing) are members of that rare and valuable class of
books which, on their first appearance, were thought obscure
even by their admirers, but which became increasingly accessible
afterwards, without losing any of their original excitement.
When *V.*, Pynchon's first novel, appeared in 1963, some of its
reviewers counselled reading it twice or not at all, and even then
warned that its various patterns would not fall entirely into
place. Even if its formal elements were obscure, *V.* still recom-
mended itself through its sustained explosions of verbal and
imaginative energy, its immense range of knowledge and incident, its extraordinary ability to excite the emotions without ever
descending into the easy paths of self-praise or self-pity that less
rigorous novelists had been tracking with success for years. By
now the published discussions of the book agree that its central
action, repeated and articulated in dozens of variations, involves
a decline, both in history broadly conceived and in the book's
individual characters, from energy to stasis, and from the vital
to the inanimate. *The Crying of Lot 49*, Pynchon's second book,
published in 1966, is much shorter and superficially more cohesive than the first book. Its reception, compared with *V.*'s almost universal praise, was relatively muted, and it has since received less critical attention than it deserves. Yet a clear account
of its total organization is now becoming possible. *Lot 49* clari-
fied many of the issues of *V.*, by inverting and developing them;
Pynchon's new novel, *Gravity's Rainbow*, will probably help to
sort out many of the difficulties of *Lot 49*. This paper is an at-

tempt at an interim progress report, with new observations, on the reading of Pynchon's second novel.

Both of the novels describe a gradual revelation of order and unity within the multiplicity of experience, but the kinds of order that the two books discover are almost diametrically opposed. Despite its cosmopolitan variety of incident and character, *V.* develops around a unifying principle that is ultimately constricting and infertile. The book's central metaphor is the thermodynamic concept of entropy, which for the moment may be defined loosely as the slowing down of a system, the calcifying decay of life and available energy on a scale that may be minute or global. Entropy is the principle within irreversible processes, the principle that, in Freud's words, opposes the undoing of what has already occurred. By extending this principle one may speculate that the universe itself must eventually suffer a "heat-death," reduced and simplified to a luke-warm system in which no energy may be used for any purpose. Pynchon used "Entropy" as the title and theme of one of his first published stories,[1] and the concept recurs, in a significantly different form, in *The Crying of Lot 49*. In Pynchon's hands entropy serves as a metaphor of exceptional range and emotional power, and in this Pynchon is not alone. The concept of entropy, whether or not it is named as such, has informed much fiction and philosophy for centuries: it is a central motif in satire, and is the historical principle behind Plato's account of four types of unjust society in the *Republic*.

*The Crying of Lot 49*, although slighter in scale than *V.*, finds the intrusive energy that is needed to reverse the process that *V.* describes. In *Lot 49* a world of triviality and "exitlessness"[2] becomes infused with energy and choice, and Pynchon seems to be demonstrating that he can balance the 500 pages of decline recounted in *V.* with some 200 pages of possible recovery in *Lot*

1. In *The Kenyon Review*, 20 (Spring, 1960), 277–292.
2. *The Crying of Lot 49* (Philadelphia: Lippincott, 1966), p. 170. Further references to this novel are inserted parenthetically into the text. To find page references in the 1967 Bantam paperback edition, subtract 8 from the reference given and multiply the result by four-fifths.

*49*. The ostensible subject of the latter novel is one woman's discovery of a system of communication, but the system refers to something far larger than itself: it fosters variety and surprise, and offers a potential access to "transcendent meaning" and "a reason that mattered to the world" (181). Extend the world of *V.* beyond the book's final chapters, and you eventually intrude on the unlit, motionless world of the later Beckett. Extend *The Crying of Lot 49*, and you soon come in sight of Prospero's island and the seacoast of Bohemia. The processes of *V.* isolate; those of *Lot 49* create community.

Almost all the incidents in *V.* enact a decline of available energy, a hardening of living beings into artificial ones, a degradation from vitality to mechanism, a transfer of sympathy from human suffering to inanimate, objective existence. In the world of *V.* there can only be few alternatives to decline, and those few are weak: some understated temporary acts of escape and love, a sudden dash into the sea as all the lights go out in a city, the reconstruction of a marriage. All the rest leads to stasis—although the book's scale and exuberance suggest that mass decline is a principle of existence in the novel but not in its creator. The central plot from which the book's various historical fantasies— Egypt in 1898, Florence in 1899, Paris in 1913, Malta in 1919 and again in the 1940s, South-West Africa in 1922, and glimpses of a score of other settings and moments—involves the search made by one Herbert Stencil for traces of the woman V., who may have been Stencil's mother, as she moves through Europe and the twentieth century, becoming ever less vital and more artificial as she grows older. In her final manifestation as "the Bad Priest" at Malta during the Second World War, V. advises young girls to become nuns, to "avoid the sensual extremes —pleasures of intercourse, pain of childbirth"—and to prevent the creation of new life. To young boys she preaches "that the object of male existence was to be like a crystal: beautiful and soulless."[3] And before her death she gives up much of her own

3. *V.* (Philadelphia: Lippincott, 1963), p. 340. Further references are given parenthetically in the text.

body to inanimate surrogates: a wig, artificial feet, a glass eye containing a clock, false teeth. A jewel is later found sewn in her navel. Increasingly lifeless and crystalline, finally killed by the mechanical engines of war in the sky over Malta, the woman V. is the most vividly realized victim of the book's pandemic processes of inanition and decline. The other victims include a ruined product of failed plastic surgery, a man with a knife-switch in his arm, a synthetic body used for radiation research, a girl reduced to a fetish, a character named Profane constantly victimized by hostile objects. The book implies a conclusion that lies beyond itself: an ending where all life and warmth have declined and disappeared, an apocalypse that arrives in total silence.

"There is more behind and inside V. than any of us had suspected. Not who, but what: what is she," asks Stencil's father in his diary (*V.*, 53). The novel *V.* is an elaborate gloss on an earlier account of a woman whom history replaced with an object: the chapter on "The Dynamo and the Virgin" in *The Education of Henry Adams*. Pynchon's Stencil, who like Adams talks of himself in the third person, searches for a symbol even more inclusive than Adams's; V. is the virgin who *became* the dynamo. The woman V. is Stencil's reconstruction of scattered and ambiguous clues and symbols, gathered into episodes told by narrators—often obviously flawed and unreliable—whom Stencil creates for the occasion. Half the novel consists of Stencil's indirect narration of the life of V., who is seldom central to the story, but slips in sideways when she is least expected. Stencil's reconstruction of V.'s fragmentary signs—an enactment in reverse of her physical disintegration—is a paradigm of Pynchon's reconstruction of twentieth-century history, a reconstruction which establishes the novel's "ground." The woman V., like Pynchon's history, is put together by design. In his Spenglerian sweep through the century (Stencil, born in 1901, is "the century's child"—*V.*, 52—as well as V.'s) Pynchon invents coincidences and patterns which suggest historical design in the novel's world. "If the coincidences are real then Stencil has never encountered history at all, but something far more appalling" (*V.*, 450).

This suggestion of will and design in history is analogous to Stencil's own "design" of V., but Pynchon makes the analogy even more complex and suggestive than a simple equation can be. To begin with, V. is not entirely a product of Stencil's reconstructions. The frame of the novel *V.* is a narrator's direct account of events in 1955 and 1956, events which include Stencil's *in*direct narrations of the life of V. (Pynchon makes certain that Stencil's narratives, compelling as they are, are taken as speculative and suspect: people speak and understand languages which they could not understand "in life," and characters in the book occasionally remark on such difficulties.) The direct framing narrative is apparently reliable, unlike Stencil's, and it gradually and increasingly provides its own, un-Stencilled, evidence of V.'s existence. "The Confessions of Fausto Maijstral," another apparently reliable narrative written by the last person who saw V. alive, has a chapter to itself, unmediated by Stencil, with a plausible account of V.'s final moments. And a relic of V., an ivory comb which in Stencil's invented narrative she had perhaps acquired decades earlier, later appears both in Maijstral's confessions and, in the hands of Maijstral's daughter, in Pynchon's direct narrative. The comb serves as a kind of optical proof that V. once existed in the world of the book. But by the time the evidence appears in the direct narrative, Stencil has gone off to Stockholm to pursue other and more tenuous threads, and the authentic clue eludes him, presumably forever. The moment when the comb reappears is a heartbreaking one, not only because the reader knows then that one neat and satisfying conclusion to the novel—a reasonably successful conclusion of Stencil's search—has been irrevocably denied, but also because the incident makes a faint and reticent suggestion about the limits of human knowledge: a suggestion that, perhaps because of its reticence, rings true.

This leads back to the matter of historical design. For the characters in the direct narration of the book, V.'s existence is never more than speculative: their evidence of her is always partial. It is only the narrator, who has no *use* for it, who has thorough knowledge of the evidence and the "truth." The characters have only partial knowledge of what in the book "in fact" exists. Now the book's Spenglerian speculation on historical design is also a reconstruction from partial evidence, for even the narrator's historical knowledge is severely limited. But by analogy with the "real" coherence of the woman V. (and the book softly but insistently presses the analogy), there may, the book suggests, be a real order and coherence to history in the world of phenomena that lies outside fiction's garden. But, as the genuine signs of V. elude Stencil—though they do exist, and Stencil has partial knowledge of some of them—so there may be a genuine transcendent coherence in the world's history, although the signs of that coherence either refuse to cooperate with our preconceptions, or elude us entirely. V. is finally a tragedy of human limitation, and like all tragedy it points towards the larger frame in which the tragic action occurs. The contradiction between human ignorance of the frame, and the frame itself, is tragedy's ultimate source, its mode of being.

## II

In contrast with the absconded signs of *V.*, the signs that appear throughout *The Crying of Lot 49* are not elusive at all. They intrude iteratively on the book's heroine until they entirely supplant the undemanding world with which she had once been familiar. In *Lot 49* the systems of interrelation and commonality that inform the book's world have consequences entirely different from the superficially similar systems in *V*. To participate in the processes of decadence in *V*. you have only to become passive, inanimate and selfish; history, which simplifies *V.*'s world, will do the rest. But in *The Crying of Lot 49* the revealed pattern offers "maybe even . . . a real alternative to the exitlessness, to the absence of surprise to life that harrows the head of everybody American you know" (170), an alternative to physical crowding and ethical vacancy, an alternative that reveals itself quietly but persistently to the passive listener, yet will not allow that listener to remain passive for long. In this second novel, published only three years after *V.*, a hidden order reinfuses Pynchon's world with energy, adds to the world's complexity, and demands not acquiescence but conscious choice.

Described briefly, in the sort of the bare outline that makes any serious plot sound ridiculous, *The Crying of Lot 49* recounts the discovery by its heroine, Mrs. Oedipa Maas, of an ancient and secret postal system named the Tristero. The manifestations of the Trystero (an alternate spelling), and all that accompanies it, are always associated in the book with the language of the sacred and with patterns of religious experience; the foils to the Trystero are always associated with sacrality gone wrong. As every person and event in *V.* is implicated in the general decline into the inanimate, everything in *Lot 49* participates either in the sacred or the profane. A major character in *V.* is named Benny Profane; in *Lot 49* there are wider possibilities (including someone named Grace). As Pynchon's work avoids the weightlessness of Nabokovian fantasy, so it avoids the self-important *nostalgie de la boue* of the social and psychological novels that occupy most of the fictional space in postwar America. Oedipa has "all manner of revelations," but they are not in the manner of most recent fiction, and certainly not the kind of revelations that her name might suggest: they are "hardly about . . . herself" (20). Pynchon writes at the end of an era in which the Freudian interpretation of an event served as a more than adequate succedanium for the event itself: it was an act of courage to name his heroine Oedipa (I shall have more to say later about the courage to risk facetiousness), for the novel contains not even a single reference to her emotional relations with her parents or her impulses towards self-creation. The name instead refers back to the Sophoclean Oedipus who begins his search for the solution of a problem (a problem, like Oedipa's, involving a dead man) as an almost detached observer, only to discover how deeply implicated he is in what he finds. As the book opens,

and Oedipa learns that she has been named executor of the estate of the "California real estate mogul" Pierce Inverarity, she
"shuffl[es] back" in her memory "through a fat deckful of days
which seemed . . . more or less identical" (11). But as she
begins to sort out the complications of Inverarity's estate she
becomes aware of moments of special significance, repeated patterns of meaning, that had not previously been apparent. Driving into the town where Inverarity's interests had been centered,
she looks down from the freeway upon "the ordered swirl of
houses and streets" and senses the possibility of a *kind* of meaning that is, for the moment, beyond her comprehension:

> she thought of the time she'd opened a transistor radio to re-
> place a battery and seen her first printed circuit. The or-
> dered swirl of houses and streets, from this high angle,
> sprang at her now with the same unexpected, astonishing
> clarity . . . [T]here were to both outward patterns a hiero-
> glyphic sense of concealed meaning, of an intent to com-
> municate. . . . [Now,] a revelation also trembled just past
> the threshold of her understanding . . . [She] seemed
> parked at the centre of an odd religious instant. As if, on
> some other frequency, or out of the eye of some whirlwind
> rotating too slow for heated skin even to feel the centrifugal
> coolness of, words were being spoken. (24–25)

At this point Oedipa's revelations are only partly defined. In the
next paragraph the narrator dismisses Oedipa's experience by
placing it in distancing quotation marks: "the 'religious instant,'
or whatever it might have been."

But a few pages later an "instant" of the same kind occurs, but
this time more clearly defined. Oedipa sees in a television commercial a map of one of Inverarity's housing developments, and
is reminded of her first glimpse of the town in which she is now:
"Some immediacy was there again, some promise of hierophany"
(31). This "promise of hierophany," of a manifestation of the
sacred, is eventually fulfilled, and her "sense of concealed meaning" yields to her recognition of patterns that had potentially

been accessible to her all along, but which only now had revealed themselves. In the prose sense, what Oedipa discovers is
the Trystero, "a network by which X number of Americans are
truly communicating whilst reserving their lies, recitations of
routine, arid betrayals of spiritual poverty"—that is, everything
profane—"for the official government delivery system" (170).
But across this hidden and illegal network information is transmitted in ways that defy ordinary logic: often, the links in the
system cross centuries, or move between the most unlikely com-
binations of sender and receiver, without anyone in the world of
routine ever recognizing that something untoward has occurred.
The Trystero carries with it a sense of sacred connection and
relation in the world, and by doing so it manifests a way of
comprehending the world. By the end of the novel Oedipa is
left alone, out over seventy thousand fathoms, left to decide for
herself whether the Trystero exists or if she has merely fanta-
sized, or if she has been hoodwinked into believing in it. On that
all-or-nothing decision, everything—her construing of the world,
and the world's construction—depends:

> how had it ever happened here, with the chances once so
> good for diversity? For it was now like walking among ma-
> trices of a great digital computer, the zeroes and ones
> twinned above, hanging like balanced mobiles right and
> left, ahead, thick, maybe endless. Behind the hieroglyphic
> streets there would either be a transcendent meaning, or
> only the earth. . . . Ones and zeroes. . . . Another mode
> of meaning behind the obvious, or none. Either Oedipa in
> the orbiting ecstasy of a true paranoia, or a real Tristero.
> For there was either some Tristero behind the appearance
> of the legacy America, or there was just America . . . .
> (181–182)

As in all religious choices, no proof is possible: the choice of
ones or zeroes presents itself "ahead . . . maybe endless," and
the watcher is left alone.

Pynchon uses religious terms and hieratic language not simply

as a set of metaphors from which to hang his narrative, not
merely as a scaffolding (as Joyce, for example, uses Christian
symbols in *Ulysses*). The religious meaning of the book does not
reduce to metaphor or myth, because religious meaning is itself
the central issue of the plot. This creates difficulties for criticism.
The Trystero implies universal meanings, and since universal
meanings are notoriously recalcitrant to analysis, it will be necessary to approach the holistic center of the book from various
facets and fragments. I hope the reader will bear with an argument that may, for a number of pages, ask him to assent to reso-
lutions of issues that have not yet been discussed.

The book refers at one point to "the secular Trystero," which
has a plausible history and a recognizable origin in ordinary human emotion and human society. During one of the few areas
of the narrative in which nothing extraordinary happens—a
"secular" part of the book—Oedipa compiles, with the help of
one of the book's prosier characters (an English professor, alas),
a history of the system that is somewhat speculative, but more
plausible than the mock-theorizing in *V.* The history of the
Trystero intersects with authentic history in a manner taken
from historical novels like *Henry Esmond* or *The Scarlet Pim-
pernel*, where an extraordinary, fictional pattern of events, one
that almost but not quite alters the larger course of history, is
presented behind the familiar, public pattern. The Trystero,
then, began in sixteenth-century Holland, when an insurgent
Calvinist government unseated the hereditary postmaster, a
member of the Thurn and Taxis family (here Pynchon blends
authentic history with novelistic fantasy—the counts of Taxis
did hold the postal monopoly in the Empire), and replaced him
with one Jan Hinckart, Lord of Ohain. But Hinckart's right to
the position, which he gained through political upheaval, not
through inheritance, is disputed by a Spaniard, Hernando Joa-
qúin de Tristero y Calavera, who claims to be Hinckart's cousin
and the legitimate Lord of Ohain—and therefore the legitimate
postmaster. Later, after an indecisive struggle between Hinckart
and Tristero, the Calvinists are overthrown, and the Thurn and

Taxis line restored to postmastership. But Tristero, claiming that the postal monopoly was Ohain's by conquest, and therefore his own by blood, sets up an alternative postal system, and proceeds to wage guerrilla war against the Thurn and Taxis system. The rallying theme of Tristero's struggle: "disinheritance" (159–160).

So far, the story, though a fantasy, is still historically plausible, requiring only a relatively slack suspension of disbelief. However the word Calavera (skull, Calvary) in Tristero's name already suggests some emblematic resonances, and the theme of disinheritance joins the Tristero's history to Oedipa's discovery of it while executing a will. Later in the history, the Trystero system takes on, *for its contemporaries*, a specifically religious meaning. Pynchon invents a severe Calvinist sect, the Scurvhamites, who tend toward the gnostic heresy and see Creation as a machine, one part of which is moved by God, the other by a soulless and automatic principle. When the Scurvhamites decide to tamper with some secular literature (specifically, the play *The Courier's Tragedy*, of which more shortly) to give it doctrinal meaning, they find that the "Trystero would symbolize the Other quite well" (156). For Thurn and Taxis itself, faced with the enmity of the anonymous and secret Trystero system, "many of them must [have] come to believe in something very like the Scurvhamite's blind, automatic anti-God. Whatever it is, it has the power to murder their riders, send landslides thundering across their roads . . . disintegrate the Empire." But this belief cannot last: "over the next century and a half the paranoia recedes, [and] they come to discover the secular Tristero" (165). The Trystero returns from its symbolic meanings into a realm that is historically safe and believable. In this passage Pynchon offers an analogously safe way to read his own book: the Trystero is a symbol for a complex of events taking place on the level of a battle in heaven, but it is merely a symbol, a way of speaking that has no hieratic significance in itself. But the novel, while offering this possibility, does so in a chapter in which nothing strange happens, where the world is Aristotelian and profane,

where the extraordinary concrescences of repetition and relation that inform the rest of the book briefly sort themselves out
into simple, logical patterns. The book offers the possibility that
its religious metaphor is only metaphor: but if the book were
founded on this limited possibility, the remaining portions of
the book would make no sense, and there would be little reason
to write it in the first place.

The potted history near the end of the novel describes the
discovery of the "secular Tristero" behind the demonic one; the
book itself describes the progressive revelation of the sacred significance behind certain historical events. It should perhaps be
mentioned that the frequent associations of the Trystero with
the demonic do not contradict the Trystero's potentially sacred
significance: the demonic is a subclass of the sacred, and exists,
like the sacred, on a plane of meaning different from the profane and the secular. When Pynchon published two chapters
from the book in a magazine he gave them the title, "The World
(This One), the Flesh (Mrs. Oedipa Maas), and the Testament
of Pierce Inverarity":[4] it is through Inverarity's will that Oedipa
completes this proverbial equation, and finds her own devil in
the agonizing ontological choice she has to make as the novel
ends. The revelation of the sacred gets underway when Oedipa
sees in the map of one of Inverarity's interests "some promise of
hierophany." The sense of the word "hierophany" is clear
enough—it is a manifestation of the sacred—but the word itself
has a history that is informative in this context. The word is not
recorded in the dictionaries of any modern European language
(the related "hierophant" is of course recorded, but "hierophany"
is not), and it appears to have been invented by Mircea Eliade,[5]
who expands most fully on the word in his *Patterns in Compara-
tive Religion* but gives a more straightforward definition in his
introduction to *The Sacred and the Profane*: "Man becomes

4. *Esquire*, 64 (Dec., 1965), 171. This title is noted on the copyright
page of the novel, while the title of another excerpt published elsewhere is
pointedly omitted.
5. Reinvented, actually: the word seems to have had a technical meaning
in Greek religion.

aware of the sacred because it manifests itself, shows itself, as something wholly different from the profane. To designate the *act of manifestation* of the sacred, we have proposed the term *hierophany*. It is a fitting term, because it does not imply anything further; it expresses no more than is implicit in its etymological content, *i.e.*, that *something sacred shows itself to us.* . . . From the most elementary hierophany . . . to the supreme hierophany . . . there is no solution of continuity. In each case we are confronted by the same mysterious act—the manifestation of something of a wholly different order, a reality that does not belong to our world, in objects that are an integral part of our natural 'profane' world."[6] This latter condition, that the objects in which the sacred manifests itself be part of the natural world, is central to *Lot 49*, because everything in the novel that points to a sacred significance in the Trystero has, potentially, a secular explanation. The pattern and the coherence may, as Oedipa reminds herself, be the product of her own fantasy or of someone else's hoax. She is left, at every moment, to affirm or deny the sacredness of what she sees.

When, as she begins to uncover the Trystero, Oedipa decides to give, through her own efforts, some order to Inverarity's tangled interests, she writes in her notebook, "Shall I project a world?" (82). But her plan to provide her own meanings, "to bestow life on what had persisted" of the dead man, soon confronts the anomaly that more meanings, more relationships and connections than she ever expected begin to offer themselves— manifest themselves. And these manifestations arrive without any effort on her part. When, by the middle of the book, "everything she saw, smelled, dreamed, remembered, would somehow come to be woven into The Trystero" (81), she tries to escape, to cease looking for order. "She had only to drift," she supposes, "at random, and watch nothing happen, to be convinced that it was purely nervous, a little something for her shrink to fix" (104). But when she drifts that night through San Francisco

6. New York: Harcourt, Brace, 1959, p. 11. Eliade's italics.

she finds more extensive and more varied evidence of the Trystero's existence—evidence far more frequent and insistent than
she found when she was actually looking for it. Like the mystic
whose revelation is dependent on his passivity, Oedipa's full
discovery of the Trystero depends on her refusal to search for it.
In the last chapter even the most surprising events leave her only
in expectant passivity: "Even a month ago, Oedipa's next question would have been 'Why?' But now she kept a silence, waiting, as if to be illuminated" (152).

Recent criticism has devoted much energy to finding detective-
story patterns in fiction, and *The Crying of Lot 49*, with its
heroine named after the first detective of them all, lends itself
admirably to this method. However, Pynchon's novel uses mech-
anisms borrowed from the detective story to produce results precisely the opposite of those in the model. Where the object of a
detective story is to reduce a complex and disordered situation to
simplicity and clarity, and in doing so to isolate in a named locus
the disruptive element in the story's world, *The Crying of Lot
49* starts with a relatively simple situation, and then lets it get
out of the heroine's control: the simple becomes complex, responsibility becomes not isolated but universal, the guilty locus
turns out to be everywhere, and individual clues are unimportant
because neither clues nor deduction can lead to the solution.
"Suppose, God, there really was a Tristero then and that she
*had* come on it by accident. . . . [S]he might have found The
Tristero anywhere in her Republic, through any of a hundred
lightly-concealed entranceways, a hundred alienations, if only
she'd looked" (179). What the detective in this story discovers
is a way of thinking that renders detection irrelevant. "The
Christian," Chesterton writes somewhere, "has to use his brains
to see the hidden good in humanity just as the detective has to
use his brains to see the hidden evil." This, in essence, describes
Oedipa's problem: she never discovers the alienation and incoherence in the world—those were evident from the start—but
she stumbles instead across the hidden relationships in the world,
relations effected through and manifested in the Trystero.

Near the middle of the book Oedipa stops searching. From this point on she becomes almost the only character in the novel who is *not* looking for something. While hierophanies occur all around her, almost everyone else is vainly trying to wrench an experience of the sacred out of places where it cannot possibly be found. As everyone in *V.* worries constantly about the inanimate, everyone in *The Crying of Lot 49* suffers from some distortion of religious faith, and almost everyone in the book eventually drops away from Oedipa into some religious obsession.[7] Their examples demonstrate the wrong turnings that Oedipa must avoid.

Mucho Maas, for example, Oedipa's husband, who works as a disc jockey, suffers "regular crises of conscience about his profession[:] 'I just don't believe in any of it'" (12). This sounds at first like a suburban cliché, but the religious language soon develops in complexity and allusiveness. Oedipa's incomprehension during her first "religious instant" reminds her of her husband "watching one of his colleagues with a headset clamped on and cueing the next record with movements stylized as the handling of chrism, censer, chalice might be for a holy man . . . [D]id Mucho stand outside Studio A looking in, knowing that even if he could hear it, he couldn't believe in it?" (25). His previous job had been at a used car lot, where although "he had believed in the cars" he suffered from a nightmare of alienation and nothingness (which also provides Pynchon with a send-up of Hemingway's "A Clean, Well-Lighted Place"): "'We were a member of the National Automobile Dealers' Association. N.A.D.A. Just this creaking metal sign that said nada, nada, against the blue sky. I used to wake up hollering'" (144). His escape from a nihilistic void takes him into the impregnable solipsism granted by LSD, and he leaves Oedipa behind him.

The drug had previously been urged on Oedipa herself by

7. One character who drops away from Oedipa, but without any religious significance to the action, is her coexecutor, the lawyer Metzger, who goes off to marry a sixteen-year-old girl. Metzger, who never takes the slightest interest in the other characters' preoccupations, seems to serve in the novel as the representative of the entirely profane.

her psychiatrist, Dr. Hilarius, who was conducting an experiment he called the Bridge—not a bridge across to community but "the bridge inward." Oedipa, who seems to merit her revelations through her knowledge of what does *not* lead to revelation, knows that she "would be damned if she'd take the capsules he'd given her. Literally damned" (17). Hilarius himself distorts the purpose of faith. In an attempt to atone for his Nazi past he tries to develop "a faith in the literal truth of everything [Freud] wrote. . . . It was . . . a kind of penance. . . . I wanted to believe, despite everything my life had been" (134–135). The strain finally sends him into paranoia and madness: fantasies of vengeful Israelis, a wish for death.

Randolph Driblette, who directs the play in which Oedipa first hears the name Trystero, suffers from the nihilistic pride that thinks itself the only possible source of order in the universe. In the play he directs, " 'the reality is in *this* head. Mine. I'm the projector in the planetarium, all the closed little universe visible in the circle of that stage is coming out of my mouth, eyes, sometimes other orifices also' " (79). (It is from Driblette that Oedipa borrows the metaphor of her notebook-question, "Shall I project a world?") In directing plays Driblette "felt hardly any responsibility toward the word, really; but to . . . its spirit, he was always intensely faithful" (152). The logical response to a world where one creates, alone, the only order— where one ignores the *data* of the word—is nihilistic despair. And the logical culmination of an exclusive devotion to the spirit is the sloughing-off of the flesh: Driblette commits suicide by walking into the sea.

John Nefastis, the inventor of a machine which joins the worlds of thermodynamics and information theory (of which more later) through the literal use of a scientific metaphor known as Maxwell's Demon is "impenetrable, calm, a believer" —in whose presence Oedipa feels "like some sort of heretic." Nefastis, the book's fundamentalist, believes his scientific metaphor is "not only verbally graceful, but also objectively true." His language recalls similar moments in the rest of the book when he refers to the visible operation of his machine as "the secular level" (105–106), and the photograph of the physicist James Clerk Maxwell that adorns the machine is, oddly enough (though the narrator does not remark on the oddity), "the familiar Society for the Propagation of Christian Knowledge photo" (86). Nefastis's unbalanced science is endorsed, shakily, by the language of belief.

At least one character, however, has something of the enlightenment that Oedipa is approaching. A Mexican anarchist whom Oedipa meets on her night of drifting, and whom she and Inverarity had first met in Mexico some years before, is named Jésus Arrabal. When he talks politics his language quickly shifts to the language of religion:

> You know what a miracle is . . . another world's intrusion into this one. Most of the time we coexist peacefully, but when we do touch there's cataclysm. Like the church we hate, anarchists also believe in another world. Where revolutions break out spontaneous and leaderless, and the soul's talent for consensus allows the masses to work together without effort. . . . And yet . . . if any of it should ever really happen that perfectly, I would also have to cry miracle. An anarchist miracle. Like your friend [Inverarity the real-estate mogul]. He is too exactly and without flaw the thing we fight. In Mexico the privilegiado is always, to a finite percentage, redeemed, one of the people. Unmiraculous. But your friend, unless he's joking, is as terrifying to me as a Virgin appearing to an Indian. (120)

The intersection of two worlds in miracles is a theme we shall return to. For the moment, it should be noted that Arrabal admits the possibility that the "miraculous" Inverarity may be "joking"—just as Oedipa has to admit the possibility that the miraculous Trystero may be a hoax, a joke written by Inverarity into his will.

Compared with the obsessions and confusions that surround most of the other characters, the religious language associated with Oedipa herself is on a different and clearer level. The word "God" occurs perhaps twenty times in the book (it appears hardly at all in *V.*), and on almost every occasion the word hovers near Oedipa or her discoveries. In her very first word, on the first page of the book, she "spoke the name of God, tried to feel as drunk as possible." When she first encounters the Trystero's emblem, a drawing of a muted post horn, she copies it into her notebook, "thinking: God, hieroglyphics" (52)—a double iteration, through the prefix *hiero*, of the Trystero's sacrality. In an early passage that anticipates the book's later, culminating reference to "a great digital computer [with] the zeroes and ones twinned above," Oedipa tries to elude a spray-can gone wild: "something fast enough, God or a digital machine, might have computed in advance the complex web of its travel" (37). When she sees the Trystero symbol in one more unexpected place she feels "as if she had been trapped at the center of some intricate crystal, and say[s], 'My God'" (92). Faced with the choice of ones and zeroes, of meaning or nothingness, she thinks, "this, oh God, was the void" (171). And there are other examples. What would simply be a nagging cliché in another kind of novel becomes here a quiet but insistent echo, a muted but audible signal.

### III

*The Crying of Lot 49* is a book partly *about* communications and signals—Oedipa's discovery of the Trystero involves the interpretation of ambiguous signs—and, logically enough, its central scientific metaphor involves communication theory (alternately called Information Theory). It is through information theory, in fact, that Pynchon establishes in this novel a richly imaginative logical link with the world of his first novel, *V.* The two novels share some superficial details on the level of plot—one minor character appears briefly in both, a Vivaldi concerto for which someone is searching in *V.* is heard over muzak in *Lot 49*—but their deeper connection lies in *Lot 49*'s extension and transformation of *V.*'s central metaphor. *V.* describes the thermodynamic process by which the world's entropy increases and by which the world's available energy declines. But the equations of thermodynamics and the term "entropy" itself were also employed, decades after their original formulation, in information theory, where they took on a wider and more complex function than they ever had before. By using information theory as a controlling pattern of ideas in his second book, Pynchon is in one way simply extending the metaphor central to his first book: but the extension also adds immeasurably to the complexity and fertility of the original idea. Thermodynamic entropy is (to speak loosely) a measure of stagnation. As thermodynamic entropy increases in a system, and its available energy decreases, information about the system increases: the system loses some of its uncertainty, its potential. In the language of information theory, however, entropy is the measure of *un*certainty in a system. As you *increase* thermodynamic entropy, therefore, you *decrease* information entropy.[8] In information theory, also, the *entropy rate* of a system is the rate at which information is transmitted. Entropy increases in *V.*, and the world slows down; in *The Crying of Lot 49* Oedipa receives more and more surprises, more and more rapidly, and entropy still increases—but now it is information entropy rather than thermodynamic, and the effect of the increase is invigorating rather than stagnating.

Metaphorically, then, the two meanings of the term "entropy" are in opposition, and it is precisely this opposition which John Nefastis tries to exploit in his machine. Oedipa finds Nefastis's account of his machine confusing, but

> she did gather that there were two distinct kinds of this entropy. One having to do with heat-engines, the other to do with communication. The equation for one, back in the '30's, had looked very like the equation for the other. It was

8. This usage conforms to that of the founder of the theory, Claude Shannon, but is disputed by other scientists. For a full discussion see Leon Brillouin's *Science and Information Theory* (New York, 1956), to which I am deeply indebted.

a coincidence. The two fields were entirely unconnected, except at one point: Maxwell's Demon. As the Demon sat and sorted his molecules into hot and cold, the system was said to lose entropy. But somehow the loss was offset by the information gained about what molecules were where. "Communication is the key," cried Nefastis. . . . (105)

When Maxwell's hypothetical "Demon" (a received term that fits neatly into Pynchon's hieratic language) sorts hot and cold molecules, he can apparently raise the temperature in one part of a system, and lower the temperature in the other part, without expending work—thereby *decreasing* the system's thermodynamic entropy, in violation of the second law of thermodynamics. But the decrease of thermodynamic entropy is balanced by an *increase* in information entropy, thereby supposedly making the whole thing "possible," when a person whom Nefastis calls a "sensitive" transmits information to the Demon that Nefastis believes is actually in his machine.[9] Nefastis mixes the language of science with that of spiritualism. The "sensitive" has to receive data "at some deep psychic level" from the Demon; the "sensitive" achieves his effects by staring at the photo of Maxwell on the machine; and so forth. The whole effect is one of Blavatskian mumbo-jumbo, but Nefastis also uses the language of belief that Oedipa is learning to understand. Feeling "like some kind of heretic," she doubts Nefastis's enterprise: "The true sensitive is the one that can share in the man's hallucinations, that's all" (107). But the implied question, raised by Oedipa's doubt, is whether Oedipa's sensitivity to the Trystero is also the product of hallucinations.

The Nefastis machine is based on the similarity between the equations for information entropy and those of thermodynamic entropy, a similarity which Nefastis calls a "metaphor." The machine "makes the metaphor not only verbally graceful, but also objectively true" (106). Pynchon has much to say elsewhere in

9. The real scientific problem behind this fantasy is described by Brillouin (ch. 13).

the book about the relation between truth and metaphor, but Nefastis's error is based on the confusion of language and reality, on an attempt to make two worlds coincide. Nefastis, the "believer," has faith in his metaphor, and believes that the truth of that faith can objectively be demonstrated and confirmed. Oedipa, on the other hand, receives no confirmation. Faith, wrote Paul to the Hebrews, is "the evidence of things *not* seen."

Besides using the association of entropy and information theory, Pynchon also exploits the theory's rule of concerning the relation of surprise and probability in the transmitting of data. Briefly, the rule states that the more unexpected a message is, the more information it contains: a series of repetitive messages conveys less information than a series of messages that differ from each other. (Of course there must be a balance between surprise and probability: a message in language the receiver cannot understand is very surprising, but conveys little information.) In *The Crying of Lot 49* there are *two* secret communications systems: the Trystero, and its entirely secular counterpart, the system used by the right-wing Peter Pinguid Society. Both circumvent the official government delivery system, but, unlike the Trystero, the Pinguid Society's system cares less about transmitting information than about nose-thumbing the bureaucracy. Oedipa happens to be with a member of the Society when he receives a letter with the PPS postmark:

> *Dear Mike,* it said, *how are you? Just thought I'd drop you a note. How's your book coming? Guess that's all for now. See you at The Scope* [a bar].
> "That's how it is," [the PPS member] confessed bitterly, "most of the time." (53)

The Pinguid Society's letters, bearing no information, are empty and repetitive. With the Trystero, in contrast, even the stamps are surprising:

> In the 3¢ Mothers of America Issue . . . the flowers to the lower left of Whistler's Mother had been replaced by

Venus's-flytrap, belladonna, poison sumac and a few others
Oedipa had never seen. In the 1947 Postage Stamp Centenary Issue, commemorating the great postal reform that
had meant the beginning of the end for private carriers [of
which the Trystero is the only survivor], the head of a Pony
Express rider at the lower left was set at a disturbing angle
unknown among the living. The deep violet 3¢ regular issue of 1954 had a faint, menacing smile on the face of the
Statue of Liberty. . . . (174)

This delicate balance of the familiar and the unexpected (note,
for example, that there are enough surprising poisoned plants, on
one of the stamps, to indicate that the even more surprising ones
which "Oedipa had never seen" are also poisonous) produces a
powerful sense of menace and dread—a sense no less powerful
for its comic aspects—while the secular Pinguid Society messages are capable only of conventionality, of repetition without a
sense of the numinous.

The unit of information in communication theory is the *bit*,
abbreviated from *binary digit*. Theoretically, all information can
be conveyed in a sequence of binary digits, i.e., ones and zeroes.
By the end of the novel, in a passage quoted above, Oedipa perceives the dilemma presented to her by the possible existence of
the Trystero in terms of the choice between one bit and another
(Pynchon always provides the possibility that the Trystero is
"only" Oedipa's fantasy, or that the whole system is a hoax written into Inverarity's will): "For it was now like walking among
matrices of a great digital computer, the zeroes and ones twinned
above . . . Behind the hieroglyphic streets there would either
be a transcendent meaning, or only the earth" (181). The signs
themselves do not prove anything: the streets are "hieroglyphic"
—an example of sacred carving—but behind the sacred sign *may*
lie what is merely profane, "only the earth." The religious content of the book is fixed in Oedipa's dilemma: the choice between the *zero* of secular triviality and chaos, and the *one* that
is the *ganz andere* of the sacred.

In Pynchon's novel, as in life, there are two kinds of repetition: trivial repetition, as in the monotony of the Pinguid Society letters, and repetition that may signify the timeless and unchanging sacred. In *The Sacred and the Profane* Eliade writes that "religious man lives in two kinds of time, of which the more important, sacred time, appears under the paradoxical aspect of a circular time, reversible and recoverable, a sort of mythical present that is periodically regenerated by means of rites" (70). Oedipa's first experience (in the book, that is) of trivial repetition occurs when she encounters a debased version of Eliade's "circular time, reversible and recoverable." In the second chapter, before she has any evidence of the Trystero, she watches television in the Echo Courts motel (the name is a grace-note on the main theme), with her coexecutor Metzger—a lawyer, once a child actor. The film on the screen turns out to star Metzger as a child, and when the film-Metzger sings a song, "his aging double, over Oedipa's protests, sang harmony" (31). At the end of the book, Oedipa wonders if the Trystero system is simply a plot against her; here, at the beginning, she suspects that Metzger "bribed the engineer over at the local station to run this[:] it's all part of a plot, an elaborate, seduction, *plot*." Time, on this occasion, seems to become even more confused and circular when one reel of the film is shown in the wrong order: "'Is this before or after?' she asked."

In the midst of the film Oedipa glimpses a more significant form of repetition: in a passage discussed above, a map in a television commercial reminds her of the "religious instant" she felt on looking over the town where she is now. But this significant repetition occurs in the midst of reports of other, sterile ones. For example, Metzger, an actor turned lawyer, describes the pilot film of a television series on his own life, starring a friend of his, a lawyer turned actor. The film rests isolated in its own meaningless circular time, "in an air-conditioned vault . . . light can't fatigue it, it can be repeated endlessly." Outside the motel room, a rock-music group called the Paranoids, who all look alike, seem to be multiplying—"others must be plugging in"—until their equipment blows a fuse.

In contrast, the reiterative evidence of the Trystero that Oedipa later discovers suggests that something complex and significant has existed almost unaltered for centuries, in Eliade's "mythical present that is periodically reintegrated." Many of the events, linked with the Trystero, that occur in the Jacobean *Courier's Tragedy* that Oedipa sees early in the book, recur in the midst of the California gold rush, and again in a battle in Italy during the Second World War. The Trystero's emblem, a muted post horn (suggesting the demonic aspect of the system: it mutes the trumpet of apocalypse), recurs in countless settings, in children's games, in postmarks, lapel pins, tattoos, rings, scrawled on walls, doodled in notebooks—in dozens of contexts which cannot, through any secular logic, be connected. Each of these repetitions, each evidence of the Trystero's persistence, seems to Oedipa a link with another world. As the Nefastis machine futilely tried to link the "worlds" of thermodynamics and communications, Jésus Arrabal talks of a miracle as "another world's intrusion into this one" (120). Those who joined the Trystero, Oedipa thinks, must have entered some kind of community when they withdrew from the ordinary life of the Republic, and, "since they could not have withdrawn into a vacuum . . . there had to exist the separate, silent, unexpected world" (92). To enter the Trystero, to become aware of it, is to cross the threshold between the profane and sacred worlds. "The threshold," Eliade writes in *The Sacred and the Profane*, "is the limit, the boundary, the frontier that distinguishes and opposes two worlds—and at the same time the paradoxical place where those two worlds communicate, where passage from the profane to the sacred world becomes possible" (25). Oedipa wonders if she could have "found the Trystero . . . through any of a hundred lightly-concealed entranceways, a hundred alienations" (179).

Yet in the middle of the fifth chapter of the book the entranceways, the alienations ("Decorating each alienation . . . was somehow always the post horn"—123), suddenly disappear: the repetitions stop. For perhaps thirty pages Oedipa receives no immediate signs of the Trystero, nothing more than some historical documents and second-hand reports. Until the middle of the fifth chapter (131, to be exact) Oedipa consistently sees the post horn as a living and immediate symbol, actively present in the daily life around her. From that point on she only hears about its past existence through documents, stamps, books—always second-hand. (This distinction is nowhere mentioned in the book, but the clean break after 131 is too absolute to be accidental.) And at the same time, all her important human contacts begin to fade and disperse: "They are stripping from me, she said subvocally—feeling like a fluttering curtain, in a very high window moving . . . out over the abyss. . . . My shrink . . . has gone mad; my husband, on LSD, gropes like a child further and further into the rooms and endless rooms of the elaborate candy house of himself and away, hopelessly away, from what has passed, I was hoping forever, for love; . . . my best guide to the Trystero [Driblette] has taken a Brody. Where am I?" (152–153). Without signs, without the repetition that all signs embody, she is left to her own devices. Until now, the repetitions *told* her of the Trystero ("the repetition of symbols was to be enough . . . *She was meant to remember.* . . . Each clue that comes is *supposed* to have its own clarity, its fine chances for permanence"—Pynchon's italics), but the simple reception of signs is insufficient for the revelation she is approaching: "she wondered if each one of the gemlike 'clues' were only some kind of compensation. To make up for her having lost the direct, epileptic Word, the cry that might abolish the night" (118).

Pynchon's reference to epilepsy recalls its traditional status as a sacred disease. A few pages earlier, Oedipa had encountered another repetition of one of the book's motifs: the destruction of a cemetery for a freeway. When she hears the cemetery and freeway mentioned again, "She could, at this stage of things, recognize signals like that, as the epileptic is said to. . . . Afterward it is only this signal, really dross, this secular announcement, and never what is revealed during the attack, that he remembers." She had been given a glass of wine made from dandelions picked once from the destroyed cemetery. "In the space of a sip of dandelion wine it came to her that she would never know how many times such a seizure may already have visited, or how to grasp it should it visit again" (95). The "message" of the epileptic seizure, the sacramental content of the wine, the persistence of mythical time behind the profane world, becomes explicit when she receives the wine once again:

> He poured her more dandelion wine.
> "It's clearer now," he said . . . . "A few months ago it got quite cloudy. You see, in spring, when the dandelions begin to bloom again, the wine goes through a fermentation. As if they remembered."
> No, thought Oedipa, sad. As if their home cemetery in some way still did exist, in a land where you could somehow walk, and not need the East San Narciso Freeway, and bones still could rest in peace, nourishing ghosts of dandelions, no one to plow them up. As if the dead really do persist, even in a bottle of wine. (98–99)

This splendid passage combines almost all the book's central motifs: the alternate world "where you could somehow walk," the persistence of the world of the sacred present, the *tristesse* of the illumination that accompanies the Trystero.

The Trystero's illuminations are conveyed through miracles, sacred versions of what Oedipa thinks of as the "secular miracle of communication" (180). The one traditional miracle most closely involved with communication is the miracle of Pentecost:

> When the day of Pentecost had come, [the Apostles] were . . . all filled with the Holy Spirit and began to speak in other tongues, as the Spirit gave them utterance. . . .

[T]he multitude came together, and they were bewildered, because each one heard them speaking in his own language. . . . And all were amazed and perplexed, saying to one another, "What does this mean?" But others mocking said, "They are filled with new wine." (Acts 2)

Pynchon names Pentecost only once, in the play-within-the-novel *The Courier's Tragedy*, where the novel's use of the Pentecost motif is parodied darkly. The gift of tongues is perverted, amidst a scene of Jacobean horror, into the tearing out of a tongue. The torturer gloats:

> *Thy pitiless unmanning is most meet,*
> *Thinks Ercole the zany Paraclete.*
> *Descended this malign, Unholy Ghost,*
> *Let us begin thy frightful Pentecost.* (68)

The feast of Pentecost is alternately called Whitsunday, after the tradition that on that day baptismal candidates wear white. The final scene of the book—a stamp auction held, surprisingly, on a Sunday—is a parody of Pentecost: "The men inside the auction room wore black mohair and had pale cruel faces. . . . [The auctioneer] spread his arms in a gesture that seemed to belong to the priesthood of some remote culture; perhaps to a descending angel. The auctioneer cleared his throat. Oedipa settled back, to await the crying of Lot 49." And the book ends. The auctioneer prepares to speak; Oedipa awaits the forty-ninth lot of the sale, a lot whose purchaser "may" turn out to be from the Trystero, thus forcing the system to reveal itself. But why the *forty-ninth* lot? Because Pentecost is the Sunday seven weeks after Easter—forty-nine days. But the word Pentecost derives from the Greek for "fiftieth." The crying—the auctioneer's calling—of the forty-ninth lot is the moment before a Pentecostal revelation, the end of the period in which the miracle is in a state of potential, not yet manifest. This is why the novel ends with Oedipa waiting, with the "true" nature of the Trystero never established: a manifestation of the sacred can only be believed in; it can never be proved beyond doubt. There will always be a mocking voice, internal or external, saying "they are filled with new wine"—or, as Oedipa fears, "you are hallucinating it . . . you are fantasying some plot" (170–171).

Oedipa's constant risk lies in that nagging possibility: that the Trystero has no independent existence, but is merely her own projection on the world outside. The center of Pierce Inverarity's interests is a town named San Narciso, and the name insistently mocks Oedipa's quest. (There is a Saint Narcissus in *The Courier's Tragedy*, so the narcissism in question is not limited to mid-century America.) The novel describes, however, Oedipa's progress away from the modes of narcissism. At the end of the first chapter Pynchon writes that Oedipa was "to have all manner of revelations[, h]ardly about Pierce Inverarity, or herself." Oedipa recalls, a few lines later, a past moment with Inverarity in Mexico when she saw an emblem of solipsism to which she responded in kind. They had

> somehow wandered into an exhibition of paintings by . . . Remedios Varo; in the central painting of a triptych . . . were a number of frail girls . . . prisoners in the top room of a circular tower, embroidering a kind of tapestry which spilled out the slit windows and into a void, seeking hopelessly to fill the void: for all the other buildings and creatures, all the waves, ships and forests of the earth were contained in this tapestry, and the tapestry was the world.[10]

(Driblette's vision of himself as director is a later version of this image.)

> Oedipa . . . stood in front of the painting and cried. . . . She had looked down at her feet and known, then, because of a painting, that what she had stood on had only been woven a couple thousand miles away in her own tower,

10. Some critics have invented pedigrees for this painting out of English literature, but Varo *was* a Spanish painter, and the painting exists. For a reproduction see *Remedios Varo* (Mexico: Ediciones Era, 1966), plate 7.

was only by accident known as Mexico, and so Pierce had taken her away from nothing, there'd been no escape.

The tower of isolation, though an expression of the self, is not a product of the self, but one of the conditions of this world:

> Such a captive maiden . . . soon realizes that her tower, its height and architecture, are *like her ego only incidental*: that what really keeps her where she is is magic, anonymous and malignant, visited on her from outside and for no reason at all. . . . If the tower is everywhere and the knight of deliverance no proof against its magic, what else? (20–21)

With this gesture towards hopelessness the chapter ends. But to its final question, the remainder of the book—with its partial revelation of what the Trystero might stand for—offers a tentative answer.

Near the end of the novel, when Oedipa stands by the sea, "her isolation complete," she finally breaks from the tower and from the uniqueness of San Narciso. She learns, finally, of a continuity that had been available, but hidden, from the beginning:

> She stood . . . her isolation complete, and tried to face toward the sea. But she'd lost her bearings. She turned, . . . could find no mountains either. As if there could be no barriers between herself and the rest of the land. San Narciso at that moment lost (the loss pure, instant, spherical . . .), gave up its residue of uniqueness for her; became a name again, was assumed back into the American continuity of crust and mantle. (177)

At this point the uniqueness of her experience matters less than the general truth it signifies: "There was the true continuity. . . . If San Narciso and the estate were really no different from any other town, and any other estate, then by that continuity she might have found The Tristero anywhere in her Republic . . . if only she'd looked" (179). Her choice now is either to affirm the existence of the Tristero—through which continuity survives, renews, reintegrates itself over vast expanses of space and time—or to be entirely separated, isolated, an "alien . . . assumed full circle into some paranoia" (182). San Narciso or America.

IV

Like every sophisticated work of fiction *The Crying of Lot 49* contains within itself guides to its own interpretation. The book offers synthesizing critical methods which are integral with the very material the methods propose to organize. Certainly this is a book that needs a *vade mecum*: its reader finds himself continuously in a dilemma analogous to its heroine's. Both are given a series of clues, signs, interconnecting symbols, acronyms, code words, patterns of theme and variation which never *demand* to be interpreted, but which always offer themselves as material that is available for synthesis and order.

The play-within-the-novel, *The Courier's Tragedy* "by Richard Wharfinger," offers in concentrated and often inverted form the main concerns of the novel as a whole. The plot of the play is quite as elaborate as that of any genuine Jacobean tragedy, and any summary here would be almost as long as Pynchon's account in the novel (q.v.). One or two points, however, call for special attention. As on every occasion when a work of art appears within another, Pynchon offers his readers the possibility that their "attendance" at the novel is analogous to Oedipa's attendance at the Wharfinger play. In the performance that Oedipa attends, and, it later develops, *only in that performance*, the director, Driblette, alters the text to conform with the version produced by Scurvhamite tampering (as discussed above), the version which actually names the Trystero. (The other editions of the play, all discussed later in the book, omit the name altogether.) The implication of this is that the naming of the Trystero on one particular night may have been directed *at* Oedipa—that the production was not simply made available

to whomever happened to buy a ticket. Underneath this suggestion (and the implications are developed in another passage
which I shall discuss shortly) is the implied possibility that the
relationship of a reader and a work of art may perhaps not be
simply an aesthetic relationship—that the work has, potentially,
a *purposive* effect.

In the action of the play itself one event casts special light on
the meaning of the Trystero system within the rest of the novel.
The eponymous hero of the tragedy, a rightful prince deposed
(disinherited, like the founder of the Trystero) and now disguised as a courier at the court of his enemy, is sent by that
enemy with a lying message to another court. But this enemy
then sends out agents—from the Trystero, in Driblette's production—after the disguised prince, with orders to murder him.
Later, the lying message is found on the dead body, but "it is
no longer the lying document . . . but now, miraculously, a
long confession by [the prince's enemy] of all his crimes" (74).
In an unexplained manner the Trystero has been associated with
a miracle: though murderers, they have somehow produced the
miraculous transformation of lies into truth. And this transformation, in which a message is miraculously different when sent
and when received, is a version of the miracle of Pentecost—
which the play has already named. The patterns of the novel
are here sketched for the novel's heroine.

But how is she—and by analogy the reader—to construe these
patterns? Is Oedipa to interpret the signs she discovers merely
as she would interpret a play in performance—or do the signs
have a meaning that "mattered to the world"? The performance
of *The Courier's Tragedy* which she attended *may* have been
directed specifically at her: her relationship with it was either
potential or actual. Pynchon elaborates on these two possibilities
in another metaphor derived from theatrical performance, this
time strip-tease:

So began, for Oedipa, the languid, sinister blooming of The
Tristero. Or rather, her attendance at some unique per-

formance . . . something a little extra for whoever'd stayed this late. As if the breakaway gowns, net bras, jeweled garters and G-strings of historical figuration . . . would fall away . . . ; as if a plunge toward dawn indefinite black hours long would indeed be necessary before The Tristero could be revealed in its terrible nakedness. Would its smile, then, be coy, and would it flirt away harmlessly backstage . . . and leave her in peace? Or would it instead, the dance ended, come back down the runway, its luminous stare locked on to Oedipa's, smile gone malign and pitiless; bend to her alone among the desolate rows of seats and begin to speak words she never wanted to hear? (54)

Pynchon here uses a metaphor from performance to describe the demands that may be made by the Trystero, and the metaphor thus transfers the problem of belief to one of its analogues, the problem of literary meaning. Pynchon joins the problem posed by the novel's *content*—the meaning of the Trystero to Oedipa—to the problem posed by the book's *presentation*—the meaning of the novel to its reader's nonliterary experience. What the passage delineates, in a version of the one-zero alternative that pervades the book, are two different concepts of art. In the first, according to which art's function is *delectare,* a novel is a superior form of entertainment which never intrudes into the world of decision and action, and whose structure and texture aspire to illuminate nothing but themselves (one might think of the later Nabokov or the stories of Borges's middle period). According to the second concept, art's purpose is *monere,* and a novel offers to its reader an example of coherence and order that rebukes the confusion of life and offers an alternative example: "the dance ended," its meaning taken out of the aesthetic realm, it offers to a reader "words [he] never wanted to hear."

These two extremes suggest a scale along which any work of fiction may be placed, a scale that measures the degree to which a work illuminates (at one end of the scale) the nature of the world outside the work, or (at the other end) the nature of the work's own language and structure. At the latter extreme is that which may be called *subjunctive fiction*, works concerned with events that can occur only in language, with few or no analogues in the phenomenal world. At the other extreme is *indicative fiction* (which includes *imperative fiction*), works that transmit, through no matter how elaborate a transformation, no matter how wide or narrow a focus, information about the emotional and physical world of nonliterary experience, including, but not limited to, the experience of language. Of course all indicative fiction has subjunctive elements, or it would be formless and not "fiction"; and all subjunctive fiction has indicative elements, otherwise it could not be understood at all.[11]

Read superficially, *The Crying of Lot 49* seems to fall near the subjunctive end of the scale. One often finds the book compared with Nabokov or Borges, and Pynchon's invention of an alternate "world," an alternate system of organization revealed through the Trystero, appears to justify these comparisons. If Van Veen can live in Anti-Terra, then Oedipa can find a Trystero. But a "subjunctive" reading accounts for too few of the novel's details and complexities, and is finally insufficient. Where Nabokov and Borges create a novelistic equivalent to *poésie pure*, Pynchon strives to remain as *impure* as possible. His novel insists on its indicative relation to the world of experience; and its proposal of "another mode of meaning behind the obvious" is not a tentative aesthetic proposal, but "words [one] never wanted to hear."

A story by Borges, from which Pynchon may have jumped off into the deeper themes of his novel, offers a subjunctive version of *The Crying of Lot 49*. Borges's "The Approach to al-Mu'tasim," in *Ficciones*, poses as a review of a novel published

11. This issue is related, of course, to the issue of probability and surprise in information theory. But while subjunctive fiction *apparently* has more "surprise," and indicative fiction more "probability," the matter in fact is far more complex. Information theory is not in any way concerned with the *value* of information—only with its quantity and the clarity of its transmission. Information theory and aesthetics are indeed related, but only tangentially.

in Bombay (and described with the usual Borgesian panoply of sources, analogues and scholarly commentary). The "reviewers" of the novel point out its "detective-story mechanism and its undercurrent of mysticism." The central figure of this novel, a student, goes in search of a woman whom he has heard about, vaguely, from a particularly vile thief. In the course of his search the student takes up "with the lowest class of people," and, among them, "all at once . . . he becomes aware of a brief and sudden change in that world of ruthlessness—a certain tenderness, a moment of happiness, a forgiving silence." The student guesses that this sudden change cannot originate in the people he is among, but must derive from somewhere else: "somewhere on the face of the earth is a man from whom this light has emanated," someone for whom he now begins to search. "Finally, after many years, the student comes to a corridor 'at whose end is a door and a cheap beaded curtain, and behind the curtain a shining light.' The student claps his hands once or twice and asks for al-Mu'tasim [the object of the search]. A man's voice—the unimaginable voice of al-Mu'tasim—prays him to enter. The student parts the curtain and steps forward. At this point the novel comes to its end."[12]

The structural analogies to *The Crying of Lot 49* are clear. The hero who sets out in search of one thing, as Oedipa sets out to give order to Inverarity's legacy; the discovery of something else entirely, as Oedipa begins to be made aware of the Trystero; the revelation of happiness and forgiveness, informed by and originating from a semi-divine object; the "detective-story and [the] undercurrent of mysticism"—all these are common to Pynchon's novel and Borges's novel-within-a-story. But Pynchon inverts the playful superficialities in Borges to create a pattern of greater intellectual depth and one deeper in emotional resource. In Borges, for example, the student *hears* his evidence

12. The translation quoted here is the one by Borges and Norman Thomas di Giovanni in *The Aleph and Other Stories* (New York: Dutton, 1970), pp. 45–52. An earlier translation appeared in *Ficciones* (New York: Grove Press, 1962). I am indebted to Professor Frank Kermode for pointing out this story.

of love and coherence amidst a scene of evil and degradation. In a corresponding episode in *Lot 49* Oedipa herself *enacts* the love and charity that Borges's hero can only witness. Oedipa's action occurs when she sees, on the steps of a dilapidated rooming house, an old sailor with a "wrecked face" and "eyes gloried in burst veins," who asks her to mail a letter bearing a Trystero stamp. After a night in which she has seen scores of signs of the Trystero, she is now flooded by a vision of the old man's whole experience of suffering, futility and isolation. She pictures to herself the mattress he sleeps on, bearing the "vestiges of every nightmare sweat, helpless overflowing bladder, viciously, tearfully consummated wet dream, like the memory bank to a computer of the lost."

> She was overcome all at once by a need to touch him. . . .
> Exhausted, hardly knowing what she was doing, she came
> the last three steps and sat, took the man in her arms,
> actually held him, gazing out of her smudged eyes down
> the stairs, back into the morning. (126)

Here Oedipa performs an act in which she takes personal responsibility for the patterns of corelation and coinherence which she has found in the world outside. Her embrace of the old sailor is a tangible manifestation of the unlikely relations for which the Tristero is an emblem. Through the Tristero Oedipa has learned to comfort the book's equivalent of that helpless figure to whom all successful quest-heroes must give succour.

But the Tristero is not simply a vehicle by which unseen relationships are manifested. Its name hides not only the unseen (and, to the secular world, illicit) relationship of the *tryst*, but also the *tristesse* that must accompany any sense of coherence and fullness. For if even the smallest event carries large significance, then even the smallest loss, the most remote sadness, contains more grief than a secular vision can imagine. When Oedipa helps the old sailor upstairs she imagines the enormous loss that must accompany his death (which she imagines as occurring when a spark from his cigarette will ignite his mattress):

> She remembered John Nefastis, talking about his Machine, and massive destructions of information. So when this mattress flared up around the sailor, in his Viking's funeral: the stored, coded years of uselessness, early death, self-harrowing, the sure decay of hope . . . would truly cease to be, forever, when the mattress burned. She stared at it in wonder. It was as if she had just discovered the irreversible process. (128)

The final metaphor, borrowed from information theory and thermodynamics, here becomes a compelling metaphor of an aspect of human experience.

"She knew," Pynchon continues, "because she had held him, that he suffered DT's. Behind the initials was a metaphor, a delirium tremens . . ." The metaphor *itself* is a delirium, a violent dissociation of what it describes. Oedipa recognizes now how deep and how complex is the indicative power of language, how much deeper than she imagined. Remembering a college boyfriend studying calculus, she forms a pun on the man's disease: " 'dt,' God help this old tattooed man, meant also a time differential, a vanishingly small instant in which change had to be confronted at last for what it was, where it could no longer disguise itself as something innocuous like an average rate; . . . where death dwelled in the cell though the cell be looked in on at its most quick." For Oedipa the possibilities of *seriousness* have now multiplied: each moment, each event, "had to be confronted at last for what it was." The movement from one element of a pun to the other is at once a comic slide and a movement towards real relation: "there was that high magic to low puns." And metaphor is at once a verbal trick and a way of talking about the truth of the world: "The act of metaphor then was a thrust at truth and a lie, depending on where you were: inside, safe, or outside, lost. Oedipa did not know where she was" (129). The problem of metaphor is here transferred in part to the reader. Metaphor—carrying over, across—is a way of signifying the true but not immediately accessible relations in the world of experience: "a thrust at truth." But metaphor acts this way only when one is "inside, safe," joined to the world in which moral and metaphoric connections, links of responsibility across time and among persons, endorsed by a hieratic vision, actually exist. If one is "outside, lost," damned to isolation and incoherence, then metaphor is nothing but a "lie," a yoking together by violence of heterogeneous concepts. Yet metaphor is, potentially, *both* a thrust and truth and a lie: the one-or-zero choice remains.

As metaphor can have either a subjunctive or an indicative meaning, so the Trystero will either leave Oedipa in peace or compel her to decision. Pynchon's novel points outside itself: the act of reading it (to use terms from communications and thermodynamics) can be either adiabatic or irreversible, either locked in the unchanging garden of fiction, or open to the shifting and uncertain world of choice, emotion, and community, either a verbal spectacle that leaves its reader in peace, or words you never wanted to hear.

The achievement of *The Crying of Lot 49* is its ability to speak unwanted words without a hint of preaching or propaganda. The book's transformation of the impersonal language of science into a language of great emotional power is a breathtaking accomplishment, whose nearest rival is perhaps Goethe's *Elective Affinities*. Equally remarkable is the book's ability to hover on the edge of low comedy without ever descending into the pond of the frivolous. The risks Pynchon takes in his comedy are great, but all the "bad" jokes, low puns, comic names, and moments of pure farce that punctuate the book have a serious function: the book, through its exploration of stylistic extremes, constantly raises expectations which it then refuses to fulfill. Its pattern of comic surprises, of sudden intrusions of disparate styles and manners, is entirely congruent with the thrust of its narrative. As Oedipa is caught unaware by the abrupt revelations that change her world, and is thus made attentive to significance she never recognized before, so the variations in the book's texture alert a reader to the book's complexity. High seriousness is difficult to sustain—nor, clearly, would Pynchon ever want to do so. A serious vision of relation and coherence must include comic relationships, and recognize comic varieties of attention.

Pynchon recognizes the limits of fiction—his comedy is in part a reminder of the fictional quality of his world—but he never lets his book become therefore self-reflective. Although he shares the painful knowledge wrought by modernism of the limits of art, and although he knows that no work of quotidian fiction—neither social nor psychological—can ever again persuade, he devotes himself to the effort that leads from pure fiction to a thrust at truth. The effort is difficult and complex, and most of the modes in which the effort has previously been attempted now seem exhausted. Pynchon's search for a new mode of indicative fiction is a lonely and isolated one, but it leads to a place where fiction can become less lonely, less isolated than it has been for many years.

### POSTSCRIPT

*Gravity's Rainbow*—all 760 pages of it—has now appeared, and tends to confirm this essay's reading of Pynchon's earlier work. The themes and methods of *V.* and *The Crying of Lot 49* also animate this third novel, yet they do so with far greater profundity and variety. *Gravity's Rainbow* is eight times as long as *The Crying of Lot 49*, and it includes at least three hundred characters, all joined to a plot that on a first reading appears uncontrolled, but which, on a second reading, reveals an extraordinary coherence. I have attempted elsewhere (*Yale Review*, Summer 1973) to suggest ways of reading this enormous novel, and will limit these remarks to the briefest conceivable account of the book, as well as to some further general observations on Pynchon's work as a whole.

It is now possible to state that Pynchon's subject is the response made by men and women to their recognition of the connectedness of the world. In *V.* the decline into entropy is the universal norm. But the central issue of the book is not this decline *per se*—if it were, the book would be little more than an ingeniously articulated conceit—but the possibility of a transcendent coherence and connectedness by which the same process of decline occurs in everything and at every scale. What Stencil finds "appalling" at the end of *V.* is the possibility that there is a design to history, that the world functions according to processes that lie outside the comfortable parameters of science or the humanistic arts. Similarly, in *The Crying of Lot 49* Oedipa recognizes the continuity that informs the apparently disconnected elements of the world, a continuity of which the Tristero is the emblem, as the woman V. was the manifestation of the earlier book's continuity. Both novels, however, oppose to their "real" connectedness the alternative possibility of false or merely mechanical relationships: in *V.*, the relations between human beings and machines, or the international conspiracies imagined or created by the people among whom V. moves; in *Lot 49*, the possibility that the Tristero is Oedipa's fantasy or an elaborate practical joke. In each case the false continuity is a symptom or cause of paranoia.

*Gravity's Rainbow* is reticulated by more systems and genuine conspiracies than one likes to imagine, ranging from an electrical grid to the bureaucracy of dead souls. Paranoia is the book's endemic disease, but Pynchon writes that paranoia "is nothing less than the onset, the leading edge, of the discovery that *everything is connected*, everything in the Creation." The book's examples of debased or mechanical connections, the analogues to the possibility of conspiracy in *The Crying of Lot 49*, involve international cartels and spy rings, even the cause-and-effect networks established by behaviorists and Pavlovians. Yet the book's final coherence, like that of the earlier book, is religious. The focus of all relationships in *Gravity's Rainbow*—its V., its Tristero, its Rome to which all hidden catacombs and public highways lead—is the V-2 rocket. The process enacted throughout the book, the analogue of entropy in *V.*, is the process (described by Max Weber) through which religious charisma yields to economic and pyschological pressure to become rationalized and routinized, to become reduced to bureaucracy. *Gravity's Rainbow* is a book about origins, and, in Weber's account, charisma in its pure form exists only in the process of originating. This process Pynchon describes most vividly in terms of the first few moments of the rocket's ascent, the originating moments through which its entire trajectory is irrevocably determined. The action of the book takes place in 1944 and 1945 (it is remarkable that the finest novel yet written of the Second World War should be the work of an author whose eighth birthday occurred on V-E Day), the originating and perhaps determining moments of contemporary history. The moral center of the book is the difficult but required task of recognizing the secular connectedness of the present scientific and political world—and the even more difficult requirement to act freely on the basis of that recognition. The secular patterns of the present, Pynchon indicates, are the product of originating moments in the past, but free action must take place here and now. The book's one-or-zero choice is the choice whether to live in the contingency and risks of freedom, or to remain trapped by the same determinism that binds the inanimate (though charismatic) rocket. The V-2 is the real descendant of the woman V.

*The Crying of Lot 49* has a story by Borges as its concealed and unacknowledged source; in *Gravity's Rainbow* Borges's name at last surfaces, and it appears often. Both Borges and Pynchon write fantasies, but while Borges's fantasies are built upon curiosities of language or mathematics, Pynchon's are extensions of man's capacity for evil and for love. Borges's language is one that is triumphantly capable of delight and astonishment, but Pynchon writes from the knowledge that language can also hurt and connect. *Gravity's Rainbow* cataclysmically alters the landscape of recent fiction, and it alters the landscape of our moral knowledge as well. It is a more disturbing and less accessible book than its predecessor, and demands even more intelligent attention, but its difficulties are proportional to its rewards. *The Crying of Lot 49* is an exceptional book, *Gravity's Rainbow* an extraordinary, perhaps a great one. The enterprise of Pynchon's fiction, its range and profundity, remain unparalleled among the novelists of our time.

EDWARD MENDELSON
*Yale University*